Chewa Traditional Religion

Chewa Traditional Religion

J.W.M. van Breugel, M. Afr.

Edited and introduced by Martin Ott

Kachere Monograph No. 13

Published by
Kachere Series
PO BOX 1037, Zomba, Malawi
kachere@globemw.net

ISBN   99908-16-34-4

First published 2001
Distributed outside Africa by
African Books Collective
http://www.africanbookscollective.com

Cover design   Deborah Kerr
Layout   Martin Ott

Printed by Lightning Source

Table of Contents

Introduction

J.W.M. van Breugel, a Dutch citizen born in 1929, arrived in Malawi in 1973. Being a Catholic priest and a member of the Missionaries of Africa (White Fathers) he was posted at several mission stations within the diocese of Lilongwe in Central Malawi. The then bishop of Lilongwe, Patrick A. Kalilombe encouraged van Breugel to conduct extensive field research. Having completed his M.A. at the School of Oriental and African Studies (SOAS) in London (1972) van Breugel embarked on a PhD programme. Geoffrey Parrinder, at that time professor at London University and author of *African Traditional Religion*, acted as tutor and supervisor. Van Breugel submitted his thesis in December 1976 under the title "Traditional Chewa Religious Beliefs and Practises. A Study in the Explanation of Evil and Suffering, and Ways of Dealing with them". He was awarded the degree of Doctor of Philosophy (Religious Studies) in 1978. The Kachere Series presents the original version of his doctoral thesis with slight corrections, editorial additions and under the title of *Chewa Traditional Religion*.[1] The spelling of the vernacular was revised to meet the criteria of the new Chinyanja/Chichewa Monolingual Dictionary.[2]

Anthropological Research under Banda

At home, in Malawi, politics on educational and cultural matters were tightened up. President Banda was convinced that social anthropology made his Malawians into a "laughing stock" and tried to prevent any research in a

---

[1] The exchange rates of Kwacha and British Pounds as given by the author (in order to give an idea about the local prices) were kept although both, the Kwacha prices and the exchange rates, have changed quite considerably since the year 1976.

[2] *Mthanthauzira mawu wa Chinyanja/Chichewa (The First Chinyanja/Chichewa Monolingual Dictionary*, ed. by Centre for Language Studies (Zomba), Blantyre: Dzuka Publishing, 2000.

culture he wanted the Malawians to get rid off. Research proposals including questionnaires, tapes and other materials used in field research had to be submitted to the secret police. Everybody who wanted to do serious research according to international academic standards was forced to do it clandestinely. Van Breugel's interest in Chewa Traditional Religion was more than suspect. Hence, his only chance to get things done, was a kind of "under cover" research, using his position as a Catholic priest and missionary to approach informants under the pretext of pastoral care. This is why in establishng the manuscript, van Breugel had to avoid mentioning the exact venues and data of his field trips including the names, age and further details of his informants (what would be a regular feature in anthropological research). He managed to smuggle his field notes to London explaining to the customs officials that the little cards contained Chichewa vocabulary. The restrictions on research included that van Breugel could not make use of "offical" sources like the National Archives and the Malawiana section at Chancellor College library in Zomba. As many other scholars confirm, it was quite dangerous to conduct research "without the President's permission".

Another problem arose from Malawian priests who did not appreciate the research of a *mzungu* (white person) on "our things". In 2001, one can hardly imagine how deep-seated the ignorance about and the resistance to research into Malawian culture was among Malawian Christians and among Malawian clergy. Bishop Kalilombe remarked: "The indigenous Malawian priests were notoriously hostile to the study of their customs by expatriate scholars! One wonders to what extent all this opposition was based on scholarship."[3] Being a guest in the Malawian church and trying to respect the sentiments of Malawian Christians, van Breugel decided to handle his research and his dissertation "on a low key". For him, the time for an open discussion on the role of African traditional religion within the Christian context was not ripe yet. After completion of his thesis, van Breugel published a summary of his findings as "The Religious Significance of the Nyau

---

[3] P.A. Kalilombe, "An Outline of Chewa Traditional Religion", in: *Africa Theological Journal* 9 (1980), no. 2, p. 51, fn 9.

among the Chewa of Malawi".[4] His educational and teaching capacities were put aside and in the following years he was involved in administrative affairs and was appointed Regional of the White Fathers being the superior of his order in Malawi. In January 1994, he left the country for good. A few copies of his thesis circulated among interested scholars in Malawi and abroad. It is only now, 25 years after the completion of his research that his thesis can be made accessible to a wider readership.

Eye-openers and Fields of Encounter

During the time of his field research van Breugel was working at Nathenje Catholic parish. In terms of traditional religion, this area was quite "traditional". Chewa institutions like initiation rites, rain prayers and *gule wamkulu* kept a strong position within popular religion. Bunda area and the Bunda Hill rain shrine complex lay within the confines of the parish boundaries belonging to the territories of chiefs *Chadza, Mazengera, and Kalumbu;* the local *Nyau* secret societes were and are famous for their influence on village life and local politics.

Van Breugel's "eye-opener" to Chewa Traditional Religion was his observation that the people around him experienced something like a continuous fear that something might go wrong. This led him to the description and analysis of the *mdulo*-complex and the fundamental distinction between the status of being ritually "hot" and ritually "cool". The necessity felt by the people to identify a "religious" cause for everything that happens prompted him to formulate his research objective as "A Study in the Explanation of Evil and Suffering, and Ways of Dealing with them". Here witchcraft functions as a central means of explanation.

A second "eye-opener" to van Breugel was his assessment that the cosmology of *Nyau* is almost entirely focused on the concept of fertility. Fecundity of the fields, of animals and of human beings was the major concern aired

---

[4] J.W.M. van Breugel, "The Religious Significance of the Nyau among the Chewa of Malawi", in: *Cultures et Développement* 17 (1985), no. 3, pp. 487-517.

out by the masked dancers, the accompanying songs, the symbolism of the masks and the taboos required for the performances.

Van Breugel encountered human beings not only as a social anthropologist, but also as a Christian and a Catholic priest. Against the often repeated argument among academics that a religious or even Christian bias would necessarily blurr the scholar's capacity to observe and to analyse the phenomena "as they are", one can substantiate that a religious "prejudice" (in the sense that H.G. Gadamer used it in his pace-setting book on hermeneutics *Truth and Method*) yields some advantages as well. In the case of van Breugel, it helped the researcher to be aware of the honesty of devotion as expressed in the different domains of Chewa Traditional Religion. Even 25 years later (when interviewed for the preparation of this publication) van Breugel turns emotional remembering the beautiful songs and prayers of the people of Central Malawi and how he was touched by their religious dedication when the prayer *Pepa Chauta, Pepa* rose to heaven accompanied by the rhythmic clapping of hands. I consider it as a unique advantage of research into African Traditional Religion that it is not only explained in terms of functionalism or structuralism, but that religion as a genuine and irreplaceable human experience holds a position among the hermeneutical tools of social anthropology. Van Breugel's background as social anthropologist and theologian qualified him best for this research topic.

Van Breugel's interest in Chewa Traditional Religion has a background which is important to know although it is not reflected in his book. It is the question as to which extent Christianity is influenced by African Traditional Religion. How deeply is Christianity rooted among the peasant Christians who worship the triune God and the ancestral spirits? Which shape has the gospel to take in order to reach the hearts of the people? These questions were put already before the age of inculturation and they give evidence that missionary activity and the reflection on what the Church is doing in the African context was not always as bad as the reputation of a culture-destroying enterprise usually suggests.

The Context of van Breugel's Research

The unique strength of this publication is the presentation of fresh field research data, especially in the domains of rain prayers, initiation, *gule wamkulu*
and witchcraft. Van Breugel provides data which had not been recorded and
published before. The author had access to some material as published and
accessible until the year 1976. His main authors for reference were J.P.
Bruwer, W.H.J. Rangeley, A.G.O. Hodgson, S.J. Ntara, T. Price, T.C.
Young, A.J. Makumbi, and J.W. Gwengwe.[5] Apart from these, he used the
different writings of M.G. Marwick as a major framework for interpretation.
Marwick did his research among the Chewa in Eastern Zambia. In Malawi,
J.M. Schoffeleers was dominating the scene. His research was predomi-
nantly done in the Lower Shire[6] and he considered the main features of
Traditional Religion to be similar in Central Malawi.[7] Nevertheless, in Central Malawi, only little field research had been conducted so far. Apart from
the political restrictions towards social anthropological research as outlined
above, the influence of the Nkhoma Synod and its strict condemnation of
"pagan" African religion had quite an impact. It was within the strongholds
of this very CCAP synod that the Catholic missionary tried to establish a
different approach. Within his own White Fathers' congregation he received
moral support and, once in a while, some academic challenge, as a few of
van Breugel's colleagues did some research as well. Fr Noel Salaun's unpublished "An Initiation to Malawi"[8] was a text of initiation and introduction
for missionaries into Malawi's culture, history and ethnology, and was based
on the author's own research. Whereas Salaun was very "modest" in his ap-

---

[5] For exact bibliographic references check the bibliographies at the end of the book.

[6] Schofelleer's two main works are "M'bona the Guardian Spirit of the Mang'anja", B.Litt.,
University of Oxford, 1966, 431 pp, and "Symbolic and Social Aspects of Spirit Worship
among the Mang'anja", D.Phil., University of Oxford, 1968, 666 pp. Most of the material,
like on worship of territorial spirits, the M'bona cult, the *Nyau* societies, the nature and
manifestations of domestic spirits, rites of appeasement, has been developed and published
in his subsequent books and articles.

[7] J.M. Schoffeleers' list of publications on African religion is quite extensive; cf. the compila-
tion in J.M. Schoffeleers, *Religion and the Dramatisation of Life. Spirit Beliefs and Rituals in Southern and Central Malawi*, Kachere Monograph, no. 5, Blantyre: CLAIM, 1997, pp. 152-156.

[8] N. Salaun, "Notes on the Achewa", polycopied, Lilongwe: Language Centre, nd., 124 pp.

proach, almost hiding his findings, A. Hovington's character was quite different. Under the assumed name of *Bibi Minus Habens* (literal translation: Lady "Not-very-bright"),[9] Hovington typescripted eight voluminous manuscripts on the "Customs of the Malawians".[10] His way of collecting data was quite embarrassing. In a kind of "burnt earth-method" he used to destroy original material (in one case even precious diaries from a mission station) stating that the information was now collected by him and that his text would now be the ultimate source for future researchers. Apart from that, his voluminous texts are a mixture of interesting and useless information, lacking sound academic treatment in the areas of reference and quotations. Claude Boucher who attended classes at SOAS at the same time had just started his own research on the different domains of Chewa Traditional Religion[11] and was still a "newcomer" when van Breugel finished his thesis.

Research on Chewa Traditional Religion after 1976

As this text is meant to be a study book for Chewa Traditional Religion, the following section gives information about the most important titles that

---

[9] Assuming that *Bibi* is the Yao (and Swahili) word for Lady, Lady "Not-very-bright" is a deliberately self-deprecating nickname intended to disarm his eventual critics. Indeed, Hovington never gave the chance for discussing or criticizing his writings.

[10] A. Hovington (spp.: Bibi Minus Habens), "An Essay of Encyclopedia: On the African Way of Life around the South West Shores of Lake Malawi and Surroundings", typescript, 8 Vols. & 1 Index, 1971-1973.
Vol. I: Physiography, History, Agriculture, Tribes (413 pp.);
Vol. II: Angoni and Yao (305 pp.);
Vol. III: De la Conception d'un Enfant à sa Naissance et jusqu'à sa Puberté (279 pp.)
Vol. IV: From the Puberty till the Marriage (450 pp.);
Vol. V: Marriage Settlement and Married Life (402 pp.);
Vol. VI: The Four Elementary Necessities of the African Material Life:
            The Bodily Wants/Feeding/Dressing/Housing (390 pp.);
Vol. VII: Religion and Moral: Among the African People of Old with Reference
            to the Present Mentality (397 pp.);
Vol. VIII: The Worshipping of the Ancestors (303 pp.).

[11] C. Boucher, "Some Interpretations of Nyau Societies. M.A., School for Oriental and African Studies", London 1976, 58 pp.; "The Matrilineal Dilemma: Chewa and Kalulu Symbolic", School for Oriental and African Studies, London 1976, 8 pp; "La dimension spirituelle des proverbes Chewa du Malawi", unpubl. typescript, 12 pp.

have been published after van Breugel had completed his research in 1976. At the end of this book an additional bibliography can be found with up-dated publications until December 2000. No clear separation between the areas of religion and culture is drawn although a recent trend in social anthropology is geared towards this direction. The section "African Traditional Religion" in the book "Religion in Malawi. An Annotated Bibliography", edited by J.C. Chakanza and K.R. Ross[12] serves as a general reference for the study of Chewa Traditional Religion. The following publications stand out among the various titles.

For the social and political history of the Chewa several books have been produced which until now have to be considered as standard texts for the subject. In 1975, K.M. Phiri submitted his doctoral thesis "Chewa History in Central Malawi and the Use of Oral Tradition, 1600-1920", an important study which unfortunately has not been published.[13] Phiri drew special attention to the research on *Nyau* in his article on "The Historiography of *Nyau*".[14] The two books of B. Pachai "The Early History of Malawi" and "The History of the Nation" provide the wider framework for any further assessment of the Chewa social and religious set-up.[15] In 1978, J.M. Schoffeleers published "Guardians of the Land" with essays on territorial cults in Zambia, Malawi and Zimbabwe.[16] Here the contributions of J.M. Schoffeleers "The Chisumphi and Mbona Cults in Malawi: A Comparative History" (147-186) and of I. Linden "Chisumphi Theology in the Religion of Central Malawi" (187-207) are of specific value.

---

[12] J.C. Chakanza & K.R. Ross (eds.), *Religion in Malawi. An Annotated Bibliography* (Kachere Text, no. 7), Blantyre: CLAIM, 1998, pp. 13-53.

[13] K.M. Phiri, "Chewa History in Central Malawi and the Use of Oral Tradition, 1600-1920", Ph. D., Univ. of Wisconsin, Madison, 1975.

[14] K.M. Phiri, "The Historiography of Nyau", in: *Kalulu. Bulletin of Oral Literature*, University of Malawi, no. 3, 1982, pp. 55-58.

[15] B. Pachai (ed.), *The Early History of Malawi*, London: Longman 1972; B. Pachai, *The History of the Nation*, London: Longman, 1973.

[16] J.M. Schoffeleers (ed.), *Guardians of the Land. Essays on Central African Territorial Cults*, Gweru: Mambo, 1979 (reprint as Kachere Text in 1999).

Several researchers conducted field research among the Chewa. Although their focus of interest is not primarily religious, they contributed considerably towards the understanding of religion as practised in the various domains of rites, ceremonies and rituals. Two researches among the Chewa of Eastern Zambia shed light on comparable aspects in adjacent Malawi. Firstly, M. Mapopa's investigation on the dramatic aspect of *gule wamkulu*,[17] and, secondly, the work of the Japanese anthropologist Kenji Yoshida on its aesthetic components.[18] In Malawi, Laurel Birch de Aguilar researched on *gule wamkulu* producing a good number of publications, among them the only academic monograph on the mask society of the Chewa in Central Malawi.[19] The specific aspect of spirit possession was under investigation by late G. Sembereka.[20] The Canadian still photographer Douglas Curran took a specific interest in the presentation of the *gule wamkulu* masks, their symbolism and aesthetic appearance.[21] His photographic representations are of excellent quality and draw attention to an aspect of culture very often overlooked. As culture and religion are as inseparable, as are music and religion, M. Strumpf's research includes the examination of the latter connection.[22] B. Morris' interest in Chewa culture is at the interface of ethnobotany, eth-

---

[17] M. Mapopa, "The Drama of Gule Wamkulu. A Study of the Nyau as practiced by the Chewa of the Eastern Province of Zambia", M.A. Diss., Univ. of Ghana, nd.

[18] K. Yoshida, "Masks and Transformation among the Chewa of Eastern Zambia", in: *Senri Ethnological Studies* (Osaka) 31 (1992), pp. 203-273; K. Yoshida, "Masks and Secrecy among the Chewa", in: *African Arts* 26 (1993), no. 2, pp. 34-45.

[19] L. Birch de Aguilar, "Masks in Social Roles", in: *Society of Malawi Journal* 47 (1994), no. 2, pp. 15-37; "Masks: Outsider and Socio-historical Experience", in: *Society of Malawi Journal* 47 (1994), no. 2, pp. 37-54; "Nyau Masks of the Chewa: An Oral Historical Introduction", in: *Society of Malawi Journal* 47 (1994), no. 2, pp. 4-17; "Masks, Society, and Hierarchy among the Chewa of Central Malawi", in: *Anthropos* 90 (1994), pp. 407-421; *Inscribing the Mask. Interpretation of Nyau Masks and Ritual Performance among the Chewa of Central Malawi*, Studia Instituti Anthropos, no. 47, Fribourg/Switzerland: University Press, 1996.

[20] G. Sembereka, "The Place of Gule Wamkulu in Dreams Attributed to Spirits, Nominal Reincarnation and Spirit-Possession: The Nankhumba Experience", in: *Society of Malawi Journal* 49 (1996), no. 1, pp. 1-31.

[21] D. Curran, "The Elephant Has Four Hearts. Nyau Mask and Rituals", in: *Iwalewa Forum 1/2000. Arbeitspapiere zur Kunst und Kultur Afrikas*, Bayreuth: Iwalewa Haus, 2000, pp. 15. The book contains 14 photographs of *gule wamkulu* masks by Douglas Curran.

[22] M. Strumpf, "Music Traditions of Malawi", Chancellor College, nd., unpubl., 17 pp.

nozoology and social anthropology.[23] His findings especially in the field of popular concepts of diseases are a major contribution to the discussion on healing, witchcraft and spirit possession, which is a major topic in Chewa religion.[24]

How culture and politics interrelate has been researched by D. Kaspin and P. Probst. Both share a special focus on *gule wamkulu*, its recent changes in modern Malawi and its impact in local politics. Whereas Kaspin includes aspects of symbolism and the relation of *Nyau* to Christianity,[25] Probst's field research covers aspects of local identity, rain shrine activities and healing.[26] Hence, from different angles, fresh data for the analysis of the religious significance of the "contemporary" Chewa cultural set-up can be obtained. J. Chakanza has collected over 2000 Chewa proverbs. His book "Wisdom of the People" is being published in Kachere Series.[27]

---

[23] B. Morris, *The Power of Animals. An Ethnography*, Oxford/New York: Berg, 1998; *Animals and Ancestors. An Ethnography*, Oxford/New York: Berg, 2000; the third of Morris' trilogy on Ethnozoology dealing with the history of conservation of mammals in Malawi is not published yet.

[24] B. Morris, "Medicines and Herbalism in Malawi", in: *Society of Malawi Journal* 42 (1989), no. 2, pp. 34-54; "Changing Conceptions of Nature", in: *Society of Malawi Journal* 44 (1991), no. 2, pp. 9-26; *Chewa Medical Botany. A Study of Herbalism in Southern Malawi*, Monographs from the International African Institute, no. 2, Hamburg: LIT 1996; "Hunting and the Gnostic Vision", in: *Journal of Human and Environmental Sciences* 1 (1996), no. 2, pp. 13-39.

[25] D. Kaspin, "Chewa Vision and Revisions of Power: Transformation of the Nyau Dance in Central Malawi", in: Jean & John Camaroff, *Modernity and its Malcontents. Ritual and Power in Postcolonial Africa*, Uni. of Chicago Press 1993, pp. 34-57.

[26] P. Probst, *Moral Discourses and Ritual Authority in Central Malawi*, Sozialanthropologische Arbeitspapiere, vol. 6, Berlin: Das Arabische Buch, 1995; "Danser le Sida. Spectacles du Nyau et Culture Populaire Chewa dans le Centre Du Malawi", in: M. Agier & A. Ricard (eds.), *Les Arts de la Rue dans les Sociétés du Sud* (Special Issue), Autrepart / Cahiers des Sciences Humaines, Nouvelle Série, vol. 1/1 (1997), pp. 91-113; "Imagination und Repräsentation: Variationen indigener Ethnographie in Malawi ", in: H. Behrend & T. Geider (eds.), *Afrikaner Schreiben zurück*, Köln: R. Köppe, 1998; "Picture Dance. Reflections on Nyau Image and Experience", in: *Iwalewa Forum 1/2000. Arbeitspapiere zur Kunst und Kultur Afrikas*, Bayreuth: Iwalewa Haus, 2000, pp. 17-32.

[27] J.C. Chakanza, *Wisdom of the People. 2000 Nyanja Proverbs*, Blantyre: CLAIM 2001.

Looking at the anthropological research conducted among the Chewa it is conspicuous that there is a "dearth of written material on the Chewa concepts of God", as J. Chakanza summarizes in his article on "Some Chewa Concepts of God".[28] The same applies to other areas of the Chewa cultural heritage, which would qualify as religious in a more specific sense. Among the few exceptions we mention the works of H.J. Sindima "Bondedness, Moyo and Umunthu as Elements of aChewa Spirituality: Organizing Logic and Principle of Life",[29] of A. Musopole on "The Chewa Concept of God and its Implications for the Christian Faith"[30] and of J. Kuppens on "Mortuary Rites and Inculturation in Malawi".[31] In order to fill the gap, students in the Department of Theology and Religious Studies, Chancellor College, Zomba, were assigned to do research into different domains of Traditional Religion in Malawi. Among those dissertions some papers offer quite interesting perceptiveness. For a complete picture the reader is again referred to the book "Religion in Malawi. An Annotated Bibliography" where the students' dissertations are integrated in the section "African Traditional Religion". A general overview on Chewa Traditional Religion is provided by W. Petermann (esp. in the field of rain rituals),[32] by P. Kalilombe[33] and by M. Ott.[34] Claude Boucher, a White Father missionary and anthropologist, conducted extensive field research in the past twenty five years, mainly on rites of passage (including birth rites, initiation, *manyumba* [introduction of chiefs and elders]), rain rituals, and *gule wamkulu*. Unfortunately he has not pub-

---

[28] J.C. Chakanza, "Some Chewa Concepts of God", in: *Religion in Malawi* 1 (1987), pp. 4-8.

[29] H.J. Sindima, "Bondedness, Moyo and Umunthu as Elements of aChewa Spirituality: Organizing Logic and Principle of Life", in: *Ultimate Reality and Meaning* 14 (1991), pp. 5-20.

[30] A.C. Musopole, "The Chewa Concept of God and its Implications for the Christian Faith", M.A., University of Malawi, 1984, 187 pp.

[31] J.J.M. Kuppens, "They Discovered the Wonders of God in their Culture. Mortuary Rites and Inculturation in Malawi", Doctoraal Scriptie, Katholieke Universiteit Nijmegen, Feb. 1992, 112 pp.

[32] W. Petermann, *Regenkulte und Regenmacher bei bantu-sprachigen Ethnien Ost- und Südafrikas*, Berlin: Reimer, 1985.

[33] P.A. Kalilombe, "An Outline of Chewa Traditional Religion", in: *Africa Theological Journal* 9 (1980), no. 2, pp. 39-51

[34] M. Ott, *African Theology in Images* (Kachere Monograph, no. 12), Blantyre: CLAIM, 2000, pp. 147-203.

lished his findings, but, for the timebeing, decided to make them available to a wider public in the Chamare museum in Mua. Claude Boucher's field researches provide a vast and rich amount of data. Until he finds time to publish, the interested reseacher has to find his way to Mua mission, to visit the Chamare museum[35] and to interview Fr. Boucher personally.

Prospects on Chewa Religion

Against the background of this comprehensive literature review it is more than recommendable to publish van Breugel's thesis. It still serves as a valid source book for the study of Chewa Traditional Religion. With the editors of the Kachere Series I hope that the text fulfills this objective for students, researchers and interested readers. There is another reason why van Breugel's reference work should be available to a wide readership. The last decade of the 20th century marked a period of drastic changes in the so-called "traditional" set-up of Chewa culture, religion and society. Many of the domains as described by van Breugel are in decline or in a process of transformation or even disappearance. The first year of the new millenium as year of releasing this volume might bear some symbolism with regard to the future of Chewa Traditional Religion. Whether one agrees or not, cultural and religious dynamics will increasingly affect the Chewa in Central Malawi, as they do in other parts of the world. Perhaps very soon van Breugel's *Chewa Traditional Religion* will be considered as a timely stock taking before it was too late. Nevertheless, it seems that the deeper layers of Chewa culture and religious imagination represent quite an interesting fusion of resistance and flexibility progressing into the new millenium. Some of van Breugel's descriptions may soon turn to be outdated historical reminiscences, others might help future researchers to disclose the hidden transcript of cultural and religious mutations.

Martin Ott

---

[35] M. Ott, "Church and Culture on Display. The Opening of the Chamare Museum in Mua", in: *Religion in Malawi* 8 (1998), pp. 41-48.

Glossary of some Chewa words

azamba	elderly women helping at child birth
bwalo	open space in the village for meetings and *Nyau* dances
Chauta/chauta	name for God/rain maker
chigayo	maize mill
chimera	maize malt
chinamwali	initiation rite for girls
ching'aning'ani	lightning weapon of a *mfiti*
chirombo	wild beast; *Nyau* dancer
Chisumphi/chisumphi	name for God/rain maker
chithumwa	charm in the form of a small sachet
chiwanda	spirit of a deceased who is not received into the spirit world because of his misdeeds
chizimba	activating agent in medicine, usually made from a human corpse
dambo	low lands with grass
dambwe	assembling place for the *Nyau*
fisi	hyena; a man called to perform ritual intercourse with a girl at the end of her initiation
gule wamkulu	*Nyau* dance
gulo	lizard with a blue head
kachisi	temple hut
khonde	veranda round the house
kudika	to abstain from sexual intercourse for a ritual purpose
kudula	to cut; causing a disaster by transgressing a sexual taboo
kulandilidwa	to be received by the spirits upon one's death
kumeta	to shave the hair
kumiyendo	place at the back of a house where provisions are kept

kutenga mwana	a ritual some weeks after the birth of a child
kutsilika	to protect with magic
kutukwana	to swear; to curse
liunde	meeting place of the *Nyau* just outside the village
Makewana	priestess at the Msinja rain shrine
makolo	ancestors
maliro	burial; a corpse
manda	grave yard
mankhwala	medicine
mdulo	mysterious disease caused by the transgression of a taboo on sexual intercourse
mfiti	witch
mfunde	rain sacrifice
(ya ku) mitu	something consecrated to the spirit of a deceased
mkazi wachitengwa	a married woman living in the village of her husband
mkuzi	string of beads around the waist
mlandu	a case or lawsuit
mpheko	two sticks rubbed together to make fire
m'pheranjiru	a sorcerer who kills out of malice or upon demand
mphinjiri	charm
mpongozi	mother-in-law; father-in-law
mtsiliko	magical protection
mwabvi	poison ordeal
mwambo, miyambo	custom
mwini	owner
mwini maliro	the maternal uncle or the elder brother of the deceased
mzimu (pl. mizimu)	spirit(s) of deceased
mzinda	the right granted to chiefs to have *Nyau* and the solemn initiation of girls
namkungwi	elderly woman in charge of the initiation of girls
namwali	a girl who has reached puberty
ndiwo	side dish of meat, fish or vegetables
nkhoswe	marriage counsellor

nsima	stiff maize porridge
nsupa	a small gourd
nthungululu	shrill shout of joy made by women
pepa	have mercy
phala	maize gruel
phungu	tutor at initiation
sing'anga	medicine man; magician
site	excavation at the bottom of the grave
siwa	abandoned house that belonged to a deceased person
tsimba	hut in which the girls are confined during their initiation
ufiti	witchcraft; sorcery in general
ula	divining lots
ulemu	sign of respect shown to chiefs and elders
woombeza ula	diviner
zolaula	songs that mention the male or female private parts

Foreword

This book is the fruit of research undertaken in Malawi from 1973 to 1976, and more specifically in the areas of Traditional Authority *Chadza, Maze-ngera,* and *Kalumbu,* all three to the south-east of Lilongwe in the Central Region. This area is still very traditional. The majority of the people follow the traditional beliefs. Only about 10% of the population is Christian (Catholic or Protestant). Within the area under survey two rain shrines are still operative (Bunda and Tsang'oma). The *Nyau* secret society is very influential in this area. I. Linden has pointed out that the *Nyau* society has been the main source of opposition to foreign influences. A former colonial District Commissioner, W.H.J. Rangeley, used to say that *Nyau* was the main factor in keeping the people backward.

The Census of 1966, which gives the latest available data, indicates that in the area under survey only one out of five children goes to school. However, one should keep in mind that very few finish primary school for the majority attend classes for one or two years only. The school attendance has gone up since 1966 and it is estimated that in Malawi as a whole about twice as many children attended school in 1973 as in 1966. The majority of the people in the area are subsistence farmers. The Chewa are a matrilineal people with uxorilocality as a rule. After a number of years some men may receive permission from their in-laws to move to their villages with wife and children. However, wife and children continue to belong to the matriline-age.

We were interested in the religious beliefs and practices of the people, in particular: what explanation does Chewa Traditional Religion offer for suffering connected with e.g. death, illness, drought or infertility, and what help does it give people in coping with suffering? We noted down all the deaths we heard of, specifying in each case what people believed was the cause of death. We collected 451 cases. We consider that a total of 451 cases is sufficient to give some indication of beliefs of the people. Death was attributed to the following causes:

Causes of death (as established in the research):

	Adult	Child	Total
God [1]	25	23	48
Diseases [2]	21	17	38
Spirits of the dead	7	2	9
Suicide and murder	8	-	8
Execution of a witch	8	-	8
Mdulo [3]	11	33	44
Poison	28	12	40
Mfiti yeniyeni [4]	20	9	29
Chizimba [5]	44	24	68
Sorcery [6]	-	-	159
Total			**451**

We have seen in the survey of 451 deaths how the Chewa attribute death in some cases to God, the spirits of the deceased and natural diseases, but in the majority of the cases to evil in man (*mdulo, ufiti,* poison, *chizimba,* sorcery). Sickness is often said to be caused by the spirits of the deceased who wish to warn or to punish their descendants. Drought is connected with God, the supreme rain-giver. Infertility is usually attributed to the spirits of

---

[1] It is a normal belief that "God takes old people to give them rest". The fact that a number of children were said to be taken by God is unusual and may be due to Christian influence.

[2] During a cholera epidemic the government carried out a campaign to enlighten the people about this disease and they got used to the idea that cholera kills.

[3] *Mdulo* is a mysterious disease caused by the transgression of a taboo on sexual relations.

[4] *Mfiti yeniyeni* (a true witch) is a person who is believed to kill in order to eat the flesh of the victim.

[5] *Chizimba* is believed to be a powerful charm because it is allegedly made from a human corpse.

[6] Here we grouped all other forms of evil magic.

the deceased, who are constituted by God as the channel through which fertility is transmitted to the living.

In this book we will successively examine the Chewa belief in God and in the spirits of the deceased and see how man can have recourse to them in prayer and sacrifice. Other chapters will deal with evil in man (in oneself or in one's fellow men) and see how the Chewa believe they can protect themselves against or purify themselves from this evil. One can often meet masked *Nyau* dancers. This *Nyau* society appears as an ancient institution which for centuries has occupied a central place in Chewa life and has proved to be the bulwark of their traditions. This *Nyau* society is connected with the Chewa veneration of the spirits of the deceased. A special chapter will examine the precise role of the *Nyau* with respect to the religious beliefs and practices of the Chewa.

Throughout the research we had the help of informants. By taking up the same questions with several informants, who did not know that the same question had been put to other people, we were able to crosscheck all the answers received. Towards the end we checked all the material once more with a few informants individually to ensure that it was correct.

J.W.M. van Breugel

Chapter 1
Concepts of God

In our survey we noted that 48 of the 451 deaths were attributed to God. The belief that God "takes old people that they may rest" was found throughout the area we studied, whereas the belief that God also "takes children" was found only in a few places, and always in the vicinity of a Christian mission school. No doubt, this belief has been influenced by Christian teaching. If then, we take only the deaths of old people, we note that those attributed to God were only 25 cases.

1. Names of God

The Chewa believe in the existence of the "Supreme Spirit" *(mzimu wam-kulu)*. All other spirits are called "lesser spirits" *(mizimu yaying'ono)*. God is known to exist because of what he does. He makes the rain fall. He gives life. He gives the sun. Different names are used for God, each name expressing a particular attribute. It is often said that "God is spirit" *(Chiuta ndi mzimu)*. He belongs to the unseen spiritual world, but as His attributes show, He surpasses all other spirits. The following names are used for God.[1]

a) Chiuta

Literally this means "the big bow". God stretches the rainbow across the sky, presiding over the fecundity which the rain brings. It is a symbol of how God shows his concern for men by giving rain. The rainbow in the sky after a downpour is also likened to the bow of a man who drives away the

---

[1] Some of the names are mentioned by S.J. Ntara, *The History of the Chewa*, Wiesbaden: Frank Steiner, 1973, p. 39; cf. also T.C. Young, "The Idea of God in Northern Nyasaland", in: E.W. Smith (ed.), *African Ideas of God*, London, Edinburgh House Press, 1961, pp. 50-52.

clouds. And as such it became a symbol of God who stops the rain when there has been enough, so that it does not spoil the crops.

b) Chauta

This name is used by many people instead of *Chiuta,* and the meaning is the same. T. Cullen Young said that the prefix *cha* indicates the notion of a person: "the Great (One) of the rainbow".[2]

c) Chisumphi

God the Giver of rain. The etymology of this name is not clear. It is used mainly with reference to rain sacrifices. It has the special meaning of God who listens to men's prayers *(womvera anthu ompepesa)*. The names *Chauta* and *Chisumphi* are also used for some rain-makers. However, the people make a clear distinction between the rain-maker and God Himself.

d) Mphambe

God the Mighty One, God Almighty. Thunder and lightning are the signs of his power. The word *Mphambe* is connected with the verb *kupambana* (to be more powerful than) and with the noun *mphamvu* (power, strength).

e) Leza (Variations: Mlezi, Lezi)

God the Sustainer of man. The word *Lezi* has the same root as the verb *kulera* which has two meanings: 1) to nourish, to nurse, to rear; 2) to be gentle, kind (e.g. *munthu oleza mtima* - a kind and patient man). *Kuleza* is the causative and emphatic form of *kulera*. This name indicates the belief that God provides for man and that He is good for man. The same idea is sometimes expressed by using the word *Tate* (father) for God. During the rain sacrifices it is said: "Is God not our Father?" T.C. Young, who mentioned the same meaning "God the Supreme Nourisher of man" said that this name arrived with the *Nkhamanga* who immigrated into Malawi at the be-

---

[2] T.C. Young, "The Idea of God", p. 51.

ginning of the nineteenth century and who connected the name *Leza* with "the lightning, the forerunner and sure sign of the onset of the rains".[3]

f) Chanjiri or Nanjiri

This means the Strong One. A related word *wojijirika* means a strong and awe-inspiring person. God can punish by withholding rain. It is interesting to note that parents have been heard to reproach a child who was spoiling food: "Be careful, do not spoil food, Chanjiri sees you" *(Chenjera, usamatero kuononga nsima, Chanjiritu akukuona).* It is sometimes said that there is a connection with the word *njiri* (warthog) which is a frightening animal lacking only tusks to turn into an elephant.

g) Namalenga or Mlengi

God the Maker of man and the world. The verb *kulenga* means to make. This same idea is also expressed by the name *Chiumbi-umbi* connected with the verb, *kuumba* (to mould).

h) N'theradi

God the Mighty One. The verb *kutha* means to be able. The suffix *di* is a strong affirmation. People use *n'theradi* as an affirmation like *ndithudi* (really, truly). Some say that this name means "the True One".

i) Matsakamula

The One who can being down rain. The verb *kutsakamula* means: to bring down, to cause to fall.

k) Mulungu

Some say that this name has some connection with the verb *kulungama* (to be straight) or *kulunga* (to put together rightly).[4] *Munthu a chilungamo* is a person who is upright.

---

[3] T.C. Young, "The Idea of God", pp. 52f.

[4] T.C. Young, "The Idea of God", p. 52.

Many older people, however, say that it is not really a Chewa name for God, but that it was introduced from elsewhere. In the last century the Christian missions adopted this word as the name for God. But in the prayer of the Bunda rain shrine the name *Mulungu* is never used. When they pray, they always use the names: *Chauta, Chisumphi, Mphambe, Leza, Namalenga, Nanjiri.* The name *Mulungu* has given rise to a misunderstanding. A. Hetherwick noted: "*Mulungu* would appear to be the spirit world in general, or the ag-

gregate of all the spirits of the dead".[5] He added: "The word *Mulungu* carried with it no idea of personality. It belongs to that class of nominatives which denotes qualities or attributes, things conceived in the abstract. It has reference to what is unseen, inexplicable, and linked with the spirit world". A. Heth-erwick seems to have taken up

Dzalanyama Mountain
- The mythical cradle of mankind -

the argument of D. MacDonald who questioned already in 1882 the suit-ability of the name *Mulungu* although his intention was clearly to convey the Christian concept of God. "In all our translations of scripture where we found the word God, we used the word *Mulungu,* but this word is chiefly used by the natives as a general name for the spirits. The spirit of a dead man is called his *mulungu,* and all the prayers and the offerings of the living are presented to such spirits of the dead. It is here that we find the great centre of native religion. The spirits of the dead are the gods of the living".[6]

A. Hetherwick seemed to conclude from the etymological analysis of the word *Mulungu* that the Chewa do not believe in a personal God. But he overlooked the fact that Mulungu is not accepted by the people as truly a Chewa word. It would seem therefore that he based his argument on insuf-

---

[5] A. Hetherwick, *The Gospel and the African,* Edinburgh: Clark, pp. 69f.
[6] D. MacDonald, *Africana, or the Heart of Heathen Africa,* 2 vols., Edinburgh: John Menzies & Co., 1881, vol. 1, p. 59.

ficient evidence. As has already been said, the real Chewa names for God are *Chiuta* or *Chauta, Chisumphi, Mphambe, Lezi, Namalenga,* etc. Of the Chewa concept of God, D.C. Scott wrote: "God is one, is a distinct person, cannot be identified with the powers of nature, nor confounded with spirits in general, who as spirits are supposed to be with Him".[7]

The argument whether or not *Mulungu* is the right word to convey the Christian concept of God has been settled today. The new ecumenical Bible translation has adopted the word *Chiuta* for God, and has dropped the word *Mulungu.* The various names for God have no plural, except *Mulungu* which in the plural becomes *milungu* and has then the meaning of "masters". The spirits of the deceased are sometimes called *milungu (ndiyo milungu yathu),* and this has mistakenly given rise to the idea that the spirits of the dead were considered gods.

As mentioned before, the names of God present some of His attributes. He created man, He nourishes him especially by making the rain fall in due time; He is the Mighty One; but also the one who is kind to man; on the other hand He is also awe-inspiring.

God was also said to be "above" *(kumwamba).* Some would say, He is "like the clouds in the sky" *(ngati thambo la m'mwamba),* others that He is like "the whole world together" *(ngati dziko lonse la pansi pano).* And again that He is "like the wind that reaches everywhere" *(ngati mphepo yofika konse).*

God was said to be the "Great One" *(wamkuluyo),* "whom man cannot approach" *(wosatha kumsendezera),* or "know much about Him" *(Chiuta ndi chinthu chosadziwika konse).* He is "not seen by man" *(wosaoneka)* and "does not change" *(wosasinthika).* Of one thing the Chewa are convinced, namely that God "listens to the prayers of man" *(Chiuta ndi mzimu omva madandaulo a anthu).*

---

[7] D.C. Scott, *A Cyclopaedic Dictionary of the Mang'anja Language,* Edinburgh: Foreign Mission Committee of the Church of Scotland, 1892, p. 403.

It is difficult to say what was the original Chewa concept of God, for undoubtedly it has been influenced by contact with the Christian missions and
with Moslem traders from the Coast.[8]

2. Creation and Fall

The following legend is widely told:

> When there was yet no living thing here on earth, *Chiuta* made a man
> and a woman, and sent them down. They alighted on a rock called
> Kaphiri-ntiwa at the Dzalanyama. That rock was still soft and they left
> their footprints on the rock when they alighted. These footprints can be
> seen still today. The same day *Chiuta* sent rain to germinate the seeds
> which had been placed there already, in order to provide food for man.[9]

On the top of the *Dzalanyama* mountains, the frontier between Mozambique
and Malawi, there is a part covered with a sacred forest, in which stands the
rock that bears a number of imprints, now believed to be the footprints of
the first man and woman.[10] The whole area is called *Msinja* and it became
the site of the great rain shrine of the Chewa.[11] Not only did the Chewa go
there to offer rain sacrifices, but also, until a number of years ago, they used
to go there to offer a thanksgiving sacrifice for the harvest.[12] People also say
that "God has stopped creating man" *(adaleka kulenga).* By this is meant that

---

[8] Cf. E.W. Smith, *African Ideas of God,* pp. 2-3; T.C. Young, "The Idea of God", p. 50.

[9] We have heard this narrative more than once. See also D.C. Scott, *A Cyclopaedic Dictionary
of the Mang'anja Language,* (1892), p. 403. D. MacDonald, *Africana,* p. 279. A Werner, *The Natives of British Central Africa,* London: Constable, 1906, pp. 10-11.

[10] The rock is called "Kaphiri-ntiwa" which means: the soft rock on which traces are left
behind. "Ntiwa" is translated by D.C. Scott as "a place which has been bruised or pressed
flat" (*A Cyclopaedic Dictionary of the Mang"anja Language,* p. 471). H.W. Langworthy in his
commentary on S.J. Ntara's, *The History of the Chewa* commented that these "imprints" are
found in many parts of Central Africa, but nowhere in such a great concentration as at
Kaphiri-ntiwa (p. 9). These apparent footprints are caused, according to Langworthy, by the
differential weathering of the granite rock in the area.

[11] As shall be seen later, rain sacrifices are offered today at the shrine of the Bunda Hill and
at Tsang'oma, which both derive from the Msinja shrine.

[12] P. Braire reported that in his time people went annually to bring such thanksgiving sacrifices at Nsinja from as far as the lakeshore. P. Braire, "Coutumes Indigènes", Rome: Archives of the Missionaries of Africa (White Fathers), Ms, 44 pages, 1927, p. 30.

God created the first ancestors and gave them the power to recreate themselves in their children. God does not need to intervene any more.

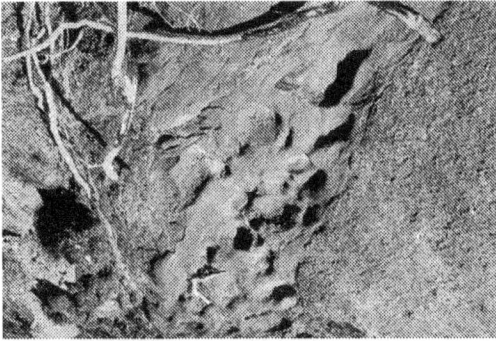

The 'mythical' footsteps at Dzalanyama

J.M. Schoffeleers reported an addition to the creation-myth given above:

> With the first man and woman came pairs of all animals as well as *Chiuta* Himself, who was accompanied by the first rains. During this first period *Chiuta*, men and animals, lived together in peace. This condition, however, was completely destroyed when man invented fire which set the grass ablaze and made the animals flee full of rage against man. *Chiuta* was rescued by the spider, who spun a thread along which He climbed to the sky. Thus driven away by the wickedness of man, God proclaimed that man would die and join Him in the sky where he would have to make rain clouds in order to quench the fires which he had invented.[13]

A. Werner reported a myth similar to the one given by Schoffeleers. However, she reported it as a myth of the Yao, the neighbours of the Chewa, and, instead of the words "God proclaimed that man would die", she wrote: "And He (God) said: When they die, let them come on high here." The myth is as follows:

> At first man was not, only Mulungu and the beasts. One morning, on visiting his trap, Chameleon found two unknown beings in it, no other than the first man and woman, who had somehow blundered into it dur-

---

[13] J.M. Schoffeleers, "The Religious Significance of Bush Fires in Malawi", in: *Cahiers des Religions Africanies* (1971), p. 274; reprint in: J.M. Schoffeleers, *Religion and the Dramatisation of Life. Spirit Beliefs and Rituals in Southern and Central Malawi*, Kachere Monograph, no. 5, Blantyre: CLAIM, 1997, pp. 22-33.

ing the night. He consulted Mulungu as to what he should do with them, and was told, "place them here, they will grow". They did grow and developed various activities, among others that of making fire by twirling a hard stick on a bit of soft wood, as is done to this day. But in the end they set the grass alight, and thus drove Mulungu from his abode on this earth. The Chameleon escaped by climbing a tree; but Mulungu was on the ground, and he said: "I cannot climb a tree". Then Mulungu set off and went to call the Spider. The Spider went on high and returned again and said: "I have gone on high nicely", and he said: "You now, Mulungu, go on high". Mulungu then went with the Spider on high. And he said: "When they die, let them come on high here". And behold, men on dying go on high in order to be slaves of God, the reason being that they ate his people here below. That is, as soon as they had found out the use of fire, they began to kill and cook buffaloes and other animals.[14]

J.M. Schoffeleers was of the opinion that the invention of fire and the subsequent conflagration of the country constituted clearly an essential element of the myth of creation. The peace among *Chiuta,* men and animals was destroyed by the fault of man. Therefore man had to die.[15] A. Werner remarked on the myth of the Yao: "This tale seems to be a very crude form of the myth in which a divine being is driven from earth by the wickedness of mankind."[16] However she did not say as did Schoffeleers that "man had to die" because of his wickedness. Some years later, in effect, commenting on yet another myth, she wrote: "I do not think any genuine native version suggests that God changed his mind (by condemning man to die) on account of men's wickedness. Where this is said one suspects it to be a moralizing afterthought, due perhaps to European influence".[17] The myth to which she was referring is the following which tries to explain the origin of death.

---

[14] A. Werner, *The Natives of British Central Africa,* p. 73; D. MacDonald reported a legend which in part is very similar to the one reported by A. Werner, in: D. MacDonald, *Africana,* vol. 1, pp. 296-297.

[15] J.M. Schoffeleers, "The Religious Significance of Bush Fires in Malawi", p. 274.

[16] A. Werner, *The Natives of British Central Africa,* p. 75. Cf. E.W. Smith in *African Ideas of God:* "It appears to be a very widespread notion in Africa that at the beginning God and man lived together on earth and talked one to the other, but that owing to misconduct of some sort on the part of man God deserted the earth and went to live in the sky" (p. 7).

[17] A Werner, *Myths and Legends of the Bantu,* London: Frank Cass, 1933 (new ed. 1968), p. 32.

After God had made man, He wanted to determine whether man would die or not. So God sent a chameleon *(bilimankhwe)* to tell man: "Even if you die, you shall come back to life again". Chameleon with his slow march took a long time to reach man. Some time after Chameleon had left God sent a lizard *(gulo)*[18] to tell man: "If you die, you shall die for good". *Gulo* ran very fast and delivered his message well before the Chameleon arrived. And so people began to die. Finally Chameleon arrived and delivered his message. People got angry with him because he had been so slow, and they said: "You have come too late, people have started already to die".[19]

In this myth no reason is given why God sent the second messenger, neither is there any indication that death came into the world because of man's fault. Death seems to be the outcome of bad luck. God as it were drew lots. He organized a race, and even kept *gulo* back for a time, but even then *gulo* outran the chameleon. Death as such is not a punishment for sin.

Even today people are afraid of the *gulo* because he is said to have brought the message of death. If someone happens to kill by accident, he immediately says: "I did not kill you, the wild cat did it" *(wakupha sindine, wakupha ndi mwanamanga)*. People detest the chameleon and sometimes they take revenge by trying to kill it by stuffing tobacco into its mouth.

We were told yet another myth which explains why it is that there are different groups of people, and why people misunderstand one another. However, there is again no mention of any fault of man.

Chiuta chose Kaphiri-ntiwa as the place where He would divide men. Some He sent to the north, some to the south, some to the east, and some to the west. That is why we find that people nowadays are different. There are different groups each with their own language. When *Chiuta* made man, there was no white man, no Chewa, nor Indian. They were all just men, without different languages or customs. But once *Chiuta* had divided them into groups, they started to speak different lan-

---

[18] The *gulo* is a big lizard with a blue head that runs very fast.

[19] We have heard this myth several times ourselves. It is also widely recorded. Cf. D. MacDonald, *Africana*, p. 288; D.C. Scott, *A Cyclopaedic Dictionary of the Mang'anja Language*, p. 419 (under the entry "nadzikambe"); A Werner, *The Natives of British Central Africa*, p. 72, and also in her later book *Myths and Legends of the Bantu*, p. 32.

guages, and they did not know what the other groups were doing. They did not know one another. The Chewa were sent by *Chiuta* to the east, in the plain.

We may summarize what has been said so far by stating that the Chewa believe that God is good, that good things like life, fecundity and rain come from Him. They do not appear to believe that death has entered the world as a punishment for some fault of man himself. The death of individuals, with the exception of the death of old people, illness and other evil are not attributed to God but to either angry spirits or evil men as will be seen in more detail when we deal with belief in the spirits of the dead and the subject of witchcraft and sorcery. God is called *Leza* and *Tate* and is thought of as good. The Chewa often say that they do not fear God, that there is no reason to be afraid of Him.

3. God and the Ancestors

Before we go any further we have to consider the relation between God, the spirits of the dead, and the living. The Chewa believe that just as God created the first ancestors and gave them the power to pass on life to their descendants, so also has he delegated them to look after these descendants and to chastise them if need be. The fact that God delegated the spirits to look after the living has often been interpreted as if He is not interested in them. This is to misunderstand the belief of the Chewa.

We were told that: "*Chiuta* does not look after men, but the spirits of the dead look after them. They alone look after them, their grandparents who have died, they look after them" *(Chiuta samasamala anthu, koma ndiyo mizimu imasamala anthu. Imasamala anthu ndiyo mizimu yokha, ndiyo imasamala anthu, agogo awo adafa kale, ndiwo amasamala ife anthu)*. But while we talked to them, it became clear that what they meant was that God does not look after men in the minute day-to-day affairs. The more important issues, like life and rain, He has reserved to Himself delegating to the spirits the task of caring for their living relatives in the smaller details of everyday life. It is a fact that in their daily preoccupations the people are much more concerned about the spirits of the dead and evil men than about God. They have no need to be afraid of Him, but have plenty of reasons to fear the evil that may be caused by spirits or evil men.

The spirits of the dead are also considered to be the intercessors with God for the living. One informant said:

Mulungu tikamupembedza podzera kwa mizimu ya makolo. Sitingathe kulankhula ndi Mzimu Wamkulu. Pafunika mizimu yaing'ono yamakolo athu ndiyo ikalank-hule ndi Mzimu Wamkulu amene ali Chiuta.

We pray to God through the spirits of the dead. We cannot speak directly to the Supreme Spirit. It is necessary that spirits of our deceased relatives speak to Chiuta, the Supreme Spirit

In normal daily life people observe a strict hierarchy and this seems to be carried over to their relationship with God. When a child has a problem it goes to its parents. Parents themselves go to their nkhoswe[20] and if these cannot solve the problem, to the village headman. If he cannot solve it they take it to the district chief. A higher authority is never approached if the solution can be given by a lesser one. Moreover, if they have to go to a higher authority, those lower down must accompany their dependents to the higher authority and speak in their name. Like a nkhoswe of the living the spirits of the dead speak for men to God. At the rain sacrifice the spirits of the dead are asked to intercede: "Speak for us" (mutinenere).

Man's relationship with God and the spirits of the dead was well explained by an informant: "Chiuta is Chiuta, we are only men. Chiuta is Mphambe, all is His, we are His as well. What should we do? We know that Chiuta is our Master, that He is good, that He loves His children. But the spirits are different, they bother us. We have to placate them and bring them offerings because they are difficult. They frighten us, but we do not fear Chiuta. He does not bother us, we love him. Chiuta is our father, He loves us his children. Would a child fear his father?" (Chiuta ndi Chiuta, ife ndife anthu chabe. Chiuta ndi Mphambe, zonse nzake, ifenso anthu. Titani ife? Chiuta timdziwa, ndi

---

[20] A nkhoswe is the guardian of the marriage. Husband and wive have one nkhoswe each who is expected to settle family problems.

mwini wathu. Ali wabwino, atikonda ife anthu ake, akonda ana ake. Mizimu iyayi,
itivuta. Titeta mizimu, tiipereka nsembe chifukwa ndi yovuta, yotiopsa. Chiuta iyayi,
sitimuopa, sativuta, timukonda. Chiuta ndi atate athu, atikonda ife ana ake. Kodi
mwana aopa atate?)

The Sacred Rain Forest at Dzalanyama

However the Chewa believe that in certain circumstances God punishes men directly by withholding rain when for instance a "rain snake" has been killed. When we asked: "Why would God punish men for that?" They said: "How can we, mere men, know about the heart of *Chiuta?* Has He called us to tell us His reasons? *Chiuta* is *Chiuta.* We are only men. We do not know at all the thoughts of *Chiuta,* the reasons why He would punish men. The reasons which *Chiuta* has are His reasons, we, mere men, do not know them" *(ife anthu tidziwe bwanji za mtima wa Chiuta? Kodi adatiitana ndi kutiuza zake? Chiuta ndi Chiuta. Ife tili anthu chabe. Sitidziwa konse maganizo ndi za Chiuta. Ife anthu achabe sitidziwa).* When we showed some surprise that God would be offended by things such as the killing of a "rain snake", while He did not seem to be offended by such things as incest, murder and stealing from poor people, they answered that God is indeed angry when people do such things, but that He leaves the punishment of such moral disorders to the spirits of the dead. The main reason why they believe that God does not punish individuals for immoral conduct is that God gives rain to everybody *(nanga bwanji sakutilanga, mvula amatipatsa tonsefe).* Only when the rains do not come, do they believe that God Himself intervenes to punish. We will consider these cases when speaking about the rain sacrifices.

Some illnesses, such as epilepsy or leprosy, are called "illnesses from God" *(nthenda ya Chauta).* However, this does not mean that these illnesses are seen as a punishment from God. The expression indicates rather that they are not seen as the work of sorcerers or evil spirits. It is somewhat like the English legal term: "Acts of God", i.e. things not caused by men.

We can sum up this section by saying that *Chiuta* is good. He is not believed to be the source of man's suffering. The Chewa think that God does not punish directly but that He has constituted the Spirits of the dead as guardians of the moral order. This idea will be developed in the chapter nine on the Moral Beliefs of the Chewa.

Chapter 2
Man's Recourse to God in Prayer and Sacrifice

A. Hetherwick wrote: "They approach *Chiuta* in prayer, but only at certain occasions. The ancestors occupy the centre of their field of vision."[1] This is true of public prayer. Individual prayers are often addressed to God. Like the woman, whose child had died and who said over and over again: "*Chiuta*, why did my child die?" *(Chiuta, chifukwa chiani mwana wanga adafa?)* A man facing danger was heard to say: "God, leave me alone. What have you done to me? Leave me alone" *(Leza, leke, wanditani Leza? Leke)*. Individual prayers like these are quite frequent, according to informants.

It is true, however, that public prayer is offered only on certain occasions and mainly for rain. Such prayers for rain are called *mfunde*. Recently *mfunde* was offered at the rain shrine at the Bunda Hill and also at the shrine of the sacred drum of the Chewa at Tsang'oma. These *mfunde* at a rain shrine have to be distinguished from the *mfunde* offered by an ordinary chief at the "temple hut" *(kachisi)* of his own village. First we shall consider the *mfunde* at the rain shrines. Afterwards we shall add a few words about the other *mfunde*. We were fortunate enough to be allowed to study the ritual at the shrine of the Bunda Hill in detail. We will describe it extensively because, so far as we know, no such description has yet been given. It is essential to give some details about the Nsinja shrine, since both, the shrine at the Bunda Hill and the one at Tsang'oma, stem from it.

---

[1] A. Hetherwick, *The Gospel and the African*, Edinburgh: Clark, 1932, p. 70.

1. The History of Chewa Rain Shrines

There is some controversy as to when the rain shrine at Msinja was established. S.J. Ntara followed one oral tradition according to which the shrine
was established at the time of migration of the Maravi eastwards towards
lake Malawi from their former homeland in the Luba country (in Katanga -
Zaire).[2] This migration under the first Kalonga is dated by H.W. Langworthy between 1200 and 1500, although he thinks that a date closer to 1500 is
more likely.[3]

According to S.J. Ntara the Maravi camped near Kaphiri-ntiwa when they
crossed the Dzalanyama Mountains, the frontier between Mozambique and
Malawi. When they saw the traces left on the rock by the first men, their
elders met to discuss what should be done.[4] They agreed that the place
should be consecrated for the worship of *Chiuta,* their God. They also decided that a certain *Mangadzi* should remain there as the priestess of the
shrine. *Mangadzi* was the mother-in-law of *Karonga* (she was the mother of
Mwali the headwife of *Karonga).*[5] After a while the people wanted to move
further eastwards and "to get away from the spirits".[6] *Mangadzi* stayed on at
Msinja with a few attendants. Henceforward she would be called *Makewana*
(*Make-wa-ana,* i.e. mother of children, or more often interpreted, mother of
the people).

Another oral tradition, reported by W.H.J. Rangeley, suggests that Msinja
was established during a later migration.[7] H.W. Langworthy accepted this

---

[2] Cf. S.J. Ntara, *The History of the Chewa,* (english translation of "Mbiri ya Achewa"), with a
commentary by H.W. Langworthy, Wiesbaden: Frank Steiner, 1973, pp. 3-10.

[3] H.W. Langworthy, "commentrary" in" S.J. Ntara, *The History of the Chewa,* p. 5.

[4] See above the myth of creation.

[5] S.J. Ntara, *The History of the Chewa,* p. 11.

[6] S.J. Ntara, *The History of the Chewa,* p. 10.

[7] W.H.J. Rangeley, "Makewana - the Mother of All People", in: *The Nyasaland Journal* 5
(1952), no. 2, pp. 31-50.

tradition as the more likely one.[8] *Karonga*[9] and a younger brother *Undi* were involved in succession dispute. *Undi* left the capital of *Karonga* and migrated towards *Maano,* his new capital in present-day Zambia sometime during the mid 1500's, taking with him most of his and *Karonga's* family. During this migration, *Undi* left a number of his relatives as chiefs along the way. He is also reported to have established a priestess, *Makewana,* at Msinja to be in charge of the rain shrine and of the spiritual centre of *Undi's* kingdom. *Undi* probably stayed there for a time himself.[10] Msinja with the *Makewana* became one of the most important religious forces in his kingdom, a symbol of his power and a stimulus to unity. On his departure from Msinja, *Undi* wanted to leave a trusted chief in the area to protect *Makewana* and to look after his interests there. He appointed *Chinsera* to this position of senior chief and protector of Msinja and *Makewana.* By the time the last *Chinsera* died, *Makewana* had established her control over the succession to this position and she directed that a certain *Kalikwikwiti* be the successor of *Chinsera.* She changed his name to *Chadza* (from *kudza* i.e. to come) because he had come to Msinja. The present incumbent to this chieftaincy is *Chadza Kwenda.*[11]

J.M. Schoffeleers presented a third theory.[12] The Kaphiri-ntiwa shrine belongs to the proto-Chewa period. The actual Chewa consist of two main groups, the *Phiri* and the *Banda.* It is now generally assumed, so J.M. Schoffeleers, that the *Phiri* came to Malawi in the course of the fourteenth century.[13] The Proto-Chewa on the contrary, are to be associated with the *Banda.* This theory in its rudimentary form was first proposed by R.A. Ham-

---

[8] H.W. Langworthy, "A History of Undi's Kingdom to 1890", PhD, Boston University, 1969; p. 184; Cf. as well H.W. Langworthy, *Zambia before 1980. Aspects of Precolonial History,* London: Longman, 1972.

[9] The name *Karonga* became a title and passed on to the successors of the first *Karonga.*

[10] H.W. Langworthy, "A History of Undi's Kingdom to 1890", p. 186.

[11] It is from him that we received permission to study the rain shrine.

[12] J.M. Schoffeleers, "The Chisumphi and M'Bona Cults in Malawi. A Comparative History". Paper read at the Conference on the History of Central African Religious Systems, Lusaka, August 31 to September 8, 1972.

[13] J.M. Schoffeleers, "Towards the Identification of a Proto-Chewa Culture", in: *Journal of Social Studies* 2 (1973), pp. 47-60.

ilton who related a dual tradition of origin to a dual population component.[14] According to him the Chewa possessed a well-known myth

Kachisi - The Temple Hut for Rain Sacrifices

describing their creation at a place known as Kaphiri-ntiwa, while at the same time another tradition ascribed their origin to a country to the north. He resolved this apparent contradiction by assigning the creation myth to a population of autochthones and the migration myth to a group of royal invaders. M.G. Marwick developed this theme by relating the distinction between autochthones and invaders to a division of functions.[15] The Banda, taken to represent the autochthones, were accredited with ritual power, particularly in the field of rain making, whereas the Phiri, representing the invaders, possessed secular authority.

The Kaphiri-ntiwa shrine came to play such an important role in the later *Phiri* states *(Karonga* and *Undi)*, that it is not surprising that we should find a number of oral traditions which ascribe the foundation of the shrine to the initiative of the *Phiri*. However, recent research suggests that at the time of the *Phiri* conquest, there were already shrines in existence, which recognized Kaphiri-ntiwa as their centre. In every case the keepers of the shrine were also regarded as secular rulers. When the *Phiri* came to power, they tried to extend their influence over these shrines.

---

[14] R.A. Hamilton, "Oral Tradition: Central Africa", in: D.H. Jones, *History and Archaeology in Africa*, 1959, p. 220.

[15] M.G. Marwick, "History and Tradition in East Central Africa", in: *Journal of African History* 4 (1963), p. 378.

There is no doubt that under *Undi* the shrine entered a period of consider-able prosperity. It was probably then that the shrine was moved from the hills to the plain below because in the hills there was a lack of arable land to support the increasing number of officials at the shrine. The shrine re-mained independent in principle but in fact it was only with the cooperation of the *Phiri* kings that tribute could be collected and that protection was as-sured. In turn the Msinja shrine enhanced the status of the kingdom and acted as an effective unifying factor for the Chewa.[16]

In 1867, Livingstone found Msinja in a very poor state. It had been ran-sacked some time before by the *Ngoni*. The sacred drum had been taken to Msekere in Mozambique for safe keeping. In the 1870's the shrine was once more sacked by the *Ngoni*. The drum was once more taken to safety to a place now called Tsang'oma where it gave rise to a new shrine.[17] The shrine at Msinja was restored to its original site in the hills, safe from the raids of the Ngoni. However, *Makewana* had attached herself to the shrine of *Tsang'oma,* where the sacred drum was kept. The shrine at Msinja never re-covered its former pre-eminence. It still has a *kachisi*, but it has become a centre for local people only. The rain cult was split between local shrines which had no other common bond than that of their common history.[18]

J.M. Schoffeleers makes the point that the most notable development in the last half-century was the adoption by some headmen of the role of the for-mer female rain makers.[19] This we see both at the Bunda Shrine and at the *Tsang'oma* shrine. The last female *Makewana* died around 1920 at *Tsang'oma.* In 1948 there was a severe drought and plans were made to elect a new *Makewana.* It was a nephew of the last *Makewana* who was chosen; he was installed on 3rd Sept 1955. The shrine at Msinja was rebuilt. The full resto-ration of the Msinja shrine failed because of a lack of co-operation on the

---

[16] For a detailed description of the cult at Msinja, see W.H.J. Rangeley, "Makewana - the Mother of All People", pp. 31-50.

[17] About 10 miles south west of the Bunda Hill.

[18] They told us at the Bunda Shrine: *Tonsefe tili ana a mai mmodzi* (We are all children of the same mother).

[19] J.M. Schoffeleers, "The Chisumphi and M'Bona Cults in Malawi", p. 12.

side of the keepers of "the sacred drum" and the chiefs, who were more interested in continuing the local shrines. All that is now left to the traditional cult is the shrine of the "sacred drum of the Chewa" at *Tsang'oma*, the one at Bunda Hill and the remnant of a shrine at Msinja. The present *Makewana* is Mr *Lorenti Makewana* of Chikuntha village, T.A. Chiseka.[20]

2. Rain Prayers at Bunda [21]

In order to study the rain cult at the Bunda Hill shrine we had to obtain permission from chief *Chadza Kwenda*. He is regarded as the "owner" *(mwini)* of the shrine. The fact that the *Chadza* chiefs were the protectors of the Msinja rain shrine gives a certain authenticity to the Bunda cult. When we asked the dignitaries at Bunda when rain sacrifices were first offered at Bunda, the only answer we could get was *kalekale* (a long time ago). In view of the fact that a human sacrifice was offered at Bunda we can put the beginning of the rain shrine before the advent of colonial administration.

There are two different ceremonies in the yearly rain ritual at Bunda Hill: (a) the bush is ritually burnt on the hill in the month of August, and (b) in Feb-

---

[20] Information obtained from Fr. R. Saffroy who knows him personally.

[21] The information concerning the rain cult at the Bunda Hill I received personally from the chiefs of the shrine. After obtaining permission from Chief Chadza Kwenda I had several lengthy interviews with these chiefs during the months of March, April and May 1976. On the first occasion there was a meeting with these chiefs that lasted a whole day. Present were chiefs Chawowa, Kamundi and Mtenje as personal representatives of *Chadza Kwenda*. Together with them were chiefs *Mwenda I, Chipambwe, Chiseka, Katakata, Mbuna, Mwenda II, Jazele Chombwe* representing *Chilowa*, and *Kamzati*. After this meeting I had several others with individual chiefs. Since I obtained the permission of *Chadza Kwenda* only in March, it was too late to assist at the *mfunde* in February. However, in that first solemn meeting everything was explained in detail. This was considered such a sacred meeting that I had to wear black clothes and take off my shoes, which is the requirement for the *mfunde* itself. Prayers were said and rain songs sung. This meeting was considered so closely linked with the *mfunde* itself, that at a certain moment people protested, accusing the chiefs of acting very wrongly; namely of praying for rains whereas there had been actually too much rain already so that the maize was rotting in the fields. I also had to offer a black hen to be sacrificed in order to atone for my presence (white skin) at the meeting. At another occasion I was told to put black mud on my face and arms.

ruary a rain sacrifice is offered if by then the rains have not yet fallen in sufficient quantity.

a) The Ritual Burning of the Bunda Hill

When the bush is completely dry in August,[22] *Chilowa* calls all the chiefs of the Bunda Shrine together at the house of *Mwenda*[23] to fix with them the date for the ritual burning of the bush. *Chadza Kwenda* is informed when the date has been fixed. The chiefs who have to be present at any such meeting are *Mwenda, Chilowa, Chipambwe, Katakata, Ching'oma, Kum'chenzi, Mliwu, Kan'chole. Jazele Chombwe,* although not a chief, has to be present as a kind of master of ceremonies. All these chiefs live around the Bunda Hill, which stands as a rather solitary hill in the midst of a vast plain.

Taboos for the chiefs involved

Chief *Chadza Kwanda* is recognized as the "owner" *(mwini)* of the shrine and he has to be kept informed of whatever happens there although he is never present at any actual meeting. During the ceremony of the burning of the bush and of the rain sacrifice *Chadza* has to stay indoors together with his wives. He has to do so under pain of "spoiling the ritual" *(kudula miyambo)* and risking causing a drought. *Mwenda,* who is the personal permanent representative of *Chadza* at the shrine, has also to stay indoors with his wife during the ceremonies, but he presides at the other meetings. The reason given by the chiefs for this was the following: *Mwenda* has to stay indoors till the one he has sent comes back. *Chilowa* is the one who is sent to pray to *Chisumphi* in the name of *Chadza* and *Mwenda. Chadza* has to stay indoors while *Chilowa,* in the name of *Chadza,* brings the sacrifice or burns the bush. They explained this by saying that *Chadza* has become like *Makewana,* the

---

[22] The rainy season is from the middle of December to April. May to the middle of August is the cool season. From the middle of August to the middle of December is the hot season. The hot season sets in rather abruptly and it is about this time that they burn the Bunda Hill.

[23] Really we should say *Mwenda I.* This is because there is another chief *Mwenda,* who is called *Mwenda II.*

priestess at Msinja. *Makewana* sends *Kamundi* to bring the sacrifice in her name. Now *Chilowa* is like *Kamundi*.

At this point it may be enlightening to report that there was another rain priest in the past. *Chauwa* of Chirenje also had to remain at home while his deputy alone performed the ritual. According to Hodgson: "Chauwa could not himself partake, as he was the director of the sacrifice".[24] We suggest the following explanation. Neither *Makewana*, nor *Chauwa*, nor *Chadza* is allowed to take part in the sacrifice and other rituals, but has to send somebody to represent them, because they are the titulars of the shrine and in the past such people were called *Chauta*, representing God the Supreme Rain-giver. These *Chauta* wore their hair long, symbolizing the rain-clouds. Their clothes had to be black instead of white, the colour of the cloudless sky, and red, the colour of fire, colours that were considered incompatible with praying for rain. The red of the bush fire and of the blood of the sacrifice had to be kept away from their sight for fear of causing the opposite effect. Even today the rain priests are identified with the rains to such an extent that red and white would have an adverse effect on them and through them on the rains.

Some other examples of the incompatibility of red and white and rain-making are the following. When there is too much rain, a white feather is planted on top of the *kachisi* (temple hut) to stop the rain. If afterwards rain is needed again, a black feather replaces the white one. When we wanted to see the "sacred drum" at *Tsang'oma* we had to take off our brown shoes and a reddish shirt. The colour of our car was red and we had to leave it far away. Otherwise "the rain would not come".

The repairing of the shrine *(kachisi)*

Before the day fixed of the ritual burning of the bush, the *kachisi*[25] has to be repaired in case it was damaged during the rainy season.[26] It is a small round

---

[24] A.G.O. Hodgson, "Notes on the Achewa and Angoni of the Dowa District of the Nyasaland Protectorate", in: *Journal of the Royal Anthropological Institute* 63 (1933), pp. 154-155.

[25] Some authors translate *kachisi* by "spirit house". In the context of the rain sacrifice, we prefer the word "temple" because the cult is directed to *Chiuta* and not only to the spirits.

hut, with doors opening towards the north, the south, the east and the west (because *Chiuta* is everywhere). The size of the *kachisi* is roughly that of a small hut in the village. The walls are made of poles and branches and the roof is thatched with dry grass. Before repairing the *kachisi* or cleaning around it, people first sit down and say a prayer: "We have come to prepare the place" *(tabwera kukonza malo)*. Normally the roof is made in the following way. A pole is planted in the soil and a framework of bamboo and branches is made with the pole as a support. Once it is ready the whole roof is lifted up and placed on the walls of the house and then thatched with grass. In the case of a roof for the *kachisi*, no pole is used as a support, but the roof is made over the head of a person. The following explanation was given for this custom. In the past they used to kill a young girl about 10-12 years old as a human sacrifice to *Chiuta*. Her body was placed in an upright position and the roof was built over her head. Even today the *kachisi* at Bunda is called *nyumba tsano* (the house of the tomb).

However, when the Colonial Administration heard of this, they said: "You should not do that, you should not kill one another. Why don't you use a living person and make him sit down and make the roof over his head". The elders thought this over and finally agreed to try it. Chief *Chiseka* suggested a certain *Kasewa*. He was chosen to take the place of the girl. He had to kneel down and have the roof build over his head. At his death this office passed on to chief *Kum'chenzi*. Until today that is how it is done.[27] When the *kachisi* has been repaired its surroundings are carefully cleaned so that the bush fire cannot reach it. If the *kachisi* happened to be burnt down by the bush fires, a disaster would ensue.[28]

The ritual of setting fire to the bush on Bunda Hill

---

[26] Recently it was suggested that it be made in more durable material.

[27] This detail about the killing of the young girl in sacrifice before the advent of the colonial administration allows us to date the Bunda cult before the beginning of the British administration.

[28] The *kachisi* at Msinji was found burnt down in August 1975. The chief who accompanied us was very angry about this and said that the rain might not come this year.

On the day fixed for the ritual burning of the bush on Bunda Hill, all the chiefs mentioned earlier assemble in the house of chief *Mwenda*. They all sit on the floor in a circle with their legs stretched out in the traditional way during a sacrifice. In the middle of their circle is a piece of a broken pot with some snuff *(fodya osira)* which has been prepared by *Mwenda* himself and which will be taken to the *kachisi* to be offered there. *Mwenda* sends them officially to the *kachisi* to perform the ritual there. Only the chiefs, with *Jazele Chombwe*, go to the *kachisi*. They sit round the *kachisi*, with their legs stretched out in front of them. *Chilowa* starts the prayer:

> Ha, please, *Chauta, Leza, Chisumphi, Mphambe, Namalenga,* we your children have come to set fire to the bush. We do not want the fire to do any harm. NN[29] if you have all come here together we are very pleased. Help us. Do not be surprised that we are making a bit of noise, we are your children. Thank you very much *(Ha, zikomo, Chauta, Leza, Chisumphi, Mphambe, Namalenga, tabwera ife ana anu kuti tiotche tchire lija. Tsono tikana kuti moto ungaononge. NN, ngati nonse mwasonkhana ife tikondwera ndithu. Tithandizeni. Ndipo musadabwe phokoso limene tili kuchita pano ndife ana anu. Ai zikomo ndithu).*

The Ritual Burning of Bunda Hill

After this prayer the new fire is made in the following manner. A *mpheko* is taken, i.e. two pieces of wood, of which the larger piece has a hole in it. The second one is like a stick which is turned and twirled in the hole until a spark is produced. No other fire is allowed on this occasion; matches, a lighter, or fire taken from the village are excluded. This *mpheko* is a sacred one for which chief *Chiseka* is responsible. It is the duty of chief *Mliwu* to get the *mpheko* and bring it with him, to start the fire and

---

[29] They insert here the names of some deceased chiefs.

to set the bush alight. When the fire begins to spread up the hill, everybody is happy. They gesture with their hands upwards towards the top of the hill shouting at the same time: "Go up, *Chibungu" (kwerani Chibungu)*. *Chibungu* is a deceased chief. They pray to his spirit to watch the fire and see to it that it burns the hill.

When the chiefs are sure that the fire is burning well and spreading up the hill, they all go back to *Mwenda's* house to make a report on how things went. At the door of the house is a large pot of water. They take water and throw it at one another, imitating the rain. Then all return to their homes. *Mwenda* and *Chadza* may leave their house towards the evening when the *nkhungulupsya* (burnt pieces of straw etc. flying in the air during a bush fire) have subsided.

Meaning of the ritual

What is the meaning of this burning of Bunda Hill? One answer given to us was that it is to clean the hill which is like the altar of the rain sacrifice. The normal method of cleaning a stretch of land is by burning the bush. A.G.O. Hodgson gives us the description of the sacrifices of *Chauwa* offered at the side of Chirenje Hill. The people still remember that sacrifices were offered at Chirenje.[30] They have been abandoned for many years now, and we have been unable to find anyone who could give us the details of the ritual. It is interesting to note that when we questioned people as to the reason why they had stopped offering rain sacrifices at Chirenje and elsewhere we were always given the same answer: "They pray for us at Bunda Hill, that is enough". The description given by A.G.O. Hodgson is curiously complicated, and it looks as if two distinct rituals were mixed and given as one. In his description we find successively the following points:

1) There was a special stretch of bush that was not burnt with the rest of the bush.
2) When *Chauwa* was about to offer a rain sacrifice he sent messengers to call the people to that stretch of bush on a fixed day.

---

[30] A.G.O. Hodgson, "Notes on the Achewa and Angoni", pp. 154f.

3) These messengers gave each village headman a maize cob with red grains to symbolize the blood of the game about to be killed.
4) *Chauwa's* deputy took a black goat and cut its throat, pouring its blood on the water of the pond.
5) *Chauwa* himself stayed in his house the whole time.
6) The deputy prayed to God that rain might fall as soon as the stretch of bush had been burnt.
7) On the day fixed the hunters assembled at the stretch of bush with their bows and arrows.
8) *Chauwa's* deputy alone was allowed to burn the bush.
9) The very bush was surrounded by the hunters so that no animal could escape.
10) Such was the reputation of *Chauwa* that rain always fell before sunset on the same day.

We think that we have two different rituals here. One of them the burning of the bush in order that rain may fall: Nos. 1, 2, 4, 5, 6, 8, 10. The other is the ritual to ensure the killing of game: Nos. 3, 7, and 9. The ritual of the burning of the bush resembles very much the ritual burning of the bush on the Bunda Hill. If we take the text as it is given by Hodgson, we find no explanation why and how the killing of game is connected with the calling of rain. If, then, we take the text of the burning of the bush by itself we have a ritual which is much the same as the one actually performed at Bunda. The only difference is that Chauwa had the bush burnt at the moment he was praying for rain, while in Bunda the bush is burnt 6 months before the rain sacrifice. The suggestion of J.M Schoffeleers, that the burning of the bush is a symbolic act, imitating black rain clouds, is perfectly acceptable in the case of Chirenje.[31] Less so in the case of the Bunda Hill, since an interval of many months will elapse before the rains. There is however a definite connection with rain calling, because at the end of the ritual the chiefs throw water at each other, an act symbolizing rain. Could it be that the basic incompatibility of fire and rain led to the performance of

---

[31] J.M. Schoffeleers, "The Religious Significance of Bush Fires in Malawi", in: *Cahiers des Religions Africaines* 10 (1971), p. 275; reprint in: J.M. Schoffeleers, *Religion and the Dramatisation of Life. Spirit Beliefs and Rituals in Southern and Central Malawi*, Blantyre: CLAIM, 1997, pp. 22ff.

these two rituals at distinct moments of the year? The ritual burning of the bush the Bunda is regarded as the ritual cleaning of a sacred place. If anybody else than the officials of the shrine were to cause fire to spread to the hill, this, they believe, would call down the wrath of *Chisumphi* and cause a drought. Such a person would have to offer two goats, a black one to be killed in a sacrifice of atonement, and the other of any colour to be given as a fine to *Chadza*, the "owner" *(mwini)* of the Bunda Hill rain shrine complex.

When the rains are late, the chiefs come together and try to find the person who set fire to Bunda Hill. When we asked the chiefs whether in such a case someone is always believed to have set fire to Bunda Hill, they answered that there could be no other reason for the rains being late. The Bunda Hill can only be cleaned ritually. Now we can understand the real meaning of the prayer of *Chilowa:* "We do not want the fire to do any harm", meaning: to the rains *(tikana kuti moto ungaononge)*. People never set fire to holy places, such as grave yards. On the contrary they take care that bush fires do not come near them. Why then has the Bunda Hill to be burnt? Why is the bush not allowed to grow there, like at those other sacred places? It would appear that it is because if it were allowed to grow there, bush fires might spread to it, with disastrous consequences.

Taboos related to the ritual

The hair of Chilowa must not be cut

Like *Makewana* at Msinja, chief *Chilowa,* the deputy of *Chadza,* in both the ritual of the burning of the bush on the Bunda and of the rain sacrifice itself, is not allowed to cut his hair.[32] Other rainmakers *(chisumphi)* also wear long hair and, when they dance and spin round, their hair stands up like "a rain cloud". In fact, the hair of *Chilowa* symbolises, we were told, the rain-clouds round the Bunda Hill *(tsitsi la Chilowa lili longa mitambo yakuda pa phiri)*.

---

[32] Cf. W.H.J. Rangeley, "Makewana - the Mother of All People", p. 33. *Makewana* never cut her hair because it was believed that she controlled the rain, and that, by analogy, if she cut her hair she would "cut the rain".

Chilowa is allowed to cut his hair only once a year at the time the Bunda is set fire to.

The safe time to burn the bush at Bunda is in August when the cold season, during which some light rain may still fall (called *chiperoni*), is over. In August the hot season begins during which rain never falls. At such a time the fire can do no harm to the rains, whereas to wait till later could be risky because the people start putting fire to the bush with the danger that such a fire might spread to the Bunda. Similarly it is safe then to cut the hair of *Chilowa*, which is like the rain-clouds round the Bunda, since at that time there are no rain-clouds round the Bunda. To cut the hair at another time would be tantamount to removing the rain-clouds and result in "cutting the rain" *(kudula mvula)*.

Taboo on sexual relations

Since the burning of the bush on the Bunda Hill marks the end of the rainy season, the sexual taboos imposed on the main dignitaries of the rain shrine, *Chadza, Mwenda,* and *Chilowa* are lifted at that same time. These chiefs, in effect, are not allowed to have sexual intercourse with their wives throughout the rainy season (from beginning of December till after the burning of the Bunda Hill). If they have intercourse, they are said to "destroy the effect of the rain ritual" *(kudula miyambo)*. Such a transgression of the taboo is looked upon as very serious indeed: "If they do it, they do very wrong. Something really very wrong will then have happened" *(akachita walakwa, pali kanthu ndithu kamene kanalakwika)*.

What is the reason for this taboo on sexual relations? To find the answer we have to go back to the customs at Msinja (the mother shrine). *Makewana* was not allowed to be married, since she was considered the "wife of *Chisumphi*" (priestess of *Chisumphi)*. However, since she was also considered as the chief of the area, she had as such to complete the initiation ritual of girls by an act of ritual intercourse with *Kamundi*. This act of ritual intercourse by a chief is considered necessary to "open the womb of the young women".[33] However, since *Makewana* was not allowed to be married, this ritual intercourse with Kamundi was referred to as "a snake who entered into her house". Neither *Makewana* nor *Kamundi* was supposed to be at that moment like normal human beings and each was well wrapped up, so that neither could see the other.[34] Kamundi was referred to as a python *(nsato)*. This was the only occasion that *Kamundi* was allowed to have intercourse with *Makewana*, who was said to be "without sex".[35]

The role of *Makewana* is taken over, as it were, by *Chadza*. For the interdiction of marriage is substituted the interdiction of sexual relationships. Chief *Chadza*, and his two delegates, *Mwenda* and *Chilowa*, are not allowed to have intercourse during the whole of the rainy season. During this time they are in a special relationship with *Chisumphi* as the priests of his shrine. Sexual activity is considered mysterious and dangerous (hot),[36] and as such it has to be kept separate from praying for rain lest sexual activity destroy the effect of the rain sacrifice. These chiefs, we were told, "do not want to perform these important duties at one and the same time, because such important things cannot go together. They are afraid that then one might destroy the other" *(amfumu aja safuna kuphatikiza udindo waukulu pa nthawi imodzi chifukwa zinthu zazikulu-zikulu sizingathe kuyendera pamodzi, chifukwa amaopa kuti zingathe kuononga)*. At the meeting in which we were given explanations about the rain shrine, chief *Mwenda* had the lower part of his body covered with a black cloth, as a symbol that he had to abstain from sexual relations.

Chiefs *Chadza*, *Mwenda* and *Chilowa* are also *eni mzinda*[37] and as such they must complete the girl's initiation with ritual intercourse. That is why *Chilowa* "must have ritual intercourse with his wife the night after the burning of the Bunda, but not at another time (i.e. before that time). If he does,

---

[33] We shall consider the ritual of the girls' initiation in chapter six *(mdulo)*.

[34] W.H.J. Rangeley, "Makewana - the Mother of All People", p. 33.

[35] Ibid. p. 36.

[36] The concept of "hot" will be considered in chapter six *(mdulo)*.

[37] *Mwini mzinda* is a chief who has the right of a *mzinda* (right to have Nyau and the girls' solemn initiations).

he would destroy the effect of the rain ritual. This is our custom" *(achilowa ayenera kuchita banja tsiku loti aotcha Bunda, koma pa nthawi ina iyayi, atachita wadula kachisi chifukwa ndi miyambo ndithu).* As *Chilowa* is regarded as the successor of *Kamundi* who had to have ritual intercourse with *Makewana* at the girls' initiation, he has now to perform this ritual by having intercourse with his wife. But the first night he can do so safely is after the ritual burning of the Bunda. Before that he would "destroy the effect of the rain ritual". After he has perfomed this ritual intercourse, *Chadza* and *Mwenda* may resume normal intercourse with their wives.

None of the other chiefs around the Bunda Hill are allowed to have the ceremonies of the girls' initiation with the required act of ritual intercourse until after *Chilowa* has had ritual intercourse.[38] But they are not forbidden to have intercourse with their wives during the rainy season. Since the effect of the rain sacrifice would be destroyed if anybody had intercourse with his wife on the night before the sacrifice, everyone is required to spend that night in the open outside *Chilowa's* house. Only young children are allowed to go with the chiefs to the *kachisi* to offer the sacrifice. All this points to the incompatibility of sexual activity and rain sacrifice.

Taboos on Nyau

The solemn dances of the *Nyau* are also forbidden in the villages around the Bunda during this same period (December until the burning of the Bunda Hill). Chief *Chadza* himself may not even look at *Nyau* dances at any time of the year.[39] The reason for this interdiction is that the *Nyau* dances are also considered incompatible with praying for rain, because, as we were told: "They sing about life and the life-giving power of men" *(Nyau zimaimba makamaka za moyo ndi mphamvu ya anthu). Nyau* and *Mfunde* (rain sacrifice) cannot take place at the same time" *(Nyau ndi mfunde sizingathe kutuluka nthawi imodzi).*

---

[38] Namely the chiefs *Chapambwe, Katakata, Ching'oma, Kum'chenzi, Kan'chole, Mwase, Mula, Kansinsi, Nsulubwa, Cheletsa, Mthiko,* and *Chatenga.*

[39] W.H. Rangeley, "Makewana - the Mother of All People", p. 34.

The burning of the Bunda appears to be the turning point in the annual cycle. It marks the definite end of the rainy season. Until then some light rain may fall. During the ritual burning of the Bunda no songs are sung and a few chiefs only go to the *kachisi*. Nobody else is allowed to accompany them. It is to be noted that the ritual burning of the bush on the Bunda Hill is done every year, whereas the rain sacrifice itself is done only if the rains do not come that year.

b) The Rain Sacrifice at the Bunda Shrine

After the chiefs have performed carefully the ritual of the burning of the bush on the Bunda Hill, they wait to see the outcome. If the rains are late, they delay any action until January. If by the end of January rain has still not fallen, *Chilowa* invites the chiefs to come together at *Mwenda's* house.

Their first task is to try to find the culprit who set fire to the bush on the Bunda, who will be fined two goats. *Mwenda* takes these two goats to *Chadza* and informs him who is the culprit. He then goes to *Chilowa* taking the black goat with him. He sprinkles it with water and smears mud on its back when he passes the pool *(dambo)* halfway between his and *Chilowa's* village. When the chiefs have decided on the date for the sacrifice they have to inform *Chadza*. In the meantime they see whether the *kachisi* needs any repairs. If the roof of the *kachisi* is in a bad state, they do not make a new one as they do in August, because at this time of the year no dry grass is available. They go to the village of Katakata where *Chilowa* simply chooses a roof. This is lifted from the house and carried to the *kachisi* to the accompaniment of rain songs. The owner of the house has no right to protest.

People are told to bring maize flour and malt *(chimera)* to the village of *Chilowa* so that sufficient food and *phala* (thin, non fermented maize porridge) can be prepared for the people who will be coming for the ceremony. The evening before the day fixed for the *mfunde* all the people come together at the village of *Chilowa*. There everybody, men and women, have to sleep out in the open. Nobody is allowed to sleep in his house, as has been said, because he would at once be suspected of having intercourse with his wife which is forbidden that evening. Should anyone break this interdiction,

the effect of the sacrifice would be destroyed and no rain would fall *(mvula si-*
ngathe kubwera, angaipitse chipembedzo). There are special songs to remind the people of this interdiction. The following is an example:

Mawa kuli mfunde	Tomorrow is the *mfunde* (3x)
tengani mbolo muyike pa denga	take your penis and put it on the roof
mawa kuli mfunde	tomorrow is the *mfunde*
mawa kuli mfunde	tomorrow is the *mfunde*

The whole night they sing and throw water at each other. Nobody is supposed to get angry when being splashed with water. Everybody is expected to be in a good mood and at peace with everyone else. This is a condition for their prayer to be heard.

Next morning very early, *Chilowa, Kum'chenzi, Ching'oma, Katakata, Chipambwe* go to the *kachisi*, together with some children, boys and girls, aged from 7 to 11 years and one or two old women, well beyond child-bearing age, who will prepare the food to be sacrificed. All the others stay in the village, singing and chanting. The womenfolk start preparing food and *phala* in readiness for the party's return from the *kachisi*. On their way to the *kachisi* the chiefs who take the black goat with them, sing rain songs while the children clap their hands and the girls produce the shrill shouts of joy called *nthungululu*. Upon arrival all sit down in a circle round the *kachisi* with their legs stretched out before them. From this moment until the end of the ceremony nobody is supposed to scratch himself or chase away a mosquito, or catch a flea. The children have to stay quiet without talking or moving around. This is the way they show respect. *Chilowa* makes the following prayer:

> Please, *Chisumphi, Leza,* pardon, *Namnjiri,* pardon, *Mphambe,* pardon, we have come to beg you, pardon, see how the people are dying with hunger, pardon, *Chauta,* pardon, *Chisumphi,* pardon, *Mangadzi,* pardon, your children are dying because they have no rain, pardon. Please give us rain today *(Ambira, Achimpsera, pardon, Asikupikana, Akululukuchenjera* [NN. people who have died - spirits of former chiefs], pardon, help us, your children, by obtaining for us rain, we are dying, pardon. Ha, the children

are dying, give us rain please, pardon, *Chauta, Namalenga,* help us, pardon).

(Zikomo, Chisumphi, Leza, pepa, Namnjiri, pepa, Mphambe, pepa, tabwera kudzadandaula, pepa, taonani anthu akutha ndi njala, pepa, Chauta, pepa, Chisumphi, pepa, Mangadzi, pepa, ana anu akutha chifukwa chosowa mvula, pepa. Tikuti mutipatse mvula lero, pepa, Ambira, Achimpsera, pepa, Asikupikana, Akululukuchenjera, pepa, thandizani ana anufe pakutigwetsera mvula, tikutha, pepa, ha, ana akutha, tipatseni mvula ndithu, pepa, Chauta, Namalenga, tithandizeni, pepa).

While *Chilowa* is saying this prayer, the other chiefs and the children continually repeat *pepa* in a low tone, while slowly clapping their hands. They also invoke the spirits of some deceased, asking them to intercede for them with *Chiuta.* All wear black, the colour of the rain-clouds. As a mark of respect they have taken off shoes or sandals. In the meantime back in his house *Mwenda* sits wrapped all in black, because he is the priest of the sacrifice *(wa ku nsembe).*

After the initial prayer *Chilowa* kills the black goat, cutting its throat with a special sacrificial knife. This is a very old knife about 15 cm long, in the shape of a lance with two blades, with a wooden handle devoid of all carvings. It is normally kept in a secret place in *Chilowa's* house. The blood of the goat is caught in a small pot held by the old women. This pot is of earthenware and made by *Mlinga,* one of the wives of *Chadza.* It is kept in the *kachisi* and can serve several years. If it is broken, *Mlinga* has to make another one. The blood is used to cook the maize porridge *(nsima)* which will be offered in the *kachisi.* Normally *nsima* is prepared with water. Together with the *nsima* some meat is also offered. *Chilowa* cuts small pieces from various parts of the goat. This meat is cooked by the old women and when ready it is placed in a *phale* (piece of broken pot). *Chilowa, Katakata, Kum'chenzi, Ching'oma, Chipambwe,* and *Jazele Chombwe,* come forward to receive the offerings. They take them into the *kachisi* and place them in a pot that is buried in the soil, with the top of the pot level with the ground. They leave the offerings there so that the spirits may accept and eat them. It is interesting to note that they offer the food to the spirits of the deceased that they may intercede for them with *Chiuta (kuti mizimu ya makolo ikamwa nd. kudya iwapepesere kwa Chiuta).*

When the chiefs leave the *kachisi*, *Chilowa* tells those present to make a fire and to roast the goat without skinning it. The fire is made with a *mpheko* as described earlier. When the meat is ready, people tear it to pieces with their hands, for they are not allowed to use a knife. Each one sees to it that he gets a piece and each must finish it quickly. If someone finishes before the others, he can take another piece or even snatch one from someone else. They have to finish the meat there and then. They eat it together with the skin and intestines. Only the bones may be thrown away. Nothing should be brought back to the village or buried. This way of eating is a symbolic act, an appeal to *Chiuta*: they are starving because the drought has brought famine to the land.

J.P. Bruwer had noticed the same way of eating a sacrificial meal: "They all started struggling to get a shred according to the customary method of eating sacrificial meat. The meat was not divided but each person simply broke off a piece. If one was slow in finishing his bit, the other immediately snatched it from his hands".[40]

When they have finished eating they all sit down once more round the *kachisi* for a final prayer. *Chilowa* says:

> *Chauta, Leza, Chisumphi, Mphambe*, please, give us rain. Our throats are dry, we are your children. We need water, we die with hunger. The crops are spoiled. Give us rain. Help us! We go now *(Zikomo. Mutipatse Mvula, ku khosi kwauma, ife ana anu. Tikufuna madzi, tikufa ndi njala. Mbeu zaonongeka. Mutipatse mvula. Tithandizeni. Tapita).*

As before, all assistants say repeatedly *pepa* and clap their hands. Clapping and singing is continued on their way back to the village. Nobody is allowed to look back. They go first to the village of *Mwenda*, at the door of whose house stands a large pot with water. He comes out of his house and sprinkles everybody with water. Afterwards all those who assisted at the cere-

---

[40] J.P. Bruwer, "Remnants of a Rain Cult among the Chewa," *African Studies* 2 (1952), p. 179.

mony sprinkle each other. From *Mwenda* they go to the village of *Chipambwe* where the same ceremony is repeated. They then return to the village of *Chilowa* where the same ritual is again repeated. Everybody throws water indiscriminately on grown-ups and children alike. Nobody gets angry. At *Chilowa* they find food and gruel *(phala)*, but beer *(mowa)* is not allowed. If the ceremony is carried out well, rain is sure to fall. It may fall while they are still at the *kachisi* or on the way back, in which case nobody runs away or takes shelter, for they are too happy and proud that their prayers for rain have been heard.

Their belief in the power of the ritual is very strong. It is remarkable that whenever they talk about rain sacrifice, they always add that rain came either at the *kachisi* or during their return to the village or as soon as they arrived at the village. This is always the final sentence of any story about rain sacrifices.

If there is too much rain, another ritual takes place. The chiefs go to the *kachisi* where they strip some of the grass off the roof and plant on top of it a white feather of a hen. Then the rains stop and there will be a break. If they want the rain to fall again, they go back to the *kachisi* to remove the white feather replacing it by a black one. The rains will start again. At these occasions they make a short prayer asking *Leza* to be kind and patient with them.

3. The Rain Sacrifice at Tsang'oma

The following is a description of the rain sacrifice at Tsang'oma. This information we received when we visited the shrine of the "sacred drum of the Chewa" in September 1975. On this occasion we met the dignitaries of the shrine: *Tsang'oma* (the keeper of the shrine), *Malemia, Kamundi, Kumsanja, Kubzikho* and *Kampini.* All these are successors to the various officials of Msinja.[41]

---

[41] A description of these officials at Msinja was given by W.H.J. Rangeley, "Makewana - the Mother of All People", pp. 37-48.

Tsang'oma calls the people together whenever there is a drought *(chilala)*. The people are asked to bring malt *(chimera)* with them. Young girls have to pound and to fetch water for the ceremony. The next morning at sunrise the dignitaries assemble and leave together for the *kachisi*, followed by children only. The *kachisi* is built in a thicket not far from the village; it is made with walls of stamped mud and a grass roof. It is about 1,5 m high and about as wide. It is big enough to allow two men to sit in it. Arrived at the *kachisi*, all kneel down and clap their hands. Then the following prayer is said:

> *Chisumphi* we have come, because our land is dried up. We have come, *Chauta, Chisumphi, Mphambe,* to pray here for rain. Have pity on us that our children may not die *(Chisumphi, tabwera ife, malinga monga ku dziko kwathu kwauma. Tabwera, Chauta, Chisumphi, Mphambe, tabwera kudzapempha mvula. Tikhululukireni kuti ana asaonongeke).*

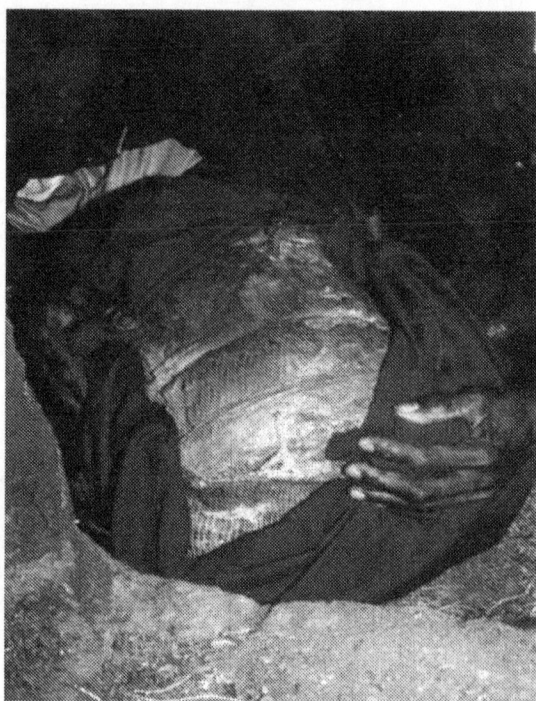

The Sacred Drum at Tsang'oma

A black goat is killed and roasted. Some of its meat is offered in the *kachisi*. The children eat the rest of it. When they have finished eating, they return singing songs. In the village stand big pots with water, from which they draw to throw at each other, soaking each other's clothes. All have to wear black clothes. On that day they are supposed to stay friendly with each other, avoiding all fighting. That is the law of Msinja, they say.

W.H.J. Rangeley reported that teeth of former *Tsang'oma* are preserved inside the drum.[42] He also gave a description of the drum. I saw the drum but was not allowed to touch it.[43] Although I could put forward questions at the meeting, we had the distinct feeling that the chiefs were cautious and reticent, especially concerning questions about Msinja, *Makewana* and the drum itself. The drum is no longer used to call people together to pray for rain, but is kept as a memorial of the past. But if it were brought out in the light, there would certainly be no rain. It was covered in a dark blue cloth, which for my benefit was moved aside a little so that I could see part of it.[44]

4. The Rain Sacrifice (*mfunde*) at Chinkhuti

The following is an eye-witness account of the *mfunde* at the Lilongwe river at Chinkhuti in 1954 given by Mr. T. Samu.[45]

> Chief *Maliri* called his people together and asked them to bring maize flour for the preparation of beer. Young girls of about 10 years of age had to stay in the enclosure where the beer was made and sing there night and day. When the beer was ready, a gourd was taken to the chief. All the people assembled, and the chief addressed them thus: "I have called you because the rain does not come and we shall die of hunger. Let us all go to appease God, for he is hard on us". With the gourd of beer and other offerings of *nsima* and meat all went to the river to a place called *Chinkhuti*, where there is a large pool of water. The people sat down. The village headman *Khundi*, draped in a large black cloth, sat next to *Maliri*. The latter prayed: "*Chiuta*, we have come together to ask your forgiveness. Here are the offerings which we bring to you, that you may

---

[42] W.H.J. Rangeley, "Makewana - the Mother of All People", pp. 40-43.

[43] W.H.J. Rangeley reported that the present-day *Tsang'oma* will not now permit the drum to be handled by visitors, and that the drum has become a money making proposition, because he charges a fee to see the drum. We had to pay 5 Kwacha. Rangeley added that according to *Tsang'oma*, only three Europeans have seen the drum. He named them and added that one of them, a Mr. Hamilton, formerly of the School of Oriental and African Studies, London, was fortunate to hear the rattle of contents in the drum when it was shown to him.

[44] No objection was made to our taking photographs of the drum. Not even when we used an electric flash, which was regarded probably as a symbol of lightning accompanying the rains.

[45] Recorded by L. Denis, "Meurs et Coutumes Indigènes", Rome: Ms, 7 Fascicles 1951-1958, Archives of the Missionaries of Africa (White Fathers), vol. 5, no. 504.

cease to be hard on us and give us rain". *Khundi* then took the offerings
and placed them in small baskets on the water. First they floated on the
water, then they were caught in the whirls and finally they disappeared in
the middle of the pool. Then *Khundi* himself, still draped in his black
cloth, also entered the water, swimming out to the middle where he disappeared for a long time. Meanwhile the people sang rain songs. When
Khundi finally emerged, the rain began to fall. Back at the village the people ate the remaining food and drank the beer.

In this account there appears a new element: *Khundi,* in a black cloth, went
into the water and stayed there. Of *Makewana* it is also said that she went
into the sacred pool at Msinja "in order to call down the rain".[46] In the water a symbolic contact is sought with *Chisumphi.* The gifts are also put on the
water and disappear in it. The female rain-makers *(chisumphi)* are also said to
enter into the water during their ritual of calling down the rain.

Finally, *Mangani* reported that at the confluence of the Diampwe and the
Linthipe rivers, offerings were also put into the water.[47] There a black goat
was killed and an offering made of meat, maize flour and clotted blood. The
offerings were placed in the water in four small baskets: two for *Chauta* and
two for the spirits of the deceased. Next morning the people came back to
see whether the offerings had been accepted. They found the baskets empty
on the shore. They then ate what remained of the meat and they sang rain
songs. They also threw small balls of *nsima (nthongo)* at one another. The
meaning of this is not quite clear, but it seems to be a variant of the water
throwing and could indicate that the rain would bring food.

In these last cases of rain sacrifices we find that the people assemble at the
water instead of at a *kachisi. Chauta* is everywhere and evidently a river is as
good as anywhere else to symbolise the presence of the giver of rain.

5. Rain Sacrifices in the Villages

---

[46] W.H.J. Rangeley, "Makewana - the Mother of All People", p. 34.

[47] L. Mangani, "The Notion of God in old Malawi", unpublished Ms, nd., 4 pp.

So far we have dealt with rain shrines. The people told us that formerly it was also common for local chiefs who had the right of *mzinda* to organize rain sacrifices on a local level.[48] Occasionally this is still done today. It was common to offer a black hen when the rains were late in coming, and, when this had no effect, to call together all the people for a rain sacrifice. This took place at the *kachisi* near the village. Some of these *kachisi* were built near the tombs of the former chiefs. The ritual is similar to that already described. Thus we find that the chief kills a black goat with a sacrificial knife. Only a chief who has a *mzinda* is allowed to have such a knife. He cuts pieces of meat from different parts of the goat to be cooked. Then all begin the prayer, sitting in a circle around the *kachisi* and facing it. People always repeat *pepa* during these prayers and slowly clap their hands. After prayer the chief stands up and offers the sacrifice by placing it into the pot buried in the floor of the *kachisi* while the people continue to sing rain songs. Back in the village the rest of the food is prepared for the children. Sometimes the chief makes a young girl offer the meat in the *kachisi*. L. Denis reported that young girls also offered pots of beer.[49]

The people believe that *Chiuta* is particularly fond of certain snakes like the python *(thunga, nsato, chilele)*. Should somebody kill such a snake, *Chiuta* would refuse to send rain. These snakes are called "masters of the rain" *(eni mvula)*. After such a killing *Chiuta* must be appeased. The one who killed the snake has to warn the chief who takes the remains of the snake, wraps them in a black cloth and throws them into a river, while praying: "*Chiuta*, pardon us, your children have done this, but do not refuse us rain" *(Chiuta, pepa, ndi ana amenewa, musatimane mvula)*. It may happen that the person who has killed such a snake hides the fact with the result that there is a real drought. The chief may suspect that someone has killed a snake and will make enquiries about it. In such a case a much more solemn sacrifice is required.

When we asked the people why rain sacrifices are not made as often as in the past, they gave two reasons. First, that it is enough for the rain sacrifice

---

[48] For instance the right to have a *kachisi*, *Nyau* and the solemn initiation of girls.
[49] Cf. L. Denis, "Meurs et Coutumes Indigènes", vol. 5, no. 635.

to be done at Bunda Hill. Secondly, according to others, that since there is so much evil around nowadays, *Chiuta* no longer listens *(akachita lero mvula sibwera chifukwa zoipa zachuluka mu dziko).* This latter reason is typical of certain older people who cannot accept that things are changing. They say that there is much more adultery *(chigololo)* committed now and that the young people no longer follow the old ways of prayer to the spirits of the dead and that many even are no longer initiated. All this may be the cause of disasters as droughts.

6. Conclusion

In chapters one and two we have seen how the Chewa conceive God. It is particularly to be noted that they consider Him as good and kind. No evil comes from His hand. He is the Master of the rains and as such may withhold the rain if people have offended Him by killing one of the rain-snakes or by burning the bush on the Bunda and so profaning a holy place. It is evident that these beliefs are not quite in keeping with the belief that *Chiuta* is good and that no evil comes from His hand. Lack of rain is one of the greatest tragedies for peasants who are dependent on a single rainy season per year. Nevertheless the belief that *Chiuta* is good and that He can be propitiated by a rain sacrifice is comforting and makes people turn to prayer.

Appendix 1: **Prayers and Songs for Rain**

Prayer 1

Chauta (God) ... pepa
Mwatimana mvula (you refused us rain) ... pepa
Ponse pauma (everywhere it is dry) ... pepa
Mutipatse lero (give us to-day) ... pepa
Tiri kudandaula (we are begging) ... pepa
Mutichitire chisoni (have mercy on us) ... pepa
Musatitaye ife ana anu (do not reject us, your children) ... pepa
Musatiumire mtima (do not be hard on us) ... Pepa
Ife ana anu (we your children) ... pepa
Mutitumizire mvula (send us rain) ... pepa

Prayer 2

Amaliri akale (Amaliri of old) ... pepa
Patseni madzi (give us water) ... pepa
Kumtunda kwauma (the land is all dry) ... pepa
Chisumphi, mutipatse mvula (Chisumphi, give us rain) ... pepa
Ndife ana anu (we are your children) ... pepa
Chauta, mutipatse nyama kumtunda (give us game of the hills) ... pepa
Ndife ana anu (we are your children) ... pepa

Prayer 3

Ife tafika pano pa kachisi (we have gathered here at the Kachisi) ... pepa
Lero 'tu tikufuna mvula (today we need rain indeed) ... pepa
Inu, mizimu ya makolo (you, mizimu of our Parents) ... pepa
Mugwirizane ndi Chauta, Chisumphi, Mphambe, Leza, Namalenga, Chan-
    giri, Ntheradi (agree with Chauta) ... pepa
Atipatse mvula (that he may give us rain) ... pepa
Tithandizeni Chauta (Chauta help us) ... pepa
Ndi mizimu yathu (and you, mizimu of our parents) ... pepa
Gwirizanani ndi Chauta (agree with Chiuta) ... pepa

Prayer 4

Tithira nsembe yopempha mvula (we bring offering asking for rain) ... pepa
Inu, mizimu ya N.N. (you, mizimu of N.N.) ... pepa
Mutinenere kwa Chauta (intercede for us with Chauta) ... pepa
Mutinenere kwa Chauta, etc. (about 6 times).

In case there has been too much rain, the following prayers were said:

Prayer 5

Ndithu (please) ... pepa
Tikhululukireni (forgive us) ... pepa
Mvula'yi yamkitsa (this rain is too much) ... pepa
Inu, mizimu ya makolo athu (you, mizimu of our parents) ... pepa

Prayer 6

Gwirizanani ndi Chauta, Chisumphi, Mphambe, Namalenga, Chanjiri, Leza,
Ntheradi (agree with Chauta...) ... pepa
Mvula'yi iyambe yadula ng'amba (may the rain start again after a spell of dry
weather) ... pepa.

Rain songs

Rain song 1

Ndi aka ndi aka (this and that [cloud])
kadza mvula (the one that will give rain)
ndi aka kamtambo (is that a small cloud)
ndi aka ndi aka (this or that cloud)
kadze mvula (which one will give rain)
kokwe koloole (may we reap and fill the grain stores)

Rain song 2

Nkokwe kolode (abundant water that drags things down)
mvula ya pano sikugwa (the rain here does not fall)
iyi ikugwa ya midzi (the rain falls elsewhere)
kokwe koloole (may we reap and fill the grain stores)

Rain song 3

Mvula yagunda m'mtambo (the storm thunders in the sky)
kulakwa ndi kudza ya matalala (it would be bad if they come with hailstones)
Mvula ndi kudza ya matalala (the storm thunders in the sky)
Kulakwa ndi kudza ya matalala (it would be bad if they come with hailstones)

Rain song 4

Njala ya makono popanda kachele [here there is famine, there are not even
kachele (small fruits of the wild fig tree)]
Popanda kachele ndi kadaoloka ndi kadapita kumwamba (without kachele
we can just as well pass across and go to the spirit world)

Rain song 5

Kalichero kanga kanka m'madzi (my small basket has been taken away by
the water)
Chilowa ndiwo kugona nao kumbuyo kwanga (I have to sleep with my back
turned to Chilowa)
Amwenda ayi kugona nao kumbuyo kwanga (I have to sleep with my back
turned to Mwenda)
de de de kanka m'madzi (floats away on the water)

*(This song refers to the obligation to abstain from sexual intercourse during the rainy
season).*

Rain song 6

Kamtemula, iyayi, sitifuna kamtambo koyera (No, Kamtemula we do not
want a small white cloud)
kokwe koloole (may we reap and fill the grain stores)
tifuna madzi (we want water)
kokwe koloole (may we reap and fill the grain stores)
isakhale ya mphepo, ya matalala (that it may not come with much wind and
hailstones)
idze yabwino (that it may come as a gentle rain).

Rain song 7

Chauta walakwa (Chauta does wrong)
Opanda mvula taima (without rain we are finished)
kamtsuko tatula (put down the small pot)
Chauta ndiye walakwa (it is Chauta who does wrong)
Opanda (mvula) taima (without rain we are finished)
Tatula kamtsuko ka madzi (we have put down the small water bucket)
Chauta ndiye walakwa (it is Chauta who does wrong)

Rain song 8

Chauta iwe (Chauta, you ...)
Ndapenyera, ndapenyera, ndalema [I have been looking, looking, and have
become tired from looking (for rain)]
Chauta iwe (Chauta, you ...)
Ndapeza mtambo woyera (I have found only a white cloud)
Chauta iwe (Chauta, you ..)
Ndapenya, ndalema (I have been looking, and got tired)
Chauta iwe (Chauta, you ..)
Mvula sikugwa (the rain is not falling)
Chauta iwe (Chauta, you ..)

Chapter 3
The Spirits of the Deceased *(mizimu)*

In the previous chapters we have considered the Chewa belief in *Chauta*, the Supreme Spirit. No evil is attributed to Him. The death of older people is said to be caused by Him, but in this case death is not considered an evil. The person's time has come, *Chiuta* takes him, that he may rest. The Chewa do not think that *Chiuta* punishes them directly for immoral conduct, since He makes the rain fall for good and bad alike. The idea is directly connected with their belief that He has left the living in the charge of their deceased relatives. In this chapter we want to consider this belief in the role which the spirits of the deceased *(mizimu/azimu)* play in the lives of the Chewa. The spirits of the deceased are also called *amanda* (those of the grave) and *atulo* (those who speak in dreams).

1. Characterisation of the Chewa Spirits

As Marwick pointed out, it is not quite accurate to speak of "ancestral spirits" in the case of the Chewa.[1] "Ancestral spirits" strictly refer to lineal senior kin. Among the Chewa, however, the group of spirits demanding attention is not limited to lineal senior kin, but is much wider, including spirits of senior relatives, those of one's own generation, and even those of one's descendants. They are commonly called *mizimu* (spirits of the dead). The *mizimu ya makolo* (spirits of deceased senior relatives) are considered to have a position of authority with regard to the family group. Spirits of younger relatives, however, have to be reckoned with also, because they too can interfere in the lives of the living. The *mizimu ya makolo* are more particularly the guardians of the ancestral customs *(miyambo)*.

---

[1] M.G. Marwick, *Sorcery in its Social Setting*, Manchester: University Press, 1965, p. 65.

Just as the headman *(mfumu)* of the village is entrusted with matters transcending the family group, so the spirits of the chiefs are entrusted with more general matters. In the case of a drought the spirits of deceased chiefs will be invoked and asked to intercede with *Chiuta,* similarly in the case of an epidemic. These spirits of deceased chiefs are called by Schoffeleers "territorial spirits" *(mizimu ya dziko)* because their interest lies with the people of a territory as such.[2]

An interesting question is whether the Chewa, a matrilineal people, refer to their matrilineal senior kin only when they speak of their *mizimu ya makolo* or whether they are bilineal when it comes to *mizimu.* When we first put this question we asked whether they venerate the spirits on their mother's side only, or also those on their father's side. It is typical of their mentality that they changed the question to: "Which spirit interferes in the life of a particular person?" A person will have to venerate a particular spirit who is thought to interfere in his life. The answer of all the informants was the same: the spirits who interfere in the life of any particular person are those of his own matrilineal group. The spirit of a father is believed to interfere in the lives of those of his own matrilineal group, i.e. his brothers, sisters and sisters' children, not in those of his own children. This is a transportation of the matrilineal customs of the Chewa into the world of the spirits. A father has no right to punish his own children. If they have to be punished, it is the mother's brother who will do so. We were told: "A spirit follows his own 'fold', lineage group, the group of his brothers and sisters, and not the 'fold' of somebody else *(mzimu umatsata khola lake, mtundu wake, achibale ake, osati khola la munthu wina ayi).*

A spirit who does not restrict himself to his own "fold" *(khola lake)* is called "a stupid spirit" *(mzimu wopanda nzeru),* because he does not know the customs. Nevertheless one has to take account of such an unwise spirit *(wopanda nzeru)* and to perform a rite in order to chase him away: "Be off, spirit without shame, you just trouble any person" *(choka iwe mzimu wopanda manyazi, ungogwira ali yense).*

---

[2] J.M. Schoffeleers, "Symbolic and Social Aspects of Spirits Worship among the Mang'anja", PhD Oxford, 1968, p. 161.

The word *mzimu* has two forms in the plural, *mizimu* and *azimu*. *Mizimu* is used for any spirit, good or troublesome alike. It is a general term without special connotation. *Azimu* is used for spirits who trouble or punish the living, e.g. a spirit who comes to a person in a dream telling him: "You buried me as you bury a child. I want *Nyau* dances and beer. I want many *Nyau* dancers and such a particular dancer has to open the dance". Such spirits are not evil but they are troublesome because they disturb the peace of the people. Both are clearly distinguished from *ziwanda* who are evil spirits who wander about to haunt and harm people. *Ziwanda* are spirits of e.g. deceased witches or murderers who are refused entrance into the world of the spirits. They cannot be placated by offerings and the only defence against them is that of magic rites and medicines *(mankhwala)*. Those spirits are feared because they are unpredictable. When they are displeased they can send illnesses and other misfortunes. They also might annoy people by requesting offerings or *Nyau* dances.

Chief Kanyenda and the Royal Stool of the Karonga

The spirits are also the guardians of the ancestral customs *(miyambo ya makolo)*. They will come to punish the living if they forget or neglect those customs. The fear of the *mizimu* makes older people very wary about changes which detract from the traditional customs. "You are forgetting our customs, you will see that the *mizimu* will take revenge" is the often repeated threat made to younger people. Older people complain, for the signs are clear: evil is rampant as younger people grow up without going through the formal initiation rituals and they do not follow the traditions. "That is the end of the country" *(ndi kutha kwa dziko lathu lino)*, the elders say.

In our survey we found only nine cases out of 451 where the spirits were believed to have caused death. M.G. Marwick reported that in his survey 3% were attributed to the spirits.[3] Here are some examples from our research:

A new stretch of road was built a few years ago which followed partly the old track and partly a new one. At a particular point where the road had to be linked with a new bridge over the Nathenje river the new track descends a rather steep slope. At this point many accidents have happened within a short time. People say that this track runs over some graves and that the spirits are so angry that they have caused four people to die in accidents, besides being responsible for many other accidents when cars crashed without causing death. It is believed that accidents will continue until the road is changed.

Another case is the one of a child who died because, as the diviner explained, its grandmother liked it so much that she came to take it with her *(gogo wake amamkonda wabwera kudzamtenga)*. This sort of reasoning is heard rather often, although we found only one case in which people actually said that a child was taken for this reason. We also found one case in which a man was said to have died because his former friends who had died wanted him to be with them. We found two cases in which people had died because, so it was said, the spirits of persons they had killed earlier came to take revenge.

The last case concerned a death in the hospital of Lilongwe. A male nurse told us that a man had died because he had been put in a bed in which a witch *(mfiti)* had died. The bed had been moved from ward to ward, but all the patients who were put in it had died *(atayesa anthu ambirimbiri onsewo nkumafa)*. According to our informant the bed had to be removed altogether.

The nine cases of our research where death was related to the influence of *mizimu* are only a very small proportion of the deaths recorded. However, a

---

[3] M.G. Marwick, *Sorcery in its Social Setting,* pp. 16-17.

much greater proportion of other (non lethal) misfortunes are believed to
be caused by the spirits. We have many such cases on record. M.G. Marwick also said that if his enquiry had included cases of lesser misfortune, the
references to the spirits would have been much higher.[4]

The *mizimu* are also believed to play a positive role: that of protecting the
living, warning them of impending danger, and of being able to give success
to their relatives' labour. The most important role of *mizimu* is that of intercessors with *Chiuta (kunenera)*. *Chiuta* is believed to be the master of life and
death, of rain and of fecundity. In all these cases the *mizimu* can speak for
the living. We have seen how at the rain sacrifices the mizimu are invoked:
"Speak for us, make rain fall for us" *(mutinenere, mutigwetsere mvula)*. As a matter of fact the offerings made at the *mfunde* are not so much intended for
Chiuta, who does not need them, as for the *mizimu*. If the *mizimu* are invoked in the right way, they will speak on behalf of the living. People believe that even when they pray directly to *Chiuta* Himself, their prayer will be
more surely heard if the *mizimu* also intercede for them. It is important to
underline this point, because a number of people mistakenly say that the
Chewa only worship the *mizimu*, and that *Chiuta* is too far away and is not
really interested in them *(Deus otiosus)*. It is difficult to say whether this belief
in the possibility of contacting *Chiuta* directly has been a development due
to influence of the Christian missions. All we can say is that the rain-rituals
with their prayers certainly date from well before the coming of the missions in the last century. It is interesting to note that during the meeting
with the chiefs of the Bunda Shrine, one of the younger men among them
brought up precisely this question of the spirits interceding for men. He
made a comparison with the belief of the Christians that Christ intercedes
for them with the Father. He said: "We too have somebody to speak for us
to *Chauta:* our *mizimu* speak for us". The other chiefs approved this way of
putting it.

The *mizimu* communicate with the living through dreams of which only the
diviner can give an authoritative interpretation, or through the raving of a

---

[4] M.G. Marwick, *Sorcery in its Social Setting,* p. 63.

person in a trance *(kubwebweta)*. They also communicate through the intervention of the diviner who consults his *ula* (lots), but not directly through visions or voices. The *mizimu* can also send e.g. snakes to warn people. If someone meets a snake called *njoka mdala* on his way he will turn back, because he believes that this is a warning by the *mizimu* that he will meet danger if he continues on his way. In the case of a person who is raving *(kubwebweta)* some older person will approach and attempt to catch what is being said, which he will then try to interpret as a message from the *mizimu*. The same is done in the case of a person who talks in his sleep.

2. The Promotion of *mizimu*

The Chewa believe that the *mzimu* survives the body after death *(mzimu utsala wamoyo munthu akafa)*. In a first reaction, the living make an effort to forget the recently passed away. This is a mechanism of self-defence. For they fear the *mzimu*, and what is feared is better forgotten. The funeral rites are designed to make the *mzimu* depart so that the living may forget the dead. At a funeral, articles that were used daily by the deceased are put in the grave. But first, they are broken or pierced, to symbolize that they are finished, that they are dead like their owner *(zatha)*. They are put there for the spirit's use so that he will not come back to fetch them.

After the funeral the house of the deceased is closed and it is pulled down following the final closing ceremony of the second shaving. This is to prevent the *mzimu* from returning to live there. If he has left a widow, she may continue to live in the house for a time, but as soon as possible a new house has to be built for her. It is deemed unsafe for her to remain on in it, for the *mzimu* may return to it during that period when he is thought to travel towards the world of the *mizimu*. This liminal period lasts till the ceremony of the second shaving, by which time he is believed to have settled in the world of the *mizimu*. After the body has been laid in the grave, all the relatives throw a handful of soil into the open grave "in order to forget the deceased".

Their attitude to the *mizimu* is ambivalent. On the one hand they are afraid of them and on the other hand they look to them as intercessors. They are afraid that they may come back to live near them in the village and to claim their debts. Every African has debts *(ngongole)* and every one remembers exactly who owes him what, remembers too every insult. No one ever loses an opportunity to ask for his due or to take revenge for an insult, and every detail is recalled. As A. Hetherwick said: "This law of revenge runs into the other world as well as right through this one".[5]

The fact that they are afraid of the *mizimu* makes people want to forget them. It also explains why they want to be as many as possible at a burial in order to face together what is mysterious and full of dread. Yet in spite of everything they look upon the *mizimu* as their *nkhoswe* (guardians) and intercessors. But even so they would prefer that they do not stay too close.

The world of the *mizimu* seems to be thought of as that of a group into which the new *mzimu* has to be received *(kulandilidwa)*. Some spirits are not received and they continue to wander about without peace. It is not so clear who it is who receives or refuses the spirits into the group. Sometimes the spirits themselves are said to receive or to refuse. One informant seemed to deny that God punishes: "God will not punish because it is not His purpose to punish men" *(Mulungu salanga anthu chifukwa si cholinga cha Mulungu kulanga anthu)*. All informants agreed that the following persons will not be received: witches *(mfiti)*, murderers, those who rob people who are poor, and those who commit incest: they are excluded and will remain *ziwanda (mfiti, ochita chigololo, kuba, kupha, sadzalandilidwa)*. These "capital sins" and the Chewa notion of retribution will be considered in the chapter on the "Moral Beliefs" of the Chewa (chapter nine).

The *mizimu* are thought to be grouped in lineages, just as the living. A young woman who lost her child, prayed to her deceased mother: "Is this not one of your children? Come and meet it, lest it get lost. Let the *agogo* (grandparents) know that your child has come. Take care of it and do not leave it in the hands of strangers".

---

[5] A. Hetherwick, *The Gospel and the African*, Edinburgh: Clark, 1932, p. 75.

After death the *mzimu* is as it were an image *(chithunzithunzi)*. It is not the same but remains similar to the person it was before. It is also said that a *mzimu* is like the wind *(ngati mphepo)*. The wind is present and although one cannot see it, one can experience it. When the wind stirs up small whirl-winds of dust *(kabvubvulu)*, the *mzimu* is said to be there. The *mzimu* is like the shadow which follows a person everywhere. When he dies, he has no shadow any more. It has gone to the world of the shadows (i.e. spirits).

The *mizimu* are said to rest *(kupumula)*. Their survival has no limit and is not dependent on the living in the sense that the offerings of the living would make any significant change. However it is important that the living honour them, for they are powerful. Since the spirits are the guardians of the customs *(miyambo)*, the best way to honour them is to be faithful to the traditions. The spirits are capricious and may make all sorts of demands on the living. The spirit of someone recently dead who is still in the liminal period is thought to be particularly susceptible. During this period he requires special attention lest he continue to trouble the living. This liminal period extends from the moment of death until the commemoration held on the anniversary of the burial *(kumeta kwachiwiri,* the second shaving). During this time while his body is decomposing, the spirit is thought to be as it were limping between the two lives. The burial ceremony is not yet completed and he has not yet been definitively sent off, his house is still standing and he may frequently come back to the village. He has not yet settled down in his new life in the spirit-world.

Even after the second shaving which brings the burial rite to a close, he has to be placated with offerings, so long as there are members of the family living whom he has personally known. Once the last of these relatives has died, all links with the living are severed, and he can rest without being disturbed by their bad conduct or negligence. Only some important chiefs may be remembered and invoked in prayer for a longer period.

The normal place where the *mizimu* are thought to stay is in the vicinity of a graveyard, a thicket with dense undergrowth and mysterious shadows. No bushfire is allowed near. From time to time the *mizimu* of those recently deceased stay at the foot of a big tree (the *mizimu* tree) in the village. As long as his former house is still standing, the *mizimu* may remain under its verandah. The living fear the *mizimu* and are not happy when they are too close. The burial rites *(maliro)* aim to make the spirit depart from the village and stay in the graveyard. When people are troubled by *azimu*, the diviner tells them to chase them away by performing certain rites and saying: "You bad spirits, be off and don't come back". The rites usually consist of washing in a solution of bad smelling roots *(nafungwe* or *bwazi)*. The bad smell is said to drive the *azimu* away.

On the whole the *mizimu* are believed to be good and to have at heart the interests of their lineage. They may be troublesome because they make demands on the living, or remind them of their duties concerning the traditions *(miyambo)*, or castigate them. There is, however, a category of spirits which is decidedly evil: the *ziwanda*. To this group belong, among others, the spirits of deceased witches *(mfiti)* or murderers. These are not "received" into the group of the *mizimu*, they will find no rest and will continue to wander about and to trouble people. The other *mizimu* are said to rest *(ipumula)* and to have peace *(ili ndi mtendere)*. Only when there is trouble among their living relatives they get annoyed *(ivutika)* and send misfortunes to remind the living of their duties. They may have to be appeased before they withdraw these misfortunes. The *ziwanda* cannot be appeased. To protect oneself against them, one must have recourse to magical rites and medicines. Especially when somebody dreams of such a bad spirit, he has to get medicine *(nafungwe* or *bwazi* roots) and boil them in water. The bad smelling vapour of these roots is supposed to drive away the bad spirit. If a married person has such a dream, both husband and wife have to wash themselves with the bad smelling solution. While performing these rites they continue insulting the bad spirit. Then they return to the house and close the door without looking back. The rest of the medicine must be thrown away at a crossroads, so that from whatever direction the bad spirit comes he will be driven away by the power of the medicine. The *mizimu* know what is happening in the villages where their relatives live. They are only interested in their own lineage. As long as everything goes well, they are believed to be happy. If, however, trouble arises, the *mizimu* are disturbed in their peace and will punish their relatives.

Under the ancestral tree

The *mizimu* are powerful *(iri ndi mphamvu)*, they are the masters of the living *(ndiyo eni anthu, ndiyo milungu yathu).*[6] The *mizimu* can help the living. They are consulted before any important work is undertaken, such as a long journey or a hunting party and at the same time their help is sought. This rite is called *kukhwisula.* It consists in an offering at the foot of the *mizimu* tree, after the diviner has been consulted and a favourable answer has been received. "Tomorrow we go hunting and we beg you to help us that we kill many animals and not come across wild animals" *(Ife mawa tili kukasaka nyama, tikupemphani kuti mutithandize kuti tikaphe nyama zambiri, ndiponso kuti tisakumane ndi zirombo).* The participants are then told to abstain from sexual intercourse *(kudika)* till after the hunting party. This taboo on intercourse is often part of the *kukhwisula* rite, because magic medicines *(mankhwala)* are often obtained in order to make doubly sure that the hunting is going to be successful. Because these *mankhwala* are powerful they often require abstention from sexual intercourse.

We have seen already that mysterious and powerful activities have to be kept separate.[7] After a good journey or some other successful work, people will say: "The spirits went with me and I was lucky" *(mizimu yinandiyendera*

---

[6] *Milungu* means masters, and not gods. *Mulungu,* in the singular, is used for God, but not the plural.

[7] See explanation of the taboos related the rain sacrifices, p. 55ff. Further explanations will be given in the chapter six *(mdulo).*

bwino, ndapeza mwayi), or "the spirit at home helped me to-day" *(mzimu wa m'nyumba wandithandiza lero)*. However powerful they are, the *mizimu* are not believed to have direct power over life or to make rain fall. This belongs exclusively to *Chiuta*, the Supreme Master. The *mizimu* can make people fall ill *(kudwalitsa)* or send all sorts of misfortunes *(kubvutitsa)*. They can also render a person sterile, e.g. a deceased child can close the womb of its mother unless an offering is made. But the spirits can intercede with *Chiuta (kunenera)* and they can obtain rain *(mizimu ili ndi mphamvu yakutigwetsera mvula)*. We have found nine cases in which the *mizimu* were said to have caused death. These cases seem to contradict the normal saying that *mizimu* do not directly kill. We think that this must be understood in the sense that the *mizimu* do not normally cause death but rather sickness and other misfortunes when their relatives neglect them or offend against the traditional customs *(miyambo)*.

3. Some Special Problems

a) Death of Small Children (Osatenga)

Small children who die before their parents have performed a special ritual called *kutenga mwana* (to take the child), by which a child is incorporated into the family, are not considered to be real human beings.[8] Their spirits will not be received into the world of *mizimu*, because they lack something essential. On the contrary a child who is "taken" will be received into the spirit world, however young it is. The spirit of a child who ha not been "taken" has to await rebirth in another child who its own mother, or her close relative conceives. In the meantime it is considered a *chiwanda* (singular of *ziwanda*).

The Chewa believe that the *mizimu* of such a child will be reborn, because such a child has not stayed long enough on earth and "has not fulfilled the purpose which God had for it" *(cholinga chimene Mulungu anafuna kwa iye anali asanachite)*. "Such a *mzimu* will be brought back by God that it may perform its work well" *(mzimu wotere Mulungu amaubweza mwamsanga kuti ugwire ntchito*

---

[8] The ritual of *kutenga mwana* will be considered in chapter six *(mdulo)*.

yake bwino). This statement was confirmed by another informant who said:
"The will of God, if a child dies very young, is that his spirit returns in the
body of a newly born child, because the will of God is not fulfilled and because it was a very young child and did not stay long on earth. That is why
God wants to bring back the spirit in the body of a child to be born soon"
*(chifuniro cha Mulungu ngati mwana afa ali wang'ono amafunanso kuti mzimu wake
uja ubwerere m'thupi la munthu wobadwa tsopano. Chifukwa sunakwaniritse chifuniro
cha Mulungu. Komanso kuti popeza ali mwana wang'ono asakhale nthawi yaitali. Chifukwa chake Mulungu amafuna kubwezera mzimu m'thupi la wobadwa tsopano).*

The above statements are particularly interesting because they introduce the
idea of a "will, a purpose of God which has to be fulfilled" *(kukwaniritssa
chifuniro cha Mulungu).* It may be going too far to read in this statement the
idea that each human being has a task to fulfil. It may merely imply that
there is a basic conviction that such children have never really been men,
that the *mzimu* still awaits birth. Moreover, since it is a child which is not
"taken" *(wosatenga),* it has no lineage and therefore cannot be received by the
mzimu, who in the afterlife are believed to be constituted in the same lineages as the living. There is no lineage to receive it in the after-life, since
there was no lineage who has received it in this life. On the other hand, a
child, however young, that has been "taken", will be received in the world
of the *mizimu* upon its death. The key to the understanding of these statements seems to be this "belonging to a lineage". Such a child that is not
"taken" will not be buried in the same way as a child that is "taken", who is
buried in the same way as any other member of the family. But a child that
is not "taken" will be carried by a few women to a very shallow grave. If its
grave were deep it "would close the womb of its mother". We were told that
such a child is still considered as somehow part of the body of the mother
and not yet really born. To bury such a child in a deep grave would be like
burying the womb of its mother, of which the child is still mysteriously a
part, and the mother would be forever sterile.

The individuality of the child is not attached to the child as such, but to a
child that has been received, i.e. has a publicly recognized place in a lineage.
That place it will receive the day it is "taken". A woman who is pregnant

with a *mzimu*, who wants to be reborn, without being physically pregnant, is in a mysterious and dangerous condition. If great care is not taken and offerings not made to appease the spirit, it may render the mother sterile. Sterility is the worst evil that can befall a woman. The people believe that such a spirit can render the woman sterile and express this by saying that she is pregnant with a *chiwanda* (a haunting spirit).

b) Mentally Deficient Persons

It is said that the *mizimu* may take possession of a mentally deficient person. The "village idiot" is treated with respect. He is said to be "of the *mizimu*". The fact that such persons often speak in a way people cannot understand makes them like those who rave *(kubwebweta)*. Certainly people have great patience with these mentally deficient, putting up with them and taking care not to treat them harshly. If they become dangerous, they will hamper their movements by fixing a big wooden log to their feet or on their shoulders. But they will not be allowed to go short of food as long as they stay in their village or in the vicinity where they are known. People put up with them and pay little attention when they cause trouble.

c) Re-incarnation

We have already seen that a child that dies before it is "taken" will be reborn in another child. When the mother is pregnant again (in such circumstances and dreams of her deceased child), she has to make an offering the next morning at the foot of a tree. At the day of the birth, the mother or a sister of the pregnant woman puts an offering at the foot of the tree which, in this case, consists of flour mixed with water, since there is no time to make beer. There are some people who think that they are a re-incarnation of some *mizimu*. These cases are rare nowadays, but people say that they were more frequent in the past. L. Denis reported that near Likuni chief *Mlima* claimed to be the re-incarnation of former chief *Mlima*.[9] "When my mother was pregnant with me", he said, "she fell ill and went to see the diviner, who told her that the former chief *Mlima* appeared to him in a dream. He said

---

[9] L. Denis, "Meurs et Coutumes Indigènes", Rome: MS, 7 Fascicles 1951-1958, Archives of the Missionaries of Africa (White Fathers), vol 6, no. 629.

that he wanted to be born again in the child with which she was pregnant and that this child will be chief *Mlima,* long since dead".

Some people believe that at their death they can become a wild animal, a wild pig, or a leopard *(munthu akafa auka chirombo, kapena nguluwe, kapena kambuku).* A leper is believed to become a hippo *(munthu wakhate akuti auka mbvuwu)* and a witch *(mfiti)* a crocodile *(ng'ona).* There are people who obtain medicine *(mankhwala)* in order to become such or such an animal. Their purpose is to impress and frighten other people. They want other people to say that they are really virile persons because they desire to become a lion or leopard. We were told that at funerals strange things happen, e.g. in one case, that the noise was heard of something moving around *(kutakataka)* in the coffin and that immediately after the burial a wild animal was seen running away.

d) Fetishism

A. Hetherwick reported that he had heard that the *mzimu* of a deceased person can be located in some object which is then set aside.[10] This object may be a gourd or a basket, or some other object. One old chief showed him a small pill box procured from some mission dispensary in which he said the *mzimu* of his predecessor was located. The medicine man *(sing'anga)* entices the *mzimu* into an object to give it a location and make it easy to approach. S.S. Murray wrote that among the northern branches of the Chewa there is a form of fetishism, where each household would have its own fetish. In this fetish, the spirits of dead relatives are enshrined to which, on family occasions, flour, beer or cloth are offered.[11] A. Werner quoted the Rev. A.G. MacAlpine saying: "We find that the Achewa have articles described as 'fetishes' and consisting of a few short pieces of wood the size of one's forefinger, bound together with a scrap of calico into the figure of a child's doll.

---

[10] A. Hertherwick, *The Gospel and the African,* Edinburgh: Clark, 1932, p. 61.

[11] S.S. Murray, *A Handbook of Nyasaland,* London/Zomba: Government of Nyasaland, 1932, p. 81.

Inside the calico is concealed a tiny box made of the handle of a gourd-cup, and supposed to contain the spirit of some dead ancestors."[12]

We tried to get some more information on this point. We found only one informant who related the following experience which he had when he was still a young man: "In 1955 I saw a man and a woman in the village of Nyama who had in their house a gourd of which they took great care because it was the dwelling of the *mizimu* of their parents. One day the woman dreamt that her mother, who had died, was talking with her. At daybreak she took the gourd and said: "I am alone, so do not reject me. If it is about the child ... I am looking after it. So what do you want? We do not want *azimu* to come. If you want to come, you must come with things only". The reason they had this gourd was that if they remembered the spirits of their relatives they could talk to them and make their requests. They had to take care of the gourd because it was the dwelling of their parents.

4. Sacrifices to the *mizimu*

Offerings are made normally only to the *mizimu* of one's own lineage, even to those of children. The quality of the offering is in proportion to the dignity of the deceased relative. To an adult one may offer a goat but to a child only a chicken. On a public occasion such as a rain sacrifice an offering may be made to the *mizimu* of former chiefs. To the spirits of other deceased offerings are not made, except in the case of a *chiwanda* who has to be chased away.

The Chewa say that their religion goes with them (*chipembedzo chimapita nawo*). On a journey, people invoke their own *mizimu*, not those of the place where they happen to be staying. When they move their village they continue to offer to the *mizimu* of the deceased in the old village, never offering to the *mizimu* of the place to which they have moved. The invocations are not addressed to the *mizimu* of the lineage in general, but to a particular person who is indicated by name. Sometimes they even address the *mzimu* of

---

their own child. Once I visited a house in whose vicinity, at the foot of a tree, a pot with offerings to a *mzimu* was buried. The owner of the house told me that it was for his child *(ndi mwana wanga)* to whom he would offer regularly.

Asked why they invoke the *mizimu* of the dead, people answer: "We appease them when they trouble us because they have no peace and cannot rest" *(titeta azimu pamene ativuta chifukwa sali ndi mtendere, sapumula)*. At the funeral and the commemoration rites, the offerings are made without the diviner asking for them. In the other cases the dead themselves ask for the offerings through the intermediary of the diviner. People think that the dead will take revenge if they are neglected. It is not wise to provoke their anger. Surrounded by enemies, their only recourse is to the *mizimu* from whom they ask protection. Without their help their work will be without success.

After a good harvest people thank the *mizimu* by putting the first maize-cob in a special place at the back of the house *(ku mnyendo)*, where provisions are usually kept. "There is plenty of maize", they say, "you have given it" *(chimanga chachuluka, munatipatsa ndinu)*. "You start to eat it" *(muyambe kudya inu)*. The next day when they find that rats have eaten some of the offerings or small ants are running over them, they say: "Let us eat now, our masters have eaten" *(tidye tsopano, eni adya)*. They are happy as they see in this a sign that the *mizimu* have accepted the offerings. As these ants and rats are supposed to be the emissaries of the *mizimu*, people get anxious if there are none. They fear that their offerings have not been accepted. Each family normally makes its offerings in their own house *kumiyendo* or at the foot of a big tree nearby. They preferably choose trees such as the *msolo (pseudolachnostylis maprouneifolia)*, because there is much shade underneath them, dark and mysterious. Offerings to the *mizimu* of a chief are made at the *kachisi* near his grave but not inside the graveyard or at the foot of the tree under which the chief used to sit. If someone dies abroad, the offerings are made in the house in which his wife and children are living, or in the house of his mother or sister, or at the foot of a tree. In such a case the house is not demolished because the *mzimu* is not supposed to come back to it. If a person falls ill far away, he may warn his relatives to consult a diviner to ascertain what to do in case a *mzimu* has caused the illness.

Nowadays the offerings are made in the following ways. On the last day of the preparation of beer, people take a small gourd of it to the tree chosen for the offering. There they pour the beer through a hole in a small pot placed upside down at the foot of the tree, saying: "Here is beer, drink it, we do not want you to come and spoil our beer" *(suwu mowawu mumwe, koma tsono sitifuna mutiipitsire mowa)*. They do this because they are afraid that otherwise the *mizimu* may spoil the beer because they have not been given their share. People will also fill a small gourd and put it in their house *ku mnyendo*. The next day when they come together to drink the beer all present pour a little at the foot of the tree.

Sharing beer between the Living and the Living Dead

On the day of the second shaving, i.e. the commemoration of the burial *(mowa wa mpalo)* they act similarily. The chief tells old people to take the beer of the *mizimu* and to pour it at the foot of the tree so that the *mizimu* may join in the *mowa wa mpalo*. This is intended to "cool down" *(kuti aziziritse)* the heart of the deceased so that he does not come back to claim beer or *Nyau* dances. The younger generation also continues to offer to the *mizimu*. They do so as follows. When they make beer they invite their grandmother or another old woman, well versed in making offerings. When the beer is ready this old woman is asked to drink the beer of the spirit *(mowa wa ku mitu)*, i.e. the small gourd which the "owner of the beer" *(mwini mowa)* had put at the *mnyendo*. Other old people of the village are also asked to drink out of that gourd. While drinking they are expected to talk loud about the beer so that the spirits may hear. The beer will then taste good. While offering this beer to the *mizimu*, they take a chicken, kill it and take out the entrails *(chiwindi)* and the lungs *(mapapu)*, which they roast and put at the *mnyendo*. Then they start drinking the beer in honour of the spirits.

The invocations are always made in the house before the actual offering at the tree. If it is a public offering, they take place in the open space of the village or near the *kachisi* where the offerings will be made. The *kachisi* built for the *mizimu* of former chiefs is a small hut opening towards the village. It is about 1,2 m wide and 1,5 m high and is often made merely with a few bamboo sticks or branches planted in the ground and supporting a grass roof. The *kachisi* is built near but never in a village. Sometimes, in a more permanent *kachisi* a bed made of a few sticks and a piece of matting is included on which the *mizimu* can rest. All *kachisi* have a pot *(chibiso)* in which the offerings are deposited: it is buried in the soil with the top of the pot level with the ground.

Nowadays there are still a few *kachisi* to be found, but not as many by far as in the past. It is remarkable that in Muslim areas the *kachisi* is still a common feature. They have integrated the traditional customs and preserved them much better than in non-Muslim areas, where the people are said to be ashamed of the *kachisi* and to have given them up because in the eyes of the educated it is a sign of backwardness. They offer at the *mizimu* tree instead. Apart from the commemoration after a burial *(maliro)* there are no set periods or days for offerings to the *mizimu*. The invocations and offerings are usually made early in the morning or at sunset, rarely during the day.

The offerings which often consist of some beer are presented in a small yellow gourd *(chipanda)* and poured into the small pot *(chibiso)* or simply on the soil itself. If there is some urgency and the offerings cannot be delayed till the beer is prepared, then a mixture of water and maize flour can be offered or even water alone, with the promise that at a later date an offering of beer will be made. The *mizimu* are thought to accept such an offering on account of the circumstances.

The offerings of food are: meat and *nsima* (stiff maize porridge), or simply maize flour: The meat is chicken (sometimes pigeon), less often goat. No other meat is offered. The animals should be fully grown and young, female or male unless one or other has been specified by the diviner, of any colour unless specified. To offer a chicken that is lame or sick is to insult the *mizimu (kutaya mizimu,* i.e. to reject).

This solid food is prepared in a *kamphika* (black earthenware cooking pot) and placed in a *phale* (fragment of a broken earthenware jar) or in a *kamphika* placed in the *kachisi* or at the foot of the tree. The *chipanda* and the *kamphika*, in which the offerings are brought can be used again for profane purposes. The other *kamphika* and the *phale* and *chibiso* may not be used again once they have been used in the *kachisi* or placed at the foot of a tree. Other offerings such as sweet potatoes, groundnuts, millet or pumpkins are sometimes made at the time of the harvest to thank the *mizimu*. Cows are sometimes offered at the burial of a chief.

In the case of a family offering the invocations are made by the family head, who can delegate another person if necessary. The diviner can also indicate the person who is to make the invocations *(kuteta mizimu)*. If there is no man present, a woman can make them. Women will make the invocation at a beer offering in the case of beer brewing. Strangers to the family cannot take an active part in the ceremony or even assist at it (invocations are made inside the hut), but they may join afterwards in the common meal or the drinking of the beer. At the public ceremony the village chief presides at the invocations. If the offering is an animal, the chief kills it outside the place where the people are gathered. He then joins the people with the animal which he cuts in pieces and places in a *kamphika*. This he hands to the person who makes the offerings. All members of the village are to be present, with the exception of children, but strangers are not allowed to assist. There are no special regulation as to clothes to be worn except during a rain sacrifice when all must wear black (or some other dark colour, dark blue for instance). There are no taboos on sexual relations except at the rain sacrifice when all have to abstain.

People, especially the older ones, still make offerings privately. We have seen old women taking some beer to a nearby tree which they pour out there, mumbling something like: "I have made beer, this is for you, drink it". Public offerings are still made at a *mfunde* (rain sacrifice). Of late in certain places people have again started to offer *mfunde* in their villages. Offerings are also made at burials and the commemoration of burials, sometimes also in the case of epidemics like chicken-pox *(chikuku)* or small-pox *(nthomba)*.

When women make beer and then, during the night, dream of a deceased relative, they will taste the beer the next morning. If it is bitter, they say that the *mzimu* has been washing himself in it. They then must distill it making *kachasu* (spirit). Before distilling it, they will put some at the *mnyendo* saying: "Spirit of NN, wash yourself in this beer" *(mzimu wa uje, usamba m'mowa umemewu)*. The next day it will be thrown away.

5. Conclusion

In the first chapter we contended that *Chiuta* does not punish immoral conduct. He has left the living in the charge of their deceased relatives, who are the guardians of the traditional customs and who punish any transgression of the traditional moral code by sending misfortunes, rarely if ever by inflicting death. They are unpredictable because they send misfortunes not only in the case of transgressions, but also when they are dissatisfied with the little thought the living gave to them. This happens especially in the case of a spirit in the liminal period who thinks that he is neglected by his living kin. The spirits are also believed to be the protectors of the living and their intercessors with *Chiuta*. They are generally believed to be good. People consult them and ask them for help in more important undertakings *(kukhwisula)*. The living still invoke the *mizimu (kupepesa)* today, although the younger generation may do it in a different way.

There exists a group of spirits who are greatly feared and who cannot be placated. They need to be chased away by magical rites. These are the *ziwanda* who have not been received into the group of the *mizimu* because of their immoral conduct during their life on earth. The "capital sins" which bar a spirit from entering the group of the *mizimu* are: witchcraft *(ufiti)*, murder, incest, and theft from poor people. These *ziwanda* are believed to continue their evil perpetrations even in the after-life. They haunt men because they are essentially evil and they cannot be propitiated because they are as it were the personification of evil. They have no mercy. This will be considered in chapter seven on *ufiti*.

The reason why small children who die before they are "taken" are said to join the world of the *ziwanda* is not quite clear. They are certainly not to be equated with *afiti*. It may be because until they are reborn they are said to haunt their mother. It is to be noted that the spirits of the dead are believed to send sickness and misfortunes as punishment for evil conduct. This punishment for evil conduct during one's life-time is an anticipation of the final condemnation for evil conduct, when the spirit of the deceased will be excluded from the group of the *mizimu* and condemned to wander endlessly without peace (cf. chapter nine on the "Moral Beliefs" of the Chewa).

The *mizimu* may be troublesome because of the demands they make, but people put up with this as they put up with the demands of living relatives. However, people do not feel comfortable if the *mizimu* remain too close to them. This is because of their fear of the mysterious and the powerful. The rites of the burial ritual are intended to "send off" the spirit, and to help the living forget him. This will be discussed in more detail in the following chapter.

Appendix 2: Invocations to the spirits *(kuteta mizimu)*

1. *In the case of an illness*

The diviner may have pointed out that the illness is caused by a *mzimu* because NN has angered the *mzimu*. All the adult members of the family of the sick person will gather in the house of the eldest sister of the deceased whose *mzimu* is said to have caused the illness. At each invocation all will answer *pepa* (pardon) and continually clap their hands as a sign of respect.

Taphika mowa uwu (we have prepared this beer) ... pepa
Si wathu (it is not for us) ... pepa
Ndi wa azimu (it is for the spirits) ... pepa
Ati afuna mowa (they said: we want beer) ... pepa
Mum'chiritse (make him get better) ... pepa
Tidzam'samala (we shall take good care of him) ... pepa
Tikupatsani mowa (we give you beer) ... pepa
Kuti mumwe'ko (that you drink of it) ... pepa

2. *Offering of beer at the commemoration of burial of a chief*

(to the spirit:)
Tasonkhana lero (we have come together today) ... pepa
Taphika mowa (we have prepared beer) ... pepa
Tifuna mtendere (we want peace) ... pepa
Tikupatsani mowa (we give you beer) ... pepa
Kuti mumwe'ko (that you drink of it) ... pepa

(to the people:)
Takuitanani nonsenu (we have called you all together)... Pepa
Titete mfumu wakale (that we appease the former chief) ... pepa
Taphika mowa (we have prepared beer) ... pepa
Titete mfumu uja (that we appease that chief) ... pepa (to the spirit:)
Takupatsani mowa (we gave you beer) ... pepa
Musabwere kutidwalitsa (do not come back bringing sickness) ... pepa
Khalani mu kachisi lanu (stay in your kachisi) ... pepa

Musabvute ana athu (do not trouble our children) ... pepa

Mukafuna mowa (if you want beer) ... pepa

Mutidziwitse bwino (let us know it gently) ... pepa

Muli ndi ana ambiri (you have many children) .... pepa

Akhale ndi mtendere (that they may have peace) ... pepa

Sitifuna mzimu wogwira munthu (we do not want a spirit who takes people)
pepa

Tikupatsani mowa (we give you beer) ... pepa

Kuti mupumule (that you may rest) ... pepa

Mugone (that you may sleep well) ... pepa.

3. A family sacrifice

Landirani mizimu (receive spirits) ... pepa

Mizimu ya makolo athu (spirits of our parents) ... pepa

Landirani mizimu wa uje (receive spirits of NN) ... pepa

Idyani (eat) ... pepa

Imwani (drink) ... pepa

Koma musatibvute ife (but do not trouble us) ... pepa

Itanani'nso anzanu (call also your fellow spirits) ... pepa

Adzadye nanu (they will eat with you) ... pepa

4. Prayer in danger

Mwauma mtima Akunyangwa (you have hardened your heart, A.) ... pepa

Tichotsereni zoopsazi (take away from us this terrible thing) ... pepa

Ife tipite (we will go) ... pepa

Maso athu ali pa inu (our eyes are on you) ... pepa

Ndi maso anu ali pa ife (your eyes are on us) ... pepa

Tisungeni (keep us well) ... pepa.

5. Prayer said by a child, designated by the diviner

Tikupatsani nsima ndi ndiwo (we give you nsima and ndiwo) ... pepa

Mutipatse mvula (give us rain) ... pepa

Tikupatsani zakudya izi (we give you this food) ... pepa

Kuti musabwerenso kudzatenga munthu (that you may not return to take a
man) ... pepa

Munthu akayenda ulendo mumyeretse m'maso kuti asadwale (when one of us goes on a journey, keep him, that he may not fall ill) ... pepa

Si uwo mowa, imwani (is this not beer, drink it) .... pepa

Tikupatsani zakudya kuti mutipatse mvula (we give you food, that you give us rain) ... pepa

6. Prayer for rain

Mwamva, inu, N.N. (listen N.N.) ... pepa

Ssonkhanani pano (come here) ... pepa

Tabwera ndi zakudya (we have come with food) ... pepa

Tati: mudye pamodzi (we mean, come and eat together) ... pepa

Chifikire pano, ife tati (the purpose of our coming here is) ... pepa

Mutipatse mvula (give us rain) ... pepa

Mvula ikukanika (rain is refused i.e. has not come) ... pepa

Tipatseni mvula (give us rain) ... pepa

Madzi (water) ... pepa

Kum mero kwauma (our throats are dry) ... pepa

Ndipo ku mudzi anthu musawathante-thante (at the village do not let people die) ... pepa

Awo ali ku ulendo muwasunge bwino (those on a journey, keep them) ... pepa

7. Prayer for intercession

Ah abanda (O banda) ... pepa

Tabwera kudzakupatsani chakudya (we have come to bring you food) ... pepa

Chimene munapempha (what you asked for) ... pepa

Ai pepani Abanda (please Banda) ... pepa

Muwauze Akwenda Phiri, atate a Mbombe, ndi anzao onse a pano (tell Akwenda Phiri, the father of Mbombe, and all his fellow-spirits from here) ... pepa

Kuti atinenere - that they intercede for us) ... pepa

Kuti asatibvutenso pansi pano (that they do not trouble us any more there below) ... pepa.

Chapter 4
Death and Burial Rites

A. Hetherwick wrote that during his many years in Africa he had witnessed many death-beds and never once had he seen death faced with anything but equanimity or even indifference.[1] A few lines further he wrote, however, that in the face of death the African, who is usually cheery, seems to be utterly overwhelmed by fate which he believes to be against him. The truth is that behind an exterior acceptance of the inevitable, there is a whole world of fears, suspicions and accusations. As our survey has shown, death is almost never regarded as something natural. In most cases it is attributed to the evil deeds of fellow-men.

1. A Person in the Village Dies

When a sick person becomes gravely ill, all the relatives have to be warned. When he enters his agony *(kuthatha ndi imfa),* as many as possible come to the house, with those who cannot find a place in the house, remaining silently in front of it. They try to comfort the dying person, who is not left lying on his mat, but is taken on the lap of one of those assisting him. A mother will hold her child and when she is tired another woman will take her place. A man will hold a man and a woman a woman. The one who supports the dying person will close his eyes and mouth each time he opens them and others will keep his arms and legs straight. The gesture of closing a dying person's mouth has been mistakenly interpreted as an attempt to kill him by suffocation. But the relatives want to ensure that he/she dies with the mouth or eyes closed and the arms and legs outstretched, for he/she has to die well *(ndi ulemu,* i.e. with dignity). For them, a dead person with mouth or eyes open is terrifying. Death is like sleeping and no one sleeps

---

[1] A. Hetherwick, *The Gospel and the African*, pp. 37-38.

with his eyes open as that would be sorcery. It would seem as if the dead person were still looking at people and this they are afraid of.

When the person is on the point of dying, some of the people present, especially his mother or wife, start weeping softly *(kusisima),* lamenting and repeating over and over again the words *mayi ine* (alas). For a child, a mother will say: "*mayi ine* (alas) ... *mwana wanga ine* (my child) ... *ndilowere kuti ine* (where can I go) ... *ndiyende bwanji ine* (how can I walk) ... *ndinalakwanji ine* (what did I do wrong) ... *mwana wanga wandisiya ine* (my child left me alone) ... *ndapalamula chiyani* (what did I do to provoke this?). For a husband, a wife will say: "*mayi ine* (alas) ... *ndakhala ine ndekha* (I stay behind alone) ... *mwandisiya ine ndekha* (you leave me alone behind) ... *andithandiza ndani* (who will help me) .... *mwamuna wanga wandisiya ine* (my husband left me alone) ... *ndilira chotani ine* (how can I cry enough)".

a) Spreading the sad News

Immediately after death, one of the dead person's brothers has to inform the chief, if he is not present. In his turn the chief sends young men to inform the chiefs of the surrounding villages. In the past these young men would take a black chicken (or black beads) to each of the chiefs as a token of their grief.[2] Nowadays this is done in two cases only, namely, when a chief dies and when a married woman dies in the village of her husband. In this latter case a messenger is sent to announce the news in her kinsmen's village.[3] Arrived there the young man starts wailing and cries: "Something terrible has happened in our village, NN died" *(ku mudzi kwathu kwachitika mabvuto, amwalira auje).*

From then on until after the burial nobody in the village and among those who will assist at the burial may eat meat *(kusala).* This is seen as a sign of grief *(chifukwa cha chisoni).* Since meat is a dish for feast days *(ndiwo ya chaka)* it would be an insult to the deceased's spirits to eat meat at his burial. It is

---

[2] Only children may eat such a chicken.

[3] The Chewa are uxorilocal people, but after a time the husband may be given permission to take his family to his own village.

also a way of avoiding suspicion of witchcraft. For a witch is said to eat the flesh of his victim, mixing it with ordinary meat so that other people will not notice it. This abstention from meat is again explained as a measure of economy. After the burial it is customary to give a meal to everybody who attends the burial and people cannot afford to give meat twice. Except nowadays perhaps, when in the case of a rich person, a goat may be killed the evening before the burial as food for the guests. But this is not common practice. The chiefs of the other villages after receiving the message gather their people and together with them go to the village of the deceased. The chief walks ahead and the men follow him single file in silence. The women walk by themselves, also single file.

b) Preparation of the Body

Meanwhile at the house of the deceased the body is washed by the men of the family in the case of a man or a grown-up boy. If the deceased is a woman or a child, it is the task of the women. In the past the hair of the deceased's head was shaved and anointed with oil. This is no longer done today. The corpse is dressed and in the case of a woman adorned with beads *(mkanda)* around neck, wrists and waist. The arms are bound in place alongside the body and the legs stretched out with the two big toes bound together to keep the legs together.

If the eyes and mouth have fallen open they are closed again. The body is placed on a big piece of new cloth, which is turned back to cover the body. The face however is left uncovered so that people may recognize the deceased. The cloth is wrapped tightly around the body and tied with a string or safety pin. In the past, the outside cloth at least had to be red for a chief, or white for an ordinary person, but nowadays any colour may be used.[4] Before wrapping the body in the cloth, strips are torn from it, which the wife and children will wear as a sign of mourning around the head *(m'cha-mulo)* or in the case of a husband around the wrist *(zithambo)*. Other relatives too may wear strips of cloth around their head or wrist. When the prepara-

---

[4] The colour red (which is the colour of life) indicates the belief that life comes from the spirits to the living through the intermediary of the chief.

tion of the body is finished, it is placed on a mat in the middle of the house, with the head nearest the door.

2. The Involvement of the Village Community

When the body has been prepared for burial, the village chief is informed and he gives the signal for the solemn proclamation of the death *(kubuma maliro)*. All the people present in the village assemble in front of the house, relatives, neighbours and strangers. The men stand together in front of the house, the women a little to the side. They all stand for a moment in silence, and then suddenly everybody begins to cry very loudly, so that they can be heard far away in the surrounding villages. This lasts for two or three minutes. The men often weep with their face hidden behind a hand while the women sometimes place their hand with fingers outstretched behind their head. Then the men sit down around the house on the verandah *(khonde)* or on that of the neighbouring houses. As many women as possible try to enter the house, where they continue the wailing. Usually one intones a few words and all join in with the *mayi ine*. At other moments everyone laments on his/her own. The men wail on their own, each one saying what comes to mind. The men shield part of their face with their hand and keep their gaze cast down. Some indulge in the most delirious weeping and gesticulations, others are more calm and composed. In the house the women keep up the wailing for many hours at a stretch. Like the proclamation itself this wailing is among the most dismal sounds I have ever heard, with nothing to compare it with.

When people arrive from other villages, they go straight to the house of the deceased without greeting anybody. Women enter the house, while the men usually stay outside in front of the house. They wail and cry out for a few minutes, and then sit down together with those already present after going over to where the chief is sitting with the relatives of the deceased and other elders in order to express their sympathy *(kupepesa)*. If anyone wants to see the deceased he can enter the house. Young men go to the graveyard to help with the digging of the grave.

The chief, the elders, and the men of the lineage of the deceased discuss the circumstances of the death, and make arrangements for the burial. They see if there is any case *(mlandu)* arising from the death. How is it that he died? Did anyone consult the diviner? Why not? Did the husband go with his wife to the hospital, or the father with the child? The eldest brother of the deceased is called the *mwini maliro* (the owner of the burial). The other brothers and sisters of the deceased are together the *eni ake maliro* (the owners of the maliro). In the case of a child, the *eni ake maliro* and the *mwini maliro* are the brothers and sisters of the dead child's mother.

Nowadays there will be a *mlandu* only in a few cases, e.g. if the relatives were not warned in time in the case of a serious illness. There will always be a *mlandu* when a pregnant woman dies. The husband will be blamed and made to pay a cow. He is said to have caused *mdulo* and so killed his wife.[5] It is sufficient to say here that it is a mysterious disease caused by the transgression of a taboo, e.g. adultery by the husband during his wife's pregnancy. A father will also have to face a *mlandu* if he did not take his child to the hospital. It must be born in mind that the Chewa are a matrilineal people and the "owners" of the child are the members of the mother's lineage *(achibale akuchikazi)*. So the husband may be blamed for the slightest negligence, real or supposed. We remember the case of a pregnant woman whose time was overdue. The young husband was worried and had asked me to take the woman to the hospital by car. The other women refused to let her go, and she had to give birth to the child in the village. Both the woman and the child died - and the husband was blamed.

As long as such a *mlandu* is not settled, permission to bury the dead is refused. The body stays in the house until at least a promise is given to have the case discussed immediately after the funeral. There may be cases in which the diviner indicated that a person has killed the deceased by witchcraft. An overt accusation of witchcraft will not happen so often nowadays because it is an offense against the law, but insinuations are made which are

---

[5] *Mdulo* will be considered in chapter six.

perfectly understood by all present. When all is settled, the chief gives permission to "bring out the body" *(kuchotsa maliro).*

People attending the burial bring presents to the *eni ake maliro* to help defray the expenses of the burial. In the past they brought objects in kind, nowadays they usually offer money. Women may still bring flour and *ndiwo* (side-dish eaten together with the *nsima*) to help prepare the funeral meal. The money offered is carefully noted down and when the body is "brought out", one person will stand up and read out how much each person or group has offered.

We already mentioned that many people attend a burial *(maliro).* This is a major event in the life of the village. Everything else has to give way to it. Meetings may be planned, but if there is a *maliro* nobody will turn up. It may happen that a series of burials during the time of planting or weeding may seriously affect the food-supply for the following year. But even if attendance at these burials entails a serious threat to the food supply, people still prefer to attend the burial rather than be branded as one who "does-not-go-to-a-*maliro*". I heard of such a series of burials that the people began complaining that they could not work in the fields. In view of this the elders decided that people could work in the fields till 10 o'clock in the morning before going to the *maliro*. This is a very rare case, the only one I have heard of so far. It shows that slowly a change of mentality is taking place. This overriding obligation to go to a *maliro* is a real problem where modern work-contracts have been introduced. Some people prefer to work far from home so that they cannot be reached in time and so cannot be expected to come for a *maliro*. One of the most common reasons for absenteeism is this obligation to attend a *maliro*. Several times I have asked informants why people have all to go to a *maliro*. That relatives, friends and neighbours go is an accepted custom everywhere. But that big crowds should spend hours and hours at a *maliro* is another question. The reasons we received can be summed up under the following headings:

1.   People want to comfort the relatives of the deceased, to distract them with dances and songs and help them forget the deceased.

2. They fear that if they do not go to the *maliro*, they may be punished. There is a tremendous social pressure to go and help at a *maliro*. I have on record several cases where the chief punished a person by forbidding people to help him with a *maliro* in his home; he had to dig the grave all by himself and prepare the coffin. The reason was that there had been persistent refusal on his part to help at other burials *(mfumu imati popeza sumapita ku maliro, tsono chita zonse wekha)*.

3. There is a great deal of work to be done at a *maliro*. To dig the grave (2 m deep), to make the coffin, to cook the food, to collect stones, to fetch water and firewood. This demands many hands, so that both men and women have to be ready to help.

4. Fear of being accused of having caused the death. A witch *(mfiti)* is believed to be afraid to go to the *maliro* of his victim. Someone who does not go to the *maliro* will readily be accused of witchcraft *(ufiti)*, since the people cannot see any other real reason for not attending.

5. There is the belief that witches *(afiti)* may come to snatch away the corpse. So many people are needed to watch the body day and night.

6. Death is something mysterious and frightening and people want to be together to face it. They are afraid of death itself, afraid of the *mizimu* who are believed to be particularly near at a *maliro*, afraid of the *mzimu* of the dead person himself, who at death entered into the liminal state. They have to honour him/her and "send him/her off" lest he/she stays in the village and accuses them of having buried him/her as they bury a child. People are also afraid of a corpse because they believe that from it emanates something mysterious and dangerous. The Chewa, like most Africans, need to be together, to do things together, to work and rejoice together. In these dangerous circumstances, when the mysterious touches them more closely they need this manifestation of solidarity and mutual encouragement.

These are the reasons which the people themselves gave. Some are more pragmatic, some more religious, but they complement each other. The "religious" element comes down to the need to "send off the *mizimu*". This we believe to be practically the only corporate act of religion nowadays for most of the people. There are not many *mfunde* nowadays in the villages.

The *maliro* seems to be the most expressive and most frequent act of corporate religion in village-life. This can explain the overriding importance given to it.

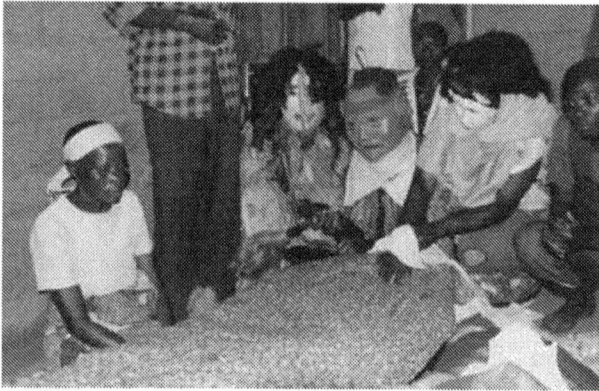

Gule wamkulu characters mourning over a corpse

If death occurs in the early hours of the morning, the burial may take place the same day, though sometimes a delay of a day is needed to allow all the relatives to arrive. If the person died late in the day, the burial will be put off until the following day. If necessary there may be a delay of a day to allow relatives to arrive. People are afraid to bury the body as long as all the relatives have not come. They may arrive after the burial and start a *mlandu*: they may refuse to mourn alleging that it is not their relative who has died. During the night there will be a vigil in the house where the body is kept conducted usually by the older women nowadays, in the past by the men. They light a fire inside the house to keep rats (emissaries of witches) away and they lie down in a circle around the body. Lamenting goes on all night. All the other people sleep out in the open or on the verandah *(khonde)* of surrounding houses. Nobody is allowed to go home and sleep indoors, he would at once be suspected of having relations with his wife, something which is forbidden during a *maliro (kudika maliro)*. Whenever a person falls ill soon after a *maliro*, someone is suspected of having violated this taboo and an attempt will be made to find him by recourse to a diviner. People believe that someone who has relations during this time insults the spirit of the deceased and will therefore be responsible for calling down the vengeance of the spirit upon the relatives.

If the deceased was a member of the *Nyau*, or if nowadays the relatives can afford to pay *(kusupa)*, *Nyau* will be danced during the night in front of the house. If there has not been enough time to prepare *Nyau,* people may sing *Nyau* songs instead.[6] For the moment it is sufficient to say that they consider *Nyau* dances important for a burial of an adult: "We accompany our deceased friend, that he may go in peace, that his spirit may sleep, and not come back to trouble us and say: you had no drums at my burial, I went like a dog" *(tikuperekeza mnzathu watisiyayo, amuke ndi mtendere, mzimu wake ugone, asadzabwerere kutigwira ndi kuti: munalibe kundiimbira ng'oma pa maliro anga, ndamuka ngati galu).*

3. The Burial

In the past there was a group of professional gravediggers *(adzukulu),* who were asked to watch the corpse during the night and to dig the grave. These were men who were not afraid of corpses. They showed fearlessness in their behaviour and displayed a certain scorn towards the dead. While digging the grave they laughed and joked and insulted everybody. They could also insult people and use all sorts of indecencies towards women. All this is done in order to show off and to prove that they knew no fear. They had certain privileges: they could go to the village and take a chicken or even a goat for their own use without risk of a court case *(mlandu).* They could put their hand in a beer pot, and the beer was theirs. These *adzukulu* were, in the minds of the people, associated with death, and therefore to be feared. "They will bury me", people said. They formed an association and people from surrounding villages would ask them for their services at a *maliro*. This custom has now disappeared. Now young men from the village dig the grave and any stranger coming to the *maliro* is welcome to join them.

The elder of the graveyard *(mkulu wa ku manda)* chooses the spot for the grave. He is an older man who is supposed to know where former graves were dug and will ensure they will not be disturbed in the digging of the new one. Normally each village has its own graveyard situated at a certain distance from the houses. It is in thick bush for it is the only place where bushfires, which destroy all undergrowth, are never allowed. People are

---

[6] *Nyau* itself will be considered in the following chapter five.

afraid to go to the graveyard, except at a *maliro*, because it is the place where the *mizimu* dwell. A person going there would immediately be accused of witchcraft *(ufiti)*, and more specifically of eating corpses. Moreover, the members of *Nyau* use graveyards as their hiding-places.

In the past, once the place for the grave was selected, an offering of flour was made by the *mwini maliro*. He poured some flour at the place where the grave was going to be dug, so that the deceased could not complain that they denied him food. People take turns to dig the grave, but the *eni maliro*, father and husband, do not join in. The grave is 2 m deep, a bit longer than the body itself, and sufficiently wide to allow two men to go down in the grave to receive the body. The grave is oriented east-west. At the bottom of the grave and along its whole length an excavation is scooped out on the south side. This is called the "site" (probably from "side") and in it the body will be laid, with the head towards the west. The body will be laid on its side. The head is towards the west because they say this is the direction form which the Chewa originally came. S.J. Ntara says that they place the head thus because *Undi* took a western direction when he left Karonga.[7] Other explanations given are the following. The houses have their door oriented towards the west and people sleep with their head nearest to the door. Death is likened to sleep. Some also say that the head is towards the west so that his *mzimu* may be attracted by the sun when it goes down in the west, that his *mzimu* may follow the sun and not come back. Once the body is laid in the "site" this is blocked off with stones so that the earth does not fall directly on the body.

Women busy themselves pounding maize to prepare enough flour for the meal to be served after the burial, or they fetch water and fire-wood. However those who belong to the family of the deceased continue to wail at the house of the deceased. The men, unless they help in the digging of the grave, sit in groups on the verandah *(khonde)* of surrounding houses, waiting for hours on end. Constantly groups of people arrive from other villages. They go directly to the house of the deceased and wail there for a while.

---

[7] S.J. Ntara, *The History of the Chewa*, Wiesbaden: Franz Steiner Verlag, 1973, p. 31.

Women try to enter the house and join the women already there. The wailing is a manifestation of grief and also a manifestation of one's innocence with respect to the death. "A *mfiti* has no sorrow". He is said not to feel sorry even when he kills one of his own children. Therefore a person who weeps genuinely cannot be the one who caused the death. While waiting for the chief to give the sign that they can "take out the body" *(kuchotsa maliro)*, small groups of men can also be seen walking up and down in the village, weeping and wailing. At a *maliro* they put on their oldest clothes, because it is a time for grief. They cannot understand how at the burial of town's people good clothes are worn. "It is as if they feast", they say. The older the clothes, the better the person expresses his grief and his innocence.

When the grave is ready, messengers are sent to the chief and the *eni ake maliro* to announce "the village is ready" *(mudzi watha)*. The grave is the new dwelling place for the deceased. On their arrival at the village these messengers start wailing as a sign that they have come to fetch the body. If all the cases *(milandu)* are settled and all the relatives have arrived, with the exception of those who cannot possibly come, the chief gives permission to "take out the body" *(kuchotsa maliro)*.

The body is rolled in a mat, tied together with pieces of bark string *(mlaza)* and reinforced with some bamboo poles by which it can be carried like a hammock. Nowadays coffins made from wood and covered with cloth are becoming more common. The body is carried out of the house, head first. In the past a hole was made in the rear-wall of the house and the body was taken through it, for the door was reserved for the living. I myself have never witnessed a corpse being taken out this way. Assembled in front of the house everybody starts wailing very loudly. The coffin is placed on a mat in front of the house and all sit down while someone reads out the list of the contributions made to the *mwini maliro* to help defray the expenses. This is done very seriously for, as we have said, everybody is expected to contribute something as token of solidarity and proof of one's own innocence.

At a Christian *maliro*, a passage from Sacred Scriptures will be read out at this point and someone will say a few words and there will be a prayer. At a non-Christian *maliro* a similar custom has been adopted with the chief or some other older men saying a few words usually of praise of the deceased and of explanation that the villagers are innocent of the death. On one occasion it was said that they had done everything they could to help the sick man: "We gave him one Cafenol in the morning, another one at noon, and again one at night, and still he died".[8] On another occasion the chief made allusions to *ufiti* without accusing anybody outright: "Some deaths are willed by *Chiuta,* some by the spirits, but some by men". On yet another occasion the chief said that the death was too sudden to be natural. "He had no time to say good-bye" *(sanalawire).* A Chewa always says good-bye when he leaves. That this deceased young man had no time to do so was a sign for them that there had been some sinister goings-on.

The coffin is placed on a bier made of poles which the young men take turn in carrying to the graveyard. In the past both the *mwini maliro* and the mother of the deceased threw flour on the corpse. A younger brother walked ahead of the procession with the basket of flour throwing some flour at intervals along the way and especially at all the crossroads, so that the *mizimu* of the deceased would find plenty of food. This, people felt, would ensure that the *mizimu* would not come back to the village to trouble them because of any neglect on their part. Whatever path he took he would find food everywhere. The people walk in a rather disorderly fashion. If any *Nyau* dancers attend the burial some of them dance around the coffin, and an animal structure may accompany the procession. A *Nyau* dancer called *Kapoli* leads the procession. Other *Nyau* dancers take up their positions at all paths leading to the village and the graveyard to chase away unwanted strangers. People sing *maliro* or *Nyau* songs. Close relatives throw themselves on the ground and roll in the dust wailing loudly. Some friends support them lest they harm themselves in their grief.

---

[8] Cafenol is a local brand of Aspirin.

When the procession reaches the graveyard those carrying the body put it down next to the grave and then lower it with ropes. Two men stand in the grave to receive the body and to place it in the "site" prepared for it. The body is buried in the "site" to prevent witches *(mfiti)* finding it. Their medicine is supposed to go straight down and so finds nothing at the bottom of the grave. In the past a small gourd with beer, *nsima,* meat, peanuts or beans was placed in the "site" together with the body to ensure that the *mizimu* had a plentiful supply of food. Other objects like a pipe, some tobacco, a bow were also left there. In the case of a woman some of her cooking pots, baskets and other objects of which she was fond might be buried with her. These objects would first be broken or pierced to symbol-

Pombo mulimire is escorting the coffin

ize that their owner had died, and they with him *(zatha).* Someone would take the bow and standing beside the grave he would imitate the gesture of one who is shooting with the bow. The bow would then be broken and handed down into the grave. Similarly a woman's pestle is broken and placed in her grave after a woman friend has gone through the gestures of crushing maize with it. In the case of a school child his copybooks would be put in the grave.

The two men down in the grave seal off the "site" with stones *(zibuma)* brought for this purpose and cement them with fresh mud. They are then helped out of the grave. Then the relatives followed by all those present, throw a handful of earth into the grave. This, they say, helps them to forget the deceased. The grave is then filled in by some of the men. On one occasion, just before earth was thrown into the grave, all the chiefs, who had been sitting at the entrance of the graveyard, were invited to leave. After the burial I asked some people what was the meaning of this invitation. The only explanation given to me at the time was that it was a mark of respect *(ulemu)*, so that the chiefs could get back to the village without being jostled by the main body of mourners. I believe that there is some deeper reason behind it. In the past chiefs never went to the graveyard itself. They accompanied the funeral procession as far as the graveyard and then let it enter without them while they sat down and waited at the entrance. I have noticed that some older men and chiefs still do precisely the same even today. The belief is that chiefs are somehow a link in the chain of life coming from the spirits of the deceased and so ensure the fecundity of their people. This is further illustrated by the taboo on sexual relations in the village during the chief's absence *(kudika mfumu).*[9] In the past the chiefs were the only ones allowed to wear red bark cloths (the other villagers had to dip their bark cloth in mud to make them black). The colour red, as well as being the colour of fire, is associated with life-giving.[10] For this reason chiefs did not go to an open grave, lest their function as a link in the chain of life be somehow diminished by the mysterious and dangerous power, which was believed to emanate from the corpse. We shall see that all those present at the burial must wash in medicated water immediately after the burial in order to eliminate this dangerous contamination, which they call the "odour of death" *(fungo la imfa).* Only then can they resume sexual relations without danger. In this context we can also point out that women in the past never went to the graveyard, but always stayed outside. Nowadays, they may enter, but even now they usually group together at the entrance; they approach the grave only when called to throw earth into the grave. A young mother may not take her baby near a corpse as long as it has not been "taken" *(kutenga mwana).*[11] The baby is so susceptible to any mysterious power emanating from the corpse that it would surely die from such contact.

Other informants said that chiefs refuse to go too close to an open grave because they fear that the power of their medicines *(mankhwala)* might be

---

[9] Cf. chapter six, when we consider the taboos of *mdulo.*

[10] See the explanation of the initiation of girls in chapter six *(mdulo).*

[11] Cf. the respective sections in chapter six

diminished in such a case. In the past children were not allowed even to see a corpse or to enter the graveyard. They were kept in a house in the village. It was believed that they would become blind on seeing a corpse. Now children need no longer stay in a house but they do not go to the grave. Because of their great grief the mother or wife of the deceased often does not go to the grave, but stay outside the graveyard and return to the village supported by friends. Some of the men stay behind to fill in the grave by pulling back the earth with their hoes. We were told that, in the past, when they had filled in about two-thirds of the grave they planted sharpened bamboo sticks in the grave and thorns as a protection against witches *(mfiti)* who might be coming to unearth the corpse. They finish off by heaping up all the remaining soil on top of the grave and in it they plant the handles of the hoes used for digging the grave. The metal blades of the hoes are removed and taken back for a ritual cleansing. The baskets used for lifting out the soil during the digging of the grave are left in the graveyard and are hung in the branches of the trees near the grave. For nothing used for the burial is supposed to be used again. The final act is to sweep the grave, so that everything is left tidy.

4. Taboos and Protection against Witches

In the past all people attending a *maliro* were forbidden to have sexual relations until after the first shaving ceremony *(kumeta maliro kachimodzi)*. This period varied, being about one week after the burial of an adult, and four weeks after the burial of a chief and about three days for a child. Nowadays only the relatives are bound to observe this taboo. The others consider themselves free once the burial itself is over. Those breaking this taboo are said to *kudula maliro* (interfere with the proper ritual sending off of the spirit). The spirits will not fail to punish them.

On leaving the graveyard all who have taken part in the funeral go straight to a stream where the men on one side (upstream), and the women on the other, wash face, arms and legs to take away the "odour of death" *(fungo la imfa)*. This will allow them to resume sexual relations later without danger. Medicine obtained from the medicine man *(sing'anga)* is poured in the water.

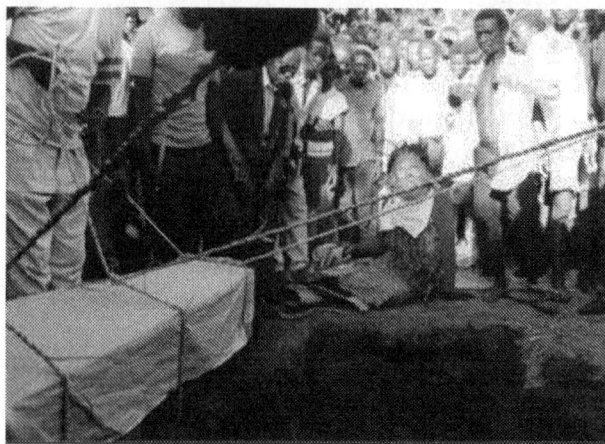

Burial

It is called *phundabwi* and consists of powder made of the *nafungwe* root which has a very bad smell. It is supposed to chase away any evil influence of death. If people did not wash, they might dream of the deceased at night. If in spite of washing someone still has dreams another will administer the medicine and say: "Leave that person, don't come back, that is jealousy, leave him, don't come back. A person who has died, must stay dead" *(musiyeni munthuyu, musabweranso, ilo ndilo jelasi, musiyeni osabweranso ayi. Munthu akafa ndiye kuti wafa)*. The metal blades of the hoes are washed with the same medicine and finally passed through fire. When all has been completed everybody walks back to the village in single file.

Back in the village an old woman (sometimes a girl in the case of a deceased child) throws a living black hen into the house of the deceased and closes the door *(kuponya nkhuku m'nyumba)*. They explain this by saying: "We are afraid of the *mzimu*, he may come back to take and kill people. It is a bad omen not to make the offerings: we would be in danger of death. To offer a chicken is to win favour" *(tiri kuopa mzimu kuti ungabwere kudzagwira ndi kufetsa anthu. Popanda kuponya nkhuku m'nyumba, ndiwo mpingu, tikutha ife anthu. Kuponya nkhuku ndiko kukoma)*. Nowadays, instead of throwing a chicken into the house, some offer one or two Kwacha.

The grave itself is protected *(kutsilika)* against a*fiti*. The *mwini maliro* waits for the people to leave the graveyard and then digs two small holes at the head of the grave and two at the foot. In each he puts some medicine obtained from the medicine man *(sing'anga)*. Sometimes a party of grave watchers is formed, who hide in the bushes near the grave in order to surprise any *mfiti* coming to feast on the corpse. M.G. Marwick described how he once took part in one of these vigils, without seeing a *mfiti*.[12] I have several cases on record of grave watchers being sent to the grave. I was told that some young people offer themselves to do this against payment. They stay at the grave till about 11 o'clock in the evening, which is the latest hour at which the *mfiti* are supposed to come. Some people told me that they believe that such young people exploited the fear of the people and made good money out of it. I heard of one occasion when some young men killed a lonely old woman in her house at night, and then reported to the people that they had found a *mfiti* who could be found dead in her house. I have 13 cases on record of people found dead whose death was interpreted as the killing of a *mfiti*. Some of these unfortunate people were even found to have been killed in the characteristic way that *mfiti* are said to be killed, namely, impaled on a pointed bamboo stick. A.G.O. Hodgson and M.G. Marwick have already reported this method of killing a *mfiti*, which is called *kumuchita chipasi* (pointed wood).[13] In 1973, one victim of such an attack managed to get to the hospital in Lilongwe. I have the story from the European doctor who was astounded to find a person in such a condition.[14]

5. The Period of Mourning

In the evening of the burial there is a *Nyau* ceremony if the *Nyau* has been invited to the *maliro*. It will continue for three consecutive nights, during which time lamentations will go on around the funeral house. Strangers may go home after the burial, but relatives *(achibale)* are expected to stay for 5 to 6 days and to continue to observe the taboos concerning sexual relations. The others had to do so in the past, but nowadays they consider themselves free once the burial itself is over. Some of the older people however still

---

[12] M.G. Marwick, *Sorcery in its Social Setting*, Manchester: University Press, 1965, p. 86.

[13] Cf. A.G.O. Hodgson, "Notes on the Achewa and Angoni of the Dowa District of the Nyasaland Protectorate", in: *Journal of the Royal Anthropological Institute* 63 (1933), p. 134; M.G. Marwick, *Sorcery in its Social Setting*, p. 86.

[14] In this particular case it was a piece of broomstick. A crowd of people had pursued the victim and was standing at the door of the hospital.

continue to observe the traditional taboo. There is wailing early in the morning and at night, in which other villagers join with the relatives. This period of mourning lasts until the "first shaving of the hair" *(kumeta maliro kachimodzi)*. No visits are made to the graveyard and anyone found going there is liable to be accused of *ufiti*. The house of the deceased person remains open till the "first shaving", but the floor is replastered with mud in order to avoid contact with death.

The husband or wife, the mother, sisters and aunts of the deceased wear a narrow strip of cloth *(m'chamulo)* around their head or around the wrist *(zithambo)*. A strip of cloth is also fixed to a pole which is stuck in the grass roof of the house. There are two separate periods of mourning. The first one lasts for 5 to 7 days for an adult, 3 days for a child and 4 weeks for a chief. It ends with the ceremony of the "first shaving" *(kumeta maliro kachimodzi)*. The second period lasts until the second shaving *(kumeta maliro kachiwiri)* which always takes place during the dry season from 6 to 12 months after the death. The time is fixed by the *mwini maliro* together with the chief. Until the *kumeta maliro kachiwiri*, the *mzimu* of the deceased is believed to be in a state of transition. The body is not yet decomposed, and the *mzimu* has not yet settled in the spirit-world definitively but hovers around the grave, his house and the village in general, being in a "liminal" state.[15] At the *kumeta kachiwiri* the people celebrate with much beer, food, and dancing, because the *mzimu* is now believed to have entered into his new definitive state. The body is now decomposed, the mourning is over, his widow is allowed to marry again. Until then the people made offerings to the *mzimu* and begged him to leave the village. Even after the second shaving *mizimu* are believed to come to the village occasionally and people beg them not to disturb the living.

a) First Shaving of the Hair (kumeta maliro kachimodzi)

At the appropriate time everybody is informed, "tomorrow is the shaving of the hair" *(kumeta maliro,* also called *mpalo)*. Many people attend because there

---

[15] We adopt here the terminology of V.W Turner, *The Forest of Symbols*, Ithaca: Cornell University Press, 1967, pp. 93-110.

is food. From that day onwards, the house of the deceased is no longer called *nyumba* (house) but *siwa* (abandoned house, or house without owner). A widow may remain in the house until another has been built for her. This has to be done as soon as possible after the start of the dry season. In such a case the house is carefully swept and the floor replastered before the widow goes back to it. All the sweepings are burnt. If the widow does not need the house, it will be closed and holes will be knocked in the walls. This is to let the *mzimu* know that he should no longer remain in the village. At the second shaving the house will be pulled down completely, because by then the *mzimu* is believed to have settled in the spirit-world. After the death of a child, the parents will continue to live in the house after replastering the floor. A widower will also continue to live in his house, but when he takes another wife he will build another house. The *mzimu* of his former wife is believed to render a marriage sterile if they live in the same house.

When all the people have arrived for the ceremony of the first shaving, everybody gathers near the house of the deceased and the shaving of the hair begins. First the wife of the deceased man is shaved (or the mother in the case of the death of a child), then all the female relatives. The men do not have their head shaved nowadays as they used to in the past. The hair is thrown on the rubbish-heap *(nthayo)*. Formerly it was carefully collected, put in a gourd and buried near the door of the *siwa*. The people all sit around the house and the *mwini maliro* makes invocations to the *mizimu* of the deceased, begging him to leave and not return to disturb the people. The people answer *pepa* as usual. After the invocations the *mwini maliro* claps his hands to draw the attention of the *mizimu*. He has brought goats and sprinkles their head and back with water to purify them. Then he says: M*zimu* wa N.N., you see these goats? They are yours. Don't come back. Leave the people in peace". These goats are now called *mbuzi ya ku mitu* (goats consecrated to *mizimu*). They are looked after by the mother or the sister of the deceased. They cannot be killed or sold. If one dies, it has to be replaced by another. In case of death the meat of the goat may be sold to buy another goat, which will then replace it as *mbuzi ya ku mitu*. Relatives may never eat its meat. Its young belong to the *mizimu*, but some may be sold to buy clothes for the children of the deceased. The goats are taken from the herd of the deceased or if he had none from those of his relatives. For a rich man cows may be consecrated instead of goats; in the case of a poor man chickens can be substituted. All the relatives are informed which animals are consecrated. If ever an animal *ya ku mitu* has to be sold, all the *achibale* (brothers and sisters) have to agree. If later on an offering has to be made to the *mizimu*, one of these animals may be taken.

One may sometimes wonder why nothing is done about the many goats one sees in the villages. In fact they usually belong to the *mizimu (za ku mitu)*. If someone kills any of these animals a case will follow because he has offended the *mizimu*. In case of an illness the diviner may say that someone has eaten a chicken *ya ku mitu* and the *mizimu* took revenge by sending the illness.

b) Second Shaving of the Hair (kumeta maliro kachiwiri)

A period of between six months to a year elapses before the second shaving *(kumeta maliro kachiwiri)*. This always takes place during the hot season when there is plenty of food and no work in the fields. It marks the solemn closing of the mourning period and is a feast for everybody with plenty of beer and food. *Nyau* are informed to get ready if their services are required. In the past they would attend only if the deceased himself had been a *Nyau* member. Now the *Nyau* will attend for everybody as long as the relatives are willing to pay. Their dance lasts four days, the final one being the day of *kumeta* itself. We shall see more about these dances of the *Nyau* in the chapter five.

On the day of the second shaving all those whose hair was cut at the first shaving will have their head shaved again. All the mourning signs *(m'chamulo, zitambo)* are now removed and burnt and the ashes are thrown away. The *mwini maliro* pours some beer into the gourd buried near the door of the *siwa* and again asks the *mizimu* not to come back and trouble the people any more. The *siwa* is then demolished and its roof burnt. A pole is placed at the emplacement of the door, and a piece of cloth is fixed to the top of it. The gourd is now at the foot of this pole. Before people start drinking the beer *(mowa wa maliro)*, the chief pours some of it in the gourd or at the foot of the *mizimu* tree and prays: "Here, have some beer, drink it, and don't spoil our beer, that it may taste good" *(suwu mowawu, mumwe, musatiipitsire mowa, ukhale wabwino)*.

Dambule - Pouring beer over the grave

A.G.O. Hodgson reported that at the final *kumeta maliro* a special performance took place.[16] The *Nyau* prepared a "corpse" at the *liunde* (their assembly place near the village) wrapping one of the dancers in a shroud with his big toes bound together. Leaves of the *mtubzi tubzi*,[17] which exude a vile odour like that of a rotten body were inserted in the shroud, and the body was then rolled in a mat. Four other *Nyau* dancers *(akasinja)* carried the body to the open space in the village *(bwalo)* where they unwrapped him and ran away. Another *Nyau* dancer *(kapoli)* stood over him with a torch, holding his breath because of the vile odour. Women came to look at the "corpse". Finally the *akasinja* returned to take the corpse away.

When a child was being mourned, a life-size figure was cut out of wood and taken to the *dambwe* (hiding place of the *Nyau*) where it was coated in black mud and left in the sun for the mud to harden. The head was then covered with gum and real hair stuck on it. The body was then wrapped in some cloths and taken to the *bwalo* by a single *Kasinja*. The women then came and examined the corpse as above. This ceremony does not seem to be per-

---

[16] A.G.O. Hodgson, "Notes on the Achewa and Angoni", p. 158.

[17] Cf. entry "Mtubzi tubzi", in: D.C. Scott, *Cyclopaedic Dictionary of the Mang'anja Language*, Edinburgh Foreign Mission Committee of the Church of Scotland, 1892, p. 472: "A shrub with a bad smell".

formed any more. At least I did not hear of it. But it appears to have been a symbolic statement of the fact that the body was putrefied. The vile smell and the cracked mud are symbols of putrefaction. The ceremony is as it were a solemn declaration of the fact that the *mzimu* has at last been finally and completely freed from the dead body, which had been holding it back somehow. The *mzimu* has now passed the liminal period and has fully entered into the world of the *mzimu*.

The *aggregation*, the last state in the transition of a person, is expressed in the symbolic presentation of the putrefied body, which is a kind of solemn declaration and a signal for much rejoicing.[18] H.S. Stannus wrote that at the second *kumeta* there was much dancing and beer drinking, expressing the idea that the "corpse has now disappeared".[19] In the past it was at the second *kumeta* that the *mwini maliro* officially told the wife of his late brother that he took her as his wife. He may tell the other wives (if any) to choose one of his other brothers. If none of the brothers intends to marry one of the widows, the *mwini maliro* tells her that she is free to marry whom she wants. In such a case the widow must give the *mwini maliro* a goat. This is called *chipindatchika* and is a sign that she is now free to marry whom she wants.

Each of the new husbands has to bring a chicken *(nkhuku)* to the house where his wife is staying. That same day, one of the children of the deceased's sister who is looking after the animals *za ku mitu,* will collect the *nkhuku*. By taking it away, the child removes the *mzimu* of the deceased. The woman and her new husband have still to get medicine from the medicine man, called *nafungwe*. These are bad smelling roots, which have to be crushed and mixed with water. On three consecutive nights they have to wash themselves completely with this water at a crossroads. On the third night they may have conjugal relations without danger. If they did not use this medicine their new marriage would certainly remain childless and, moreover the *mzimu* of the former husband would come to disturb them.

---

[18] Cf. V.W Turner, *The Forest of Symbols*, pp. 93-111.

[19] H.S. Stannus, "Notes on some Tribes in British Central Africa", in: *Journal of the Royal Anthropological Institute* 40 (1910), p. 315.

6. Some Special Death Cases

a) Death of a Child

A stillborn child or one which has survived for less than a week is carried by a few women (the grandmother and some others) in a broken pot and put down somewhere near the graveyard at the foot of a tree. The pot is closed with a clod of earth and no food is offered because the child had not learned to eat. The same procedure is followed in the case of a completely deformed child. While still alive it is put in a pot, carried to a tree in the bush near the graveyard, and the pot is closed with a clod of earth. Afterwards the women go to bathe at the river. There is no wailing, except by the mother herself who weeps "silently" so as not to be heard. Nowadays the child's corpse is often wrapped in a cloth and put in a shallow grave dug by the women.

A child who dies before being ritually introduced into the lineage *(kutenga)* is buried in a shallow grave by womenfolk alone. The little corpse is not called a corpse *(maliro)* but unripe *(nsenye)*. If the child dies at about one month old, men may do the digging but they do not attend the burial. Only the parents and the grandmother will cry over it *(kulira)*. In its grave they may put the carrying cloth of the child *(mbereko)* and some food. Only the mother is shaved and there is no second shaving. All children who have been ritually introduced into the lineage are buried as grown-up people.

b) Death of a Pregnant Woman

While the grave is being dug, the *mwini maliro* and the chief of the village try to find a man who is not easily frightened. He has to go to the graveyard and hide himself. Once the people have brought the body and have lowered it into the grave, they must withdraw to a certain distance from where the grave is out of sight. The man comes out of hiding, jumps down into the grave and stabs the woman's abdomen with his knife. He then climbs out of the grave and runs away, imitating the cry of a hyena. The people then return to continue the funeral. The reason given for this is that there are really two deaths, and that the *mzimu* of the child must be helped to leave the womb.

c) Death of a Twin

The burial follows the normal procedure. But each evening for a week the mother must rub the head of the surviving child with medicine, the bad smell of which is intended to chase away the *mzimu* of the dead child who might come to claim his twin. If, later on, the child cannot sleep and cries during the night, the mother will repeat the treatment.

d) Death of a Chief

In the past, the chiefs of the surrounding villages used to descend with their men to ransack the village as soon as they heard about the death. The villagers used to try to keep the death secret for a while in order to gain sufficient time to place their belongings in safety. This raid was meant to symbolize the need for authority, and to show that without a chief there is only disaster.

e) Death of a Leper or of a Victim of Small-Pox (nthomba)

They were not buried in the ground but left hanging from a tree in the graveyard so that the earth would not be contaminated by the disease. Nowadays they favour burial of these persons but they leave the grave open so that the evil can come out without contaminating the soil.

7. Conclusion

The Chewa attribute illness and death to various agents and make every effort to discover those responsible. Even among Christians this mentality is still prevalent. In moments of crisis this deep-seated conviction, built up by centuries' old traditions, may surface. An atmosphere of fear and distrust is created which becomes particularly acute in circumstances such as a sudden and unexpected death, many deaths occurring in a relatively short period of time, a death after a beer party and deaths connected with pregnancy and childbirth.

The husband is often the person accused. In the case of illness the husband will be particularly anxious to send messages to inform the relatives of his wife in due time. He will also do his best to get his wife or child to a hospital, especially if he has taken his wife to live in his own village *(mkazi wa-chitengwa)*. The Chewa are a matrilineal people and, at least in the early years of marriage, uxorilocal. The owners of the children are the brothers and sisters *(achibale)* of the mother, and the husband owes explanation to them. The fact that the husband is often accused is inherent in the system in which the husband is looked upon as a stranger whose services are needed but whose interests lie with his own *achibale* and the children of his own sisters.

A burial is a major event in the life of the village. Everything else has to give way to it and every effort is made by relatives and acquaintances to be present. The funeral rites are an act of corporate religion. A deceased person has passed from the world of the living and is in a transition to the world of the *mizimu*. Using the terminology of V. Turner we could classify the funeral rites as follows:[20]

1. *Separation.* The person has died and has left the world of the living. The rites of burial underline this. There exists an overriding desire on the part of the living "to forget" the dead. Their prayer is: "Go and do not come back".

2. *Marginal state, liminality.* During the time of transition the situation of the spirit of the deceased is ambivalent. He is as it were in the process of becoming a *mzimu*, but he is still to some extent held back by his body, which is undergoing the process of decomposition. During this period the spirit of the deceased is believed to be particularly susceptible and unpredictable in his reactions towards the living. The rituals accompanying this state consist in continuous mourning and concerted prayer: "Don't come back to trouble us". This is the period during which the

---

[20] V.W. Turner, *The Forest of Symbols*, pp. 93-110.

relatives are particularly afraid to be visited by dreams concerning the deceased. They protect themselves by having recourse to bad-smelling medicine believed to "drive away" the spirit.

3. *Aggregation.* The spirit is believed to have settled in his new home, and to have fully acquired his new status. His body is now decomposed. The symbolic presentation of the putrefied body is as it were the ritual declaration that the spirit had reached the world of the *mizimu.* There is much rejoicing. The mourning signs are burnt, the widow can remarry, the house is demolished. From now on the spirit is believed to come back no more except to protect, to warn of an impending danger, or to punish if traditional customs *(miyambo)* are not observed. The people are still afraid of him, but at least he is not so unpredictable as during his state of transition.

The period of mourning is the time that people remember the deceased more vividly and suffer more acutely the loss of a husband, wife, mother friend, etc. With the passing of time this acute suffering disappears. The reaction against this suffering is the desire to "forget", to have the memory of the deceased recede and not "come back".

Death with its accompanying decomposition is dangerous to the living. There is the belief that the "odour of death" is particularly dangerous for chiefs, women and children. After a burial all present at it have to undergo a ritual washing with medicated water which ensures that no danger will follow from resumed sexual relations. This and the need for *kudika maliro* (the taboo on sexual relations) confirm Chewa beliefs that death (symbolized by the "odour of death") is dangerous to life especially to the passing-on of life. The wailing during the *maliro* expresses grief and innocence with regard to the death of the deceased. The belief in a *mfiti* who kills in order to feast on the corpse of his victim will be described in chapter seven (Witchcraft).

The grief and the fear of death, of the *mizimu*, and of sinister powers of *ufiti* are made tolerable by the fact that they can be given communal expression at the burial: Fear and grief that cannot be expressed lead to intolerable tension. The religious element at the burial consists in the various rites by which the spirit is accompanied through his liminal state until he reaches his new status of *mzimu*. In the following chapter we shall consider the *Nyau*, which plays such an important role in the funeral rites as we mentioned already. M. Wilson makes a reflection while describing funeral rites of the Nyakyusa which will help us to understand part of the "anomalies" of the *Nyau* presence at a *maliro*. She writes: "Having no confident expectation of happiness in a future life, they turn at burials to a realization of present life in its most intense quality, to a war dance, to sexual display to show their strength, to lively talk, and to the eating of great quantities of meat".[21]

---

[21] M. Wilson, *Rituals of Kinship among the Nyakyusa*, London: OUP, 1957, p. 30.

Appendix 3: **Some *maliro* Songs**

Chauta jenjee, ali maso ndipo adatenga.
Chauta, he was alive and now you have taken him.

Chauta, Chauta, tsoka ndidachita ine, wawononga.
Chauta, Chauta, alas to me, you have taken him.

Kumanda kuononga kuononga anyamata okoma ochiseka ochigwira pa-kamwa.
In the grave fine young men lie dead who used to laugh and joke.

Wapita, wapita, wapita, chaona mnzako chapita mawa chidzaona iwe.
He is gone, He is gone, He is gone, what happened to your friend, may happen to you tomorrow.

Dzulo analipo, dzulo analipo, mbale wanga yee.
Yesterday he was still here, yesterday he was still here, my brother alas.

Munthu ukapita, munthu ukapita, ukhale bwino ndi ana.
When you have gone, when you have gone, be kind to your children.

Siyo ndege yagwa, hoo, siyo ndege yagwa, hoo.
See how the plane crashed, see how the plane crashed.

Njira ya kumanda yopanda taima, njira ya kumanda.
On the road to the grave, there is no "Stop!", on the road to the grave.

Eni ake a nyumba iyi kodi adanka kuti? Ali chete, chete ku manda, Ali chete, chete ku manda.
Where is the owner of this house? He is silent, silent in his grave. He is silent, silent in his grave.

Chapter 5
Nyau

Among the authors who have described *Nyau*, D.C. Scott was the first to do so, but he seemed to have confused it with the *Unyago* of the Yao.[1] E. Foà gave a short description of a *Nyau* dance which he considered as an apparition of the spirits of the dead.[2] R.S. Rattray mentioned that it was a dance of grass animals who were believed to be re-incarnations of the dead. He added that it was difficult to get information about it because the people refused absolutely to speak about it.[3] H.S. Stannus was more precise: it is a dance of men only, who are often naked, while women sing. Children are not allowed to be present. The animal figures are made of grass and bamboo, they are life-size and completely enclose the dancers. These constitute a society with a secret language. Membership was reserved to those who had given proof of bravery and endurance. The dance is called "the big dance" *(gule wamkulu)*.[4] A.G.O. Hodgson added a description of some animal structures.[5] W.H.J. Rangeley gave us the most detailed description of the *Nyau* in the Central province so far. His study is particularly interesting in that he gave us a detailed description of a number of *Nyau* masks and animal structures.[6] M. Tew made a synthesis of all literature existing at that

---

[1] D.C. Scott, *Cyclopaedic Dictionary of the Mang'anja Language*, Edinburgh Foreign Mission Committee of the Church of Scotland, 1892, pp. 84 and 678.

[2] E. Foà, *La Traversée de l'Afrique du Zambése au Congo Francais*, Paris: Plon, 1900, pp. 40-44.

[3] R.S. Rattray, *Some Folk-Lore Stories and Songs in Chinyanja*, London: Society for the Promotion of Christian Knowledge, 1907, pp. 178-179.

[4] H.S. Stannus, "Notes on some Tribes in British Central Africa", in: *Journal of the Royal Anthropological Institute* 40 (1910), pp. 197, 314, 334.

[5] A.G.O. Hodgson, "Notes on the Achewa and Angoni of the Dowa District of the Nyasaland Protectorate", in: *Journal of the Royal Anthropological Institute* 63 (1933), pp. 146-152.

[6] W.H.J. Rangeley, "Nyau in Nkhotakota District", in: *Nyasaland Journal* 2 (1949), no. 2, pp. 35-49 (part I), 3 (1930), no. 2, pp. 19-33 (part II)

date.[7] A.J. Makumbi in his study of Chewa customs relating to funerals gave some interesting incidental references to *Nyau*.[8] J.M. Schoffeleers wrote on the Mang'anja of South Malawi where a form of *Nyau* can be found with certain similarities with the *Nyau* of the Chewa.[9] In his study on Proto-Chewa Culture the same author made important points with regard to the historical past of the *Nyau*.[10] I. Linden gave us a historical study of the conflict between the *Nyau* and the Christian missions.[11]

In this study I intend to consider above all the religious significance of the *Nyau*. As the *Nyau* is a secret society, it was difficult to gain access to it and to discuss with members of the *Nyau* their beliefs. Eventually I had to go through a form of "initiation" in April 1976. The word *Nyau*[12] is not only used for the association, but also for the dancers, their dance, their masks and animal structures.

1. *Nyau* - the Heart of Chewa Identity

The *Nyau* as a secret association of dancers using masks and animals structures exists mainly among the Chewa. Some Ngoni and Yao communities, isolated among the Chewa, have adopted it.[13] The Ngoni and Tumbuka who live to the North of the Chewa don't have *Nyau*. To the South, among the Mang'anja, a form of *Nyau* is found, which, although similar, remains in many respects different from the *Nyau* of the Chewa. Tradition has it that

---

[7] M. Tew, "People of the Lake Nyasa Region", in: D. Forde (ed.), *Ethnographic Survey of Africa*, London: OUP, 1950, pp. 47-48.

[8] A.J. Makumbi, *Maliro ndi Miyambo ya Achewa*, Blantyre/Cape Town, 1955, passim.

[9] Cf. J.M. Schoffeleers, "Symbolic and Social Aspects of Spirits Worship among the Mang'anja", Ph.D. Dissertation, Oxford, 1968, pp. 307-415.

[10] Cf. J.M. Schoffeleers, "Towards the Identification of a Proto-Chewa Culture", in: *Journal of Social Science* (University of Malawi) 2 (1973), pp. 47-60.

[11] I. Linden, *Catholics, Peasants and Chewa Resistancce in Nyasaland 1889-1939*, London: Heinemann, 1974, pp. 117-137.

[12] Sometimes the spelling *Nyao* is in common as well.

[13] Cf. A.G.O. Hodgson, "Notes on the Achewa and Angoni", p. 146, and W.H.J. Rangeley, "Nyau in Kotakota District", p. 35.

the Mang'anja and the Chewa lived together as one people at Kaphiri-ntiwa; this explains the similarities between them. Later they were divided into a number of tribes. The Mang'anja, under Kaphwiti, left the main group and travelled south.[14] Since then they have been influenced by other tribes thus acquiring certain features that do not exist among the Chewa.

After the Ngoni invaded the country in the last century, a period of great insecurity followed, during which the *Nyau* dance became rare. With the restoration of peace and the establishment of the colonial administration the people readily revived many of their old cherished traditions. A.G.O. Hodgson reported in 1933 that under the colonial administration the number of *Nyau* members had greatly increased, although, he felt, the dance itself had diverged to some extent from its original purpose and degenerated into mere amusement. W.H.J. Rangeley used the same term "degeneration" in 1949 when the *Nyau* had started enlisting boys of 8 to 10 years old.[15] In the past *Nyau* membership had been reserved for men of mature age, having one child or more.

The fact that the *Nyau* started to enlist boys was, according to W.H.J. Rangeley and I. Linden, a reaction of the *Nyau* associations against the steadily growing influence of the mission schools.[16] The missionaries forbade the Christians and catechumens to go to the *Nyau* dance because of its immoral implications. In villages where there was no *Nyau* association Christian influence was unopposed, whereas the problem became acute wherever *Nyau* associations were established. Any effort to prevent the Christians and Catechumens from attending the dance was interpreted by the *Nyau* as an attempt to challenge the authority of the chief and to break down the village structure. The chiefs looked upon the Missions as destroying their former prestige and the advantages attached to their position. These feelings still exist today in areas where the *Nyau* is strong and where

---

[14] Cf. A.G.O. Hodgson, "Notes on the Achewa and Angoni", p. 146.

[15] W.H.J. Rangeley, "Nyau in the Kotakota District", pp. 39, 48.

[16] Cf. W.H.J. Rangeley, "Nyau in the Kotakota District", pp. 38, 48, and I. Linden, *Catholics, Peasants, and Chewa Resistance in Nyasaland*, p. 121.

the Mission has not been able to gain a strong following.[17] The anti-school attitude still continues here and there. It was this attitude that was branded by W.H.J. Rangeley, himself a District Commissioner, as the major obstacle to the development of schools. He wrote that the *Nyau* was certainly responsible for the backwardness of people.[18] The conflict is well presented by I. Linden. However he also implies that the conflict between the *Nyau* and the Missions was in part a conflict between the Ngoni chiefs and the *Nyau*. The Ngoni chiefs took the side of the Missions because they felt that the *Nyau* was undermining their own authority. According to I. Linden this was particularly true in Mua and Mtakataka where chief *Kachindamoto* took every opportunity to prosecute the *Nyau*.[19]

a) The Nature of Nyau

It has often been said that the *Nyau* is a secret society whose membership is selective and restricted. W.H.J. Rangeley wrote that originally only men of mature age could be members of the *Nyau* society, and that the introduction of boys into the *Nyau* was only a policy to counteract the influence of the mission-schools.[20] The practice of introducing mere boys into the *Nyau* still exists today. Some see *Nyau* as a kind of primitive Masonic brotherhood with its special vocabulary and rigid restriction to initiates only. Others consider *Nyau* exclusively under its folkloric aspect. They see it as some sort of carnival organized to enhance some popular ceremonies, such as funerals. In T.C. Young's and H.K. Banda's "Our African Way" both ideas are mentioned.[21]

---

[17] This is confirmed by our own experience in an area where the *Nyau* is particularly strong. We have examples of schools that had to be closed because the chiefs forbade youngsters to attend.

[18] W.H.J. Rangeley, "Nyau in the Kotakota District", p. 35.

[19] Cf. Linden, I., "Chewa Initiation Rites and *Nyau* Societies: the Use of Religious Institutions in Local Politics at Mua", in: T.O. Ranger & J. Weller (eds.), *Themes in Christian History of Central Africa*, London: Heinemann, 1975, pp. 30-44.

[20] W.H.J. Rangeley, "Nyau in the Kotakota District", p. 48.

[21] T.C. Young & H.K. Banda, *Our African Way of Life*, London: Lutterworth, 1946, pp. 24f.

N. Salaun is the only one so far to point out that *Nyau* is "an integral part of the structure and life of the tribe in the sense that in the old days all the boys had to go through the *Nyau* initiation before marriage."[22] Not to be initiated would mean that the young man "would never have adult male status. He would never be considered a full member of the clan, and he would never have any influence in village life". The initiation of the young men into the *Nyau* was as necessary as the *chinamwali* initiation of the young women. N. Salaun stressed the point that the initiation of a young man into the *Nyau* has to be understood not as an optional incorporation into a private association but as a true initiation, a formal incorporation into the clan itself. I tend to agree with N. Salaun that originally *Nyau* was the form of initiation for all young male Chewa. A man who is not initiated is even today looked upon by the members of the *Nyau* as not fully an adult. He is not really a Chewa, as many informants have told us.[23] A man who does not belong to the *Nyau* society is "like a small child who does not know anything at all" *(ngati mwana wang'ono wosadziwa chili chonse)*. "They are children, all they do is childish" *(ndi ana, zonse zimene amachita ndi zachibwana-bwana)*. Many young men go to the *Nyau*, even today, notwithstanding the influence of the schools, because they want to become men. They do not want to remain in some way strangers to the life of the clan. They want to know the things that men know. Moreover, if indeed *Nyau* initiation was something obligatory for all young men, part and parcel of the structure of the clan, then it is understandable that the chiefs protested when the mission forbade the Christians and catechumens to be initiated. This was seen as a way of undermining the very structure of the tribe.

On the other hand it is also true that the *Nyau*, as it exists today, is a secret society whose membership is restricted to initiates only. Some sort of secret language is employed, the places where they assemble are forbidden to anyone else, their activities are secret, the identity of the dancers is concealed with masks. Revelation of these secrets is severely punished. During the

---

[22] N. Salaun, "Notes on the Achewa", polycopied, Lilongwe: Language Centre, nd., p. 77. W.H.J. Rangeley in "Nyau in the Kotakota District", p. 48, disagrees with Salaun's opinion.

[23] After my own "initiation" it was even said in a meeting that I was a Mchewa as well as they are.

dances the identity of the dancer is carefully concealed. If the identity of the dancer were to be revealed the effect of the mysterious and the suggested re-incarnation of the *mizimu* of the departed would be destroyed. Another reason currently given is that women would not be able to guard the secrets and abide by the severe rules concerning secrecy.[24]

In the past, death was the normal punishment for such indiscretion and even today punishment is greatly feared. Cases are judged by the *Nyau* members *(akulu a Nyau)* and are not brought to the chief's court. Even if a *Nyau* member has committed some outrageous act the case is not judged by the chief. "They are *Nyau*, we cannot judge the *Nyau*" *(ndi zirombo, sitingathe kuona za zirombo). (Zirombo* are wild animals, and it is a name for the *Nyau* dancers). One chief told us that when a person revealed something about the *Nyau*, he was killed in the past, and that even today they succeed in punishing him in some way *(ngati munthu aulula za Nyau kale amaphedwa, komanso si kale lokha ayi, ngakhale lero amakhoza kuchita naye kanthu)*. Another person was for a long time unwilling to talk to me saying: "I may get a knife in my back". This fear to reveal anything concerning *Nyau* remained a serious obstacle to be overcome throughout my research.

The ritual performance of the *Nyau*, the *gule wamkulu* is the most popular dance of the Chewa. It is not an ordinary dance, but rather a ritual dance. It has a religious significance and is performed at funerals, commemorations of funerals, and whenever a particular *mzimu* expresses in a dream the desire that *Nyau* be danced in his honour. In addition it is danced at the initiation of girls *(chinamwali)*. Some say that this *Nyau* performance at *chinamwali* is a later development.[25] A *Nyau* dance opens with a dance by the chiefs who are present. All people watch while the chiefs thus pay their homage to the *mizimu* of the departed. They are followed by the *Nyau* dancers. Not all the initiated take part in the dance, the active dancers being only a small group, with the rest acting as audience, joining in the singing and clapping of hands. The drummers also form a special group. The identity of the dancers

---

[24] A.G.O. Hodgson, "Notes on the Achewa and Angoni", p. 151.

[25] Cf. A.G.O. Hodgson, "Notes on the Achewa and Angoni", p. 146.

themselves is completely hidden when they dance. Anyone disclosing anything would be liable to a heavy penalty.

Chadzunda

The women stand on one side of the *bwalo*. Their presence is neces-
sary to such an extent that people say that without the singing of the women there can be no *gule wam-kulu*. They answer the songs of the men by way of chorus. They may be in constant movement, being pursued by some masked dancers and then returning to their places. Women however cannot be mem-
bers of the *Nyau* association itself. W.H.J. Rangeley reported that the reason is that they are "basically impure".[26] The mysterious and the dangerous is the prerogative of men. When we considered the rain sacrifices, we saw that *Makewana* was considered a person without sex.[27] Neither she, nor any other rain priestess like *Chauta* and *Chisumphi* was allowed to be married. The underlying reasoning is always the same.[28]

The Chewa consider all mysterious powers in terms of "hot" or "cool". Something that is "hot" must not be brought in contact with something that is "cool". The mysterious powers would destroy one another. One such mysterious power is the power to give life. Sexual activity makes a person

---

[26] W.H.J. Rangeley, "Nyau in the Kotakota District", p. 38.

[27] W.H.J. Rangeley, "Makewana - the Mother of All People", in: *The Nyasaland Journal* 5 (1952), no. 2, p. 36.

[28] See the respective sections in the chapter six on *mdulo* where we shall develop this point much more in detail.

"hot". A menstruating woman is also "hot" and dangerous to what is "cool", and vice versa. In the context of the *Nyau* dance, the dancers themselves are "cool" because they are in close contact with the *mizimu* of the departed whom they represent and who are "cool". We shall see that the *Nyau* dancers must observe the taboo on sexual activity all the time of the *gule wamkulu*, for otherwise "hot" and "cool" would clash and they would contract or cause other people to contract *mdulo*, a disease which is a punishment for bringing "hot" and "cool" together. Women, then, are considered basically "impure", as W.H.J. Rangeley put it. They are often "hot" because of menstruation. Only old women, who are beyond child-bearing, can be allowed near the *Nyau*, such as the *namkungwi* (leader of the girl's initiation) and those other old women whose role is to bring food and water to the *Nyau* members at the *dambwe*. With respect to the rain sacrifice, the *Makewana* embodied as it were the rain shrine and therefore had to be always "cool". The rain is thought to be "cool", and the power to obtain rain is also "cool".[29]

b) The Origin of the Nyau

A.G.O. Hodgson reported that the most prevalent explanation of the origin of *Nyau* was that when God made the country and its people, he also gave them *Nyau*.[30] Consequently, he wrote, the life of the people is bound up with it. We ourselves have heard from a good number of informants that originally *Nyau* was given by God to the women as their dance. Tradition has it that the dance is as old as mankind and that God gave the dance to the women. At first it was something innocent, but men took it away from the women and changed it into something frightening, affirming that the dancers were wild animals in order to install fear in the women and children. When one woman said that they were only men, she was killed because she revealed the secret. The women then gave way because the men were stronger than they were, and they resolved to stay silent. Now everybody says that the *Nyau* are *zirombo* (wild animals) re-incarnating the *mzimu* of the departed.

---

[29] Cf. the respective sections in chapter six on *mdulo*.

[30] A.G.O. Hodgson, "Notes on the Achewa and Angoni", p. 146.

However, the women have now their own *Nyau* dance. They call it *zitun-gulule* or *chinkhombe*. It is danced during the day and never at night. It is danced at the funeral of women, sometimes at the funeral of a man. The dancers dress in men's trousers and shirts, or wear a man's jacket over their own dress. They also conceal their head in a sort of cloth mask and carry a stick or even an axe. They are not frightening and children sometimes move freely between them. Some of the smaller children are afraid because they think that they are real *Nyau*. The dressing-place of the women *(manda* or *dambwe)* is the house of the *namkungwi* (leader of the girls' initiation) or even the house of the chief. They sing *Nyau* songs and other people answer as at the *Nyau* dance. They are also called *zirombo* of the women *(zirombo za anthu aakazi)*. While they dance, women beat the drums and other older women may join in their dance. Men and women look on and give them coins *(ku-supa)* which they throw on a towel placed there for that purpose. I was told that there are many places where such dances take place, the purpose of which is to fulfil the original idea of the *Nyau* dance. Their "masked danc-ers" can easily be recognized to be just ordinary living persons and do not pretend to represent the *mizimu* of the dead.

At this point it is interesting to note that in some areas at the initiation of girls the *namkungwi* (leader of the initiation) takes the girls to the *liunde* of the *Nyau* at night when there are no men around. They show them the *Nyau* structures and say: "these were ours" *(zimenezi zidali zathu)*. It is impossible to discover the origin of this tradition. Is it just a reaction of the women to the oppressive character of the male *Nyau*? Is it a "degeneration" of *Nyau*? The men apparently do not mind it, they watch it in good humour and join in the laughter and applause.

A.G.O. Hodgson's remark that *Nyau* originated at the time God made the land and the people, could mean that, as far as tradition goes, it has always been with the Chewa. Some informants told us that the Chewa brought *Nyau* with them during their migration from their homeland. It is generally accepted that they originated from Katanga, and even earlier from some-where in West Africa. It is a fact that masked dancers are also found there.

Nevertheless the Chewa have, over the years, developed their own beliefs concerning the significance of *Nyau*.

W.H.J. Rangeley reported another version.[31] During a period of famine a certain Nyanda invented the *Nyau* dance in order to obtain food from the women. Other young men joined him, continuing the dance even after the famine was over, because it pleased the people so much. At his death the other dancers proposed to dance *Nyau* at his funeral because he had liked the dance so much during his life time. It thus became the traditional way of honouring the dead, especially the chiefs and other members of the *Nyau*.

N. Salaun gave still another version.[32] A man Akundaliro and a woman Akumatewa thought it good to use animal structures and masked dancers to frighten the girls at their initiation. *Nyau* was also a means of adding solemnity to the occasion. This presupposes that *Nyau* already existed in the life of the people. It would account for the introduction of the *Nyau* as an element in the initiation of girls, but would not explain the origin of *Nyau* itself. It does concur with the statement of many that *Nyau* was first a funeral dance and later also became an initiation dance at the *chinamwali* (initiation of girls).

One chief in particular told us the following story: The one who made the Chewa dance, the *Nyau*, is *Makewana,* the rain priestess at Msinja, who, as we have seen, also acquired considerable secular power. When she noticed, the story goes, that the chiefs were not sufficiently respected by the people, she said that it was important to start *Nyau* which until then had not existed. *Makewana* chose a number of chiefs and gave them the right to have a *bwalo* (the dancing place of the *Nyau*). When they had started *Nyau*, she saw that much more respect was being paid to the chiefs.

This story could be interpreted as placing greater emphasis on initiation during which the initiates are told to respect the chief and learn the various

---

[31] W.H.J. Rangeley, "Nyau in the Kotakota District", pp. 36f.

[32] N. Salaun, "Notes on the Achewa", p. 77.

signs of respect. Even today this is an important item of the instructions given to the initiates and any of them lacking in respect is severely punished in order to make him change his ways.

So far we have been dealing with legends. M. Schoffeleers in his historical study of the Proto-Chewa suggested that *Nyau* societies are in all probability older than rain shrines, going back in time to a hunting and food-gathering economy.[33] They formed part of the Proto-Chewa culture. In the organization of this proto-Chewa cult rain shrines were associated with *Nyau* societies. With the advent of the centralizing efforts of the Phiri (1400-1600 A.D.), who seemed to have been particularly hostile to the *Nyau*, these became gradually divorced from the rain shrines and withdrew to the villages. After the Phiri had succeeded in controlling the shrines, these shrines came to be associated with the interests of the ruling aristocracy. The *Nyau* on the other hand became representative of village interests and a factor of resistance. The Phiri never quite succeeded in integrating the Proto-Chewa village system into their centralized political entities, and they had to be content with a type of political organization which left the Proto-Chewa considerable power on the local level. The *Nyau* became a primary agent in the defence of Proto-Chewa political interests. They continued to operate, acting both as a powerful focus of Chewa ethnicity and as an active force of resistance to the imposition of centralization. With the advent of the Ngoni invaders and, a little later, of the colonial power, *Nyau* once more became a potent factor of resistance. This is illustrated e.g. in the conflict of the *Nyau* and the Christian missions.[34]

---

[33] J.M. Schoffeleers, "Towards the Identification of a Proto-Chewa Culture", pp. 47-60.

[34] The conflict of the *Nyau* and the Christian missions is recounted by I. Linden, *Catholics, Peasants, and Chewa Resistance in Nyasaland*, pp. 117-137.

2. Persons, Sites, and Moments of Performance

a) The Chiefs - Owners of the Land

Nyau is closely connected with the chiefs. The chiefs who are the "owners of the land" *(eni ake dziko)* are also the "owners" of the *Nyau*. The chief directs and controls the *Nyau* with the assistance of two "officers": the *wa ku bwalo* and the *wa ku dambwe* whom we shall consider later. He can not, however, interfere with the *Nyau* ritual itself because this is fixed by the ancestors *(makolo)*. Traditionally, the chief is the spiritual head of the community, part of whose function it is to direct such matters as the selection of burial grounds, maintenance of the *kachisi* (spirit temple), and the selection of the *mizimu* tree. He also presides over prayers and sacrifices to *Chiuta* (rain sacrifices) and to the *mizimu* of former chiefs (territorial spirits). His duty is to preserve among his people the sacred traditions and practices as laid down by the ancestors *(makolo)*. He also has to provide a decent funeral for any departed in order to prevent his spirit from causing harm to the community.

The *Nyau* is a way of placating the *mizimu* of the departed and of assuring their intercession with *Chiuta*. The *Nyau* dance *(gule wamkulu)* is, as a matter of fact, called "our great prayer to the mizimu" *(pemphero lathu lalikulu la mizimu)*. In the following pages we shall consider this religious meaning of the *Nyau* dance and try to determine what relation it has with the *mizimu* and in how far it can be called a prayer. Since the chief is the spiritual head of the community, he is also the head of the *Nyau* community. Not all the chiefs have the right to have *Nyau*, but only those who have obtained the right of *mzinda*. *Mzinda* is the right to have *Nyau* and to hold initiation ceremonies. In the past there were only a few of the more important chiefs, the "owners of the land" *(eni ake dziko)* who had *mzinda*. But gradually they granted the right of *mzinda* to other chiefs as well. They granted it either to their relatives or against payment of a tribute: goats, slaves, or more recently money. Once granted the right of *mzinda* is considered given forever. However, even today not all village chiefs have obtained *mzinda*.

The chief himself does not necessarily participate in the *Nyau* dances, but he is the "owner" and the leader of the association. Any offence against the *Nyau* is an offence against the chief himself. He directs when and for whom the dance will take place, where the secret place *(dambwe)* will be situated. He must be informed of everything that happens at the *dambwe*. He decides about the admission of new members into the association. He also receives tribute at the occasion of initiation. When he has chosen the place where the *Nyau* will dance *(bwalo)*, he goes there at night together with the medicine man *(sing'anga)* and some elders to bury the skull of a former chief together with some medicine *(nchiri)*. This is a dedication of the *bwalo* to the *mizimu*. Nowadays medicine only is often buried.

b) The Nyau Officers

The chief alone is the "owner" of the *Nyau*. However, he entrusts the organization and supervision to some older men. But even in that case he himself has the last word. Usually there are two such "officers". One is in charge of the *dambwe (wa ku dambwe)* who supervises the preparation of the animal structures and the initiation of new members. The other one is in charge of the *bwalo (wa ku bwalo)* and is responsible for the drums. If necessary he borrows them from other villages. It is he who invites other *Nyau* groups to come to the dance, organizes the dance, ensures that the *bwalo* is prepared before the dance and that all traces are removed after the dance. For in order to maintain the mystery, no trace is supposed to be left of what has been happening.

The *namkungwi* is an old woman in charge of the girls' initiation. She is not really a member of the *Nyau*, but since she is the only woman to work closely together with the chief and the elders, she is supposed to know about the secrets of the *Nyau*.

There are always six drummers involved, according to the necessary number of drums. There is a long one, about 2 m long, the *mpanje,* and a big one, about 1 m long and almost 1 m wide, the *ndewere* or *mbalule*. Then there are four smaller ones: two about 60 cm long, the *mbandambanda* or *mtiwizo,* and two about 45 cm long, the *kamkumbe*. Before the dance the drums are warmed with fire to avoid any dampness of the skin.

c) *Animal Structures and Masked Dancers*

Chimkoko

The animal structures are made like an open barrel from wicker and covered with sacks or husks of maize-cobs. They have a head, sometimes complete with horns, and a tail. The bottom of the structure is left open so that a man can enter into it to carry it. In-side the structure is a crossbar which the man inside grasps in his hands and by means of which he can carry the structure and manoeuver it. There are three small holes, one in front and one on each side, so that the man can see where he is go-ing. The enclosed person is completely hidden from view. The structure reaches down to his ankles, and his feet are painted with ashes or mud. Some structures are carried by one person only, some enclose four men, and some from 8 to 10 or even more. There are a number of different structures, called *zirombo* (wild animals). All have their own particular sig-nificance. We shall consider them in detail later (cf. pp. 156ff).

There is also a great variety of masked dancers. They are also called *zirombo* (wild animals). The identity of the dancers is always concealed for they wear masks of wood or of cloth. Various other materials such as sacks, strips of cloth, leaves or grass are worn around the head and in various parts of the body. Those parts of the body which are not covered are usually painted with ashes or mud. Some dancers are almost naked, others wear elaborate "costumes". Most of them are frightening. They all have a precise role to perform. They do not use ordinary speech but either make animal-like sounds or shout in a very high pitched voice. A detailed description of dancers and their particular meaning will be given later (cf. p. 156ff).

The dancers may appear during the day in the village. Some come to terrify the women and children and to steal chickens. Others come to entertain and dance in front of the women. At a particular funeral of a chief, dancers were continually running through the village, leaping across fences and making strange sounds.

d) The Places where the Nyau-dancers Gather

We have to distinguish the *dambwe,* the *liunde,* and the *bwalo.* The *dambwe* is the secret place where animal structures are prepared and where the initiation of boys takes place. It is usually situated in thick bush, often in a graveyard. Nobody who does not belong to the *Nyau* community is allowed to go near it. If, despite this prohibition, someone should go there deliberately, he would be severely beaten (even today) and fined. In the past he would have been killed. If he went nearby accidentally he would be fortunate to get away with only a fine; he would have to promise not to disclose anything he had seen. Usually paths leading to a *dambwe* are marked with branches put across them, or small pieces of cloth are left hanging in the branches of the trees. Women are never allowed to come near, except some older women who have to bring food and water to the dancers. But even they are supposed to leave everything at the "entrance". Women never take part in the activities at the *dambwe.*

The *liunde* is a place near the village were the *Nyau* from different villages foregather with their animal structures and the apparel of the individual dancers in order to prepare everything for the dance. Often the *liunde* is just a place under trees fenced off with tall dry grass *(masekera)* or with mats. It can be likened to a back-stage from which the various performers come to perform on the *bwalo,* and to which they return after their dance. In principle dancers transport the animal structures from the *dambwe* to the *liunde* at night, but, in fact, they can frequently be seen during the afternoon. When there is to be a dance, *Nyau* communities are invited to combine their efforts, each preparing a certain number of structures. They can be seen coming from different directions, some from afar, all converging on the same village. On its way from the *dambwe* to the *liunde* an animal structure is always accompanied by a group of men and boys. Someone leads the procession with a flag, and everyone is expected to leave the road and let them pass. The men who have not been initiated, and all women and children, have to run away and stay at a distance. Those who accompany the structure sing *Nyau* songs. Non-initiated are never allowed at the *liunde* when it is in use. If there is an elephant structure *(njobvu)*, it has a *liunde* all to itself.

The *bwalo* is the open space in the village where the dance takes place. It is often surrounded by big trees. Under one of these trees the skull of a former chief is buried with some medicine as a way of dedicating the *bwalo* to the *mizimu*. Often a new chief chooses a new site for the *bwalo*, abandoning the old one at the death of the former chief. Before a dance takes place the *bwalo* is carefully cleaned *(kulambula)*.

From the *liunde* to the *bwalo* the dancers proceed one by one. Each one performs his own dance. Some structures gyrate *(kuzweta)*, while others, which are too big or too long, move forward and backward or from side to side. All the dances are accompanied by the beating of drums and a great variety of *Nyau* songs. The women answer as a chorus. There is *nthungululu* (a shrill trill produced by women while beating their hands against their lips). Some structures imitate the sound of the animal they represent. When the dance is finished all the structures and dancers withdraw to the *liunde,* where their apparel is hidden till the next day's performance. At the conclusion of the dances, the animal structures may be burnt. However, they will often be kept at the *dambwe* for future use. There are also secret caves which hold a number of structures which are kept from year to year. We know of one enterprising chief who has built a sort of big shed where he keeps a few *zirombo* which he hires out to the various associations on demand, e.g. during the rainy season when it is impossible to make new structures. After the dances the *Nyau* members take a ritual bath with water in which medicine has been mixed. We shall return to this when we speak about the taboo on sexual intercourse for dancers during a *Nyau* performance. Normally it is impossible to take pictures of *Nyau* structures or masked dancers. One would certainly risk being beaten up and fined and probably have one's camera ruined. For a long time I was unable to take any photographs. However, after my "initiation" I was allowed to do so. The chief himself presented the various dancers. On that occasion there was also a group of young boys who had made their own small animal structure. As it was so well made, I wanted to take a picture of it as well, but the chief forbade this saying that it was not a real *chirombo*. The boys were sent back.

e) Moments of Performance

The *Nyau* dance can take place at any time of the year at the occasion of a funeral of a chief or of a member of the *Nyau* association. It can also take place at the funeral of any adult whose relatives ask for the dance and can afford to pay for it. In April 1976 it costs 5 Kwacha (2.50 Pounds Sterling) to have a *mkala* (small structure enclosing one man) at a funeral. At a funeral there will usually be only a few structures, if any, together with a number of masked dancers.

Normally, one may find *Nyau* at more important funerals. Much will depend on the social status of the deceased. For a chief, many structures may come, even the *njobvu* which is the biggest and most important structure of all. Nowadays in some areas there will even be some dancers at the funeral of a child. We know of one area, where some *Nyau* dance takes place practically every week.

The really big dance *(gule wamkulu)* does not take place at a funeral but at the commemoration of a funeral. Because it is so expensive to have a *gule wamkulu*, several villages will group their funeral commemorations. The *gule wamkulu* takes place in the period after the harvesting and before the start of the rains, that is especially from August to November. Plenty of beer will be provided. Moonlight also is an important factor of determining the date for a dance for complete darkness would make the dance impossible. During this season there may be almost continuous dancing going on in the area. The *Nyau* associations combine efforts and travel from *mzinda* to *mzinda*. During this period one can hear the drums almost every evening somewhere in the distance, now in one place now in another.

A complete *Nyau* performance *(gule wamkulu)* lasts four days with dances on three consecutive nights. The first two nights they last only a few hours but on the third and final night dancing goes on throughout the night (this is called *mchezo)*. The closing ceremony takes place during the afternoon on the fourth day *(za masana)*. The darkness and the impressiveness of the animal structures create an atmosphere of mystery and fear. The rhythm of the drums, the songs, the clapping of hands, the trilling *(nthungululu)* of the women cause a magical attraction to all who hear them.

3. *Nyau's* Involvement during Initiation

This section discusses the involvement of *Nyau*-dancers during the boys' initiation. The role of the *Nyau* at the girls' initiation *(chinamwali)* will be described in chapter six. Any young man wishing to be initiated must be introduced by a sponsor *(phungu),* who will normally be a relative, already belonging to the *Nyau* community. The application is first accepted by the *wa ku dambwe* and ultimately by the chief. A fee has to be paid: a goat, some chickens and money. The goat and the money are a tribute to the chief. The chickens will be eaten at the *dambwe.* M. Tew proposed the theory that the initiation is a "formal incorporation into the matrilineal kin group and separation from the father's kin group".[35] The two reasons she gives are the following: The father is not allowed to be present and the boy is presented to his sponsors by his mother. However, this does not seem to be really the case. The *Nyau* communities are wider than the matrilineal kin-group, cutting right across the lineage divisions. Moreover, although a marriage is uxorilocal at the beginning, it often becomes virilocal after a few years. After having lived with his parents-in-law for some years (often until after the birth of about two children) the husband is allowed to take his family to his own village, his *kwathu kwenikweni.* It would seem, therefore, that the *Nyau* community into which a young man will be initiated is more often the one in which he will find his father and other paternal uncles.

---

[35] M. Tew, "People of the Lake Nyasa Region", p. 47.

It was alleged by the Christian missions that the *Nyau* had been applying unfair pressure on everyone including Christians and catechumens to accept initiation. As a result of these complaints, the colonial administration laid down the regulation, which the chiefs accepted, that no boy needed to join the *Nyau* against his own will.[36] As a matter of fact the rule has remained a dead letter. Actually it is sometimes difficult to know who decides on the initiation: the relatives under pressure from the *Nyau* or from fear of offending the ancestors or the boy himself who wants to know. Some put a pride on knowing what "real men" know. For they want to be men like all other men in the village and are afraid to stay almost a stranger in their own village. Even today a good number of boys, Christians or catechumens, go to the *Nyau* to "buy their way" *(kugula njira)*. Without this they could be victimized by *Nyau* members and would not be free to travel in the countryside whilst *Nyau* structures are being moved from village to village and during the dances. In this case of *kugula njira* they might not go through the whole initiation, for a brief minimum instruction would ensure them freedom of movement for the future. Often the important part of *kugula njira* is the payment of a tribute to the chief.

What follows is the disscription of a *Nyau* initiation as it is performed nowadays. In the past it was much more severe, according to all accounts. The following description is based on the information given by several young men who told me about their own initiation. Accounts of the initiation in the past were collected by missionaries and incorporated into a report sent to the colonial administration. A copy of this dossier is in the possession of the author. However, I shall not make use of it in the following description, because upon checking the details with informants, I discovered that they represent extreme methods which are no longer followed today. Moreover, I suspect this dossier to be coloured slightly because it was drawn up with a view to impressing the administration with the "immorality" of the *Nyau*.

---

[36] Cf. the minutes of the meeting between the Administration and the Chiefs in Lilongwe on 27.4.1929, file on *Nyau*, Archives, Bishop's House, Lilongwe.

a) *Arrival at the dambwe*

Initiation takes place when the *Nyau* members are at the *dambwe* preparing their *zirombo*. This will usually be some time between September and November. The boy to be initiated is taken by his *phungu*, who before they reach the *dambwe* blindfolds him and carefully instructs him to keep absolute secrecy concerning all he will see or hear. When the two approach the *dambwe*, the *phungu* calls out to warn the members at the *dambwe* that they have arrived. They sing the following song to invite them to come forward:

Mwana alira'yo abwere, adzaone, yeee.   Let that weeping child come near and see, yeee,
Mwana alira'yo adzaone chinyama, yeee.   that weeping child see a huge beast, yeee.

As he enters the bush, the others fall upon him and beat him with sticks. If up to the present he has been cheeky he will be punished. This punishment is an essential element of the initiation. It is meant as a punishment for his bad behaviour in the village and at home. It also stresses the fact that it is necessary to grow up and to abandon childish behaviour. He must be disciplined and has to conquer fear if he is to be a genuine member of the adult community. A.G.O. Hodgson mentioned a symbolic burial of the initiate to indicate that he enters upon a period of transition.[1] His mother has been invited by his *phungu* to tell whether she has any remarks concerning the behaviour of her son: has he insulted her, said such and such a thing, refused to do such and such a thing.

The punishment meted out to the boy can be quite serious. He may be severely beaten *(kukwapula)*, made to go into the water very early in the morning when the water is very fresh, and be repeatedly submerged. He may also have his genitals tied with a cord which binds several boys together, up to 10 or more. They then are made to run or are pulled in different directions. This is called *kuchita fulang'onga*. When I observed that this could maim these boys for life, *Nyau* members answered that they knew how to do it without maiming them, but that it was very painful. They might also refuse food to

---

[1] Cf. A.G.O. Hodgson, "Notes on the Achewa and Angoni", p. 136.

the boy. One or other form of punishment might be continued throughout the period of initiation.

b) Instructions

Blindfolded the boy is made to enter into an animal structure. When he has overcome his fear of the *chirombo* he is shown how it is made. During his stay at the *dambwe*, which may last up to one month, he is taught all about the making of these structures. *Nyau* members teach him the special vocabulary used in connexion with the various materials used to construct the images and the secret language which is used whenever a member of the *Nyau* wants to find out whether someone is initiated. The following are a few examples of the expressions in use. We have collected about 100 of such expressions.

Chalale	stands for *makoko*	=	husks of maize cob
Mtoto (i.e. paint)	stand for *dothi*	=	soil, or *thope* i.e. mud
Nthiti (i.e. rib)	stands for *mtengo*	=	branch or bamboo stick.
Nkhweza	stands for *khonje*	=	sisal string
Mafuta (i.e. oil)	stands for *chipala*	=	ashes
ubweya (i.e. fur)	stands for *udzu*	=	grass.

Any person using the wrong word at the *dambwe* is fined. He must bring a chicken which will be killed and eaten by the members of the *Nyau*. He continues to learn other secret words and expressions *(mikuluwiko)* such as: *Wapsya pwetekere ku mundakwa make chenjerani* which means: "there is a dance tomorrow". Then there are riddles such as the following one: "Where do the *zirombo* come from?" Answer: "They come from the *munda* (field)". "When they come from the *munda* they are at?" "At the *nkhokwe* (grainstore)". And so it goes on, with the answers being given: "at the *dzala*, at the *bwalo*, at the *manda*, at the *mtototo*". Such riddles are used especially to find out whether someone is a member of the *Nyau* or not.

Instruction is also given him on how to behave as an adult. The boy is taught to show respect *(ulemu)* to his parents and elders and especially to the chief. He also learns many good things calculated to turn him into a useful member of the community. For this is the main aim of the initiation. Said one chief: "If a boy was cheeky before he went to the *dambwe,* they will beat him because they want him to change his former bad behaviour. When he comes back to the village, he has really changed" *(ngati munthu anali wamwano napita ku dambwe amam'menya chifukwa amafuna kuti asinthe makhalidwe amene anali nawo kale. Tsono ayi akabwera kumudzi amasintha ndithu).*

He is taught the facts of life and the names of the organs of man and woman. Information on marriage and the taboos regulating marital intercourse will be given to the young man at the marriage instructions. A point strongly insisted upon is that he is no longer allowed near the place where his parents sleep, under pain of incurring *mdulo.*[2] He is also taught that in the absence of his parents he may not take food from one of the cooking pots, lest he contracts *masaya* (an imaginary disease of the cheeks). He must pay respect to his parents and avoid rudeness to his mother. When his father tells him to do something, he must obey quickly. If he sees an older man carrying a heavy load he should offer to carry it for him.

Besides all this, he is also taught the *Nyau* songs and certain expressions which are less edifying, such as *kutukwana* (to curse people while using words referring to male or female organs). He is also told to go practically naked and steal chickens at the village. He must obey his *phungu* implicitly in all this. N. Salaun wrote: "experience has shown that very often a boy is changed in a few days under their influence."[3]

c) Medicine Given to the Initiate

The *phungu* kills a chicken. He then takes a branch, with which they make the animal structures (from the *chabzera* tree), and impales the chicken on it. The chicken is roasted and the branch is extracted and given to the initiate who eats what is stuck to it. The bones of the chicken together with the branch itself are burnt and ground. Salt is added to the powder which is

---

[2] Cf. the respective section in chapter six on *mdulo.*
[3] N. Salaun, "Notes on the Achewa", p. 82.

then put into the boy's food. Should he refuse to eat *khundabwi,* as it is called, he is supposed to become mad if he dances *Nyau.*

d) Kumeta (to shave the initiate's hair).

On the day fixed, the *phungu* shaves the boy's hair. This day is called *mpala.* They also tell him that while the *zirombo* are dancing at the *bwalo,* he must continually spit on the *bwalo.* If he does not do so he will wake up with nightmares during the night or become mad.

The initiation is now over. He has been taught *Nyau* songs, expressions, the way the structures are made, the way he should dance. He will be closely supervised in the coming weeks by his *phungu* to see whether he puts into practice all that he has been told. If he does not do so, he will be punished.

4. The Religious Significance of *Nyau*

a) Symbolic Representation of the Invisible Spirit World

The *Nyau* dance has a specific religious significance namely; it is the symbolic representation of the invisible spirit world. It is surrounded by many regulations concerning secrecy in order to preserve the full effect of the mystery, and to keep the people believing that these strange and frightening figures which suddenly erupt from the bush, or rather from the graveyard *(manda)* where the *dambwe* usually is into the village, represent the *mizimu* of the dead. The dancers themselves are identified with the *mizimu* to such an extent that many of their customs appear as part of this process of identification. They have to undergo a transformation like a deceased person whose body decomposes in the grave. They are in a marginal state which is symbolically characterized by "reversals", a behaviour which is the opposite of what their behaviour would be at the village:

- They leave the village and live at the *dambwe* situated at the graveyard where normal people never go.
- They speak a secret language.

- They have to observe taboos on sexual relations because they have to remain "cool" by reason of their close contact with the spirits of the dead.
- They curse freely *(kutukwana)* which in normal life would be taken as an indication of being a witch *(mfiti)*.
- They fight, chase and assault women.
- They go about practically naked, are dirty, and paint themselves with mud and ashes.
- The avoidance rules between father-in-law and son-in-law are suspended.
- They shout obscenities at one another without respect for the difference of generation and social status.
- During the dance they shout obscenities at the women, and especially at the mother-in-law *(mpongozi)*.
- They steal chicken from the village.

Instead of the normal norms of decency, respect to be paid to elders, sense of shame, self-control, which are all very pronounced in normal life, we find at the *dambwe* and at the dances precisely the opposite code of behaviour. The *Nyau* dancers even handle human skulls and human hair, which in normal circumstances would be tantamount to witchcraft. They howl and make animal-like cries. When they commit offenses, no juridical action can be taken against them, because by definition spirits *(zirombo)* are outside the law.[4] After the dance all traces of what has taken place must be removed because spirits are not supposed to leave traces behind. The *mizimu* are alternatively believed to be a comfort to their living relatives and a danger to them because they may punish them for they are the guardians of the ancestral customs *(miyambo ya makolo)*. This double role is also assumed by the *Nyau* dancers. At a funeral they may come to comfort the mourners, but at the same time may appear threatening, violent, and devastating.

At the *Nyau* initiation we again find this double role. The dancers inculcate right behaviour and responsible adult attitudes and at the same time they

---

[4] Cf. W.H.J. Rangeley, "Nyau in the Kotakota District", p. 44.

Chinkoko-madziansatsi

punish previous bad behaviour. At the girls' initiation the *Nyau* come to punish and to frighten. They symbolically bury the initiates in order that from now on they may be adults, having left their childhood behind them. At a funeral the *Nyau* dancers represent the *mizimu (zimafanizira mizimu)* who receive the spirit of the deceased person in their midst. Although the term "dance" is used *(kubvina)* when they speak of the *Nyau*, it is really more a "mime" which aims at explaining the presence and the activity of the *mizimu*. There are a great variety of dancers. Each dancer, animal structure or masked dancer embodies an aspect of their belief in the world of the *mizimu*. To a certain extent we can speak of a "mystery-play" by means of which the traditional beliefs of the people are kept alive. At the end of this chapter we shall consider the individual characters one by one, and what they are meant to express.

People use the expression: "*Nyau* is our great prayer" *(Nyau ndiyo pemphero lathu lalikulu)*. When however we asked informants how they conceived this and what they prayed for at the *Nyau* dance, they found it difficult to answer the question. One said that *Nyau* was not a prayer, because while they were dancing they did not pray for rain. Prayer for rain is *mfunde*. He obviously identified prayer with prayer for rain. This particular informant was one of the chiefs of the Bunda rain shrine. Another said that *Nyau* was not a prayer but *kulira*. *Kulira* is the term used for wailing at a *maliro* (which actually has the same root as *kulira*). Thus the *Nyau* is an integral part of the funeral rites. Others stated that *Nyau* was danced because the *mzimu* of the dead wanted it. It was a way of placating them.

b) Placating the mizimu

The dance is performed to please the *mizimu,* and by doing so, to appease them *(kupepesa ndi kuikondwetsa).* Often the dance is perfomed "at the express demand" of the *mizimu.* They are believed to ask for *Nyau* dances in dreams. The *Nyau* dance is also a way of asking the *mizimu* at a funeral not to come back and make people suffer *(Nyau pa maliro ndi pemphero kut: mizimu isabwerenso kudzaononga anthu).* At a funeral dance a goat is killed and some of the meat taken and cut into small pieces. It is roasted and some of it given to the *mizimu* at the tree. The rest is eaten by the dancers. They make this offering to indicate that they dance to honour the *mizimu* of the deceased person. Before someone dies, he may ask that *Nyau* dance at his *maliro* saying that he wants such and such a mask or structure. His relatives will carry out his wishes, for they are afraid that otherwise the spirit of the dead man be angry and come to trouble the living. The mask mentioned by the person before his death will be the first to dance and songs connected with that dancer or structure will be chosen. Moreover, the people will keep their distance from that particular mask or structure because, they say, he represents the *mizimu* of the deceased person. If they were not to execute his "last will" the *mzimu* would come back and say: "I want a dance, you have buried me as if I were a small child" *(ine mwadiika ngati mwana wang'ono),* and he would cause someone to fall ill. It is possible that nowadays the religious aspect has somehow become secondary and that the dance is seen as a popular form of entertainment.[5] Nevertheless the religious meaning persists:

- The dance is repeatedly called: our great prayer to the spirits of the dead *(pemphero lathu lalikulu la mizimu).*
- It is also called: dance of the deceased *(gulu la anamwaliri),* its purpose is to give homage to the deceased *(kuchitira ulemu kwa amwaliri).*
- The dancers are said to come from the bush or the river and to represent the spirits of the dead.
- At the *bwalo* of the dance the skull of a former chief was buried (nowadays medicine only) in order to dedicate the *bwalo* to the spirits of the dead. The former chiefs and the other spirits of the dead of the village

---

[5] A.G.O. Hodgson, "Notes on the Achewa and Angoni", p. 146.

are said to gather under the tree near the *bwalo* during a *Nyau* performance to receive the homage *(ulemu)* of the living.

One particular informant explained the *Nyau* dance in the following way:[6]

> The aim of the dance is to ensure that the spirit of the deceased is well
> received in the world of the *mizimu*. The *mizimu* are supposed to have
> been very fond of the *Nyau* dances while they were alive. *Nyau* is part of
> the tradition handed down by the ancestors. Someone who has not been
> faithful to the traditions of old is not well received by the *mizimu*. He is
> like a stranger to the tribe. But someone who was fond of what the
> *mizimu* have been fond of, who has been faithful to the traditions, and
> who above all at his death was accompanied by the singing and dancing
> of the *Nyau*, shall be received as a true member of the tribe. Therefore
> the living accompany the deceased with their dances and songs during
> his passage into the spirit-world, and introduce him to the ancestors as a
> true member of the tribe.

The *Nyau* dances form an integral part of the funeral ritual in the case of
adults. This is why older people urge youngsters so strongly to join the
Nyau, in order to ensure the homage *(ulemu)* of the *mizimu* and to help a deceased during his passage to the *mizimu* world. Moreover, when a *mzimu* returns to visit the living, these should be ready to receive him with *Nyau*
dances and songs of which he was so fond. In this way the dead partake in
the joy of the living. *Nyau* is a means to please the *mizimu*, who then in turn
will be more merciful towards the living.

c) Continuation of Life in the Clan

Nyau is also a prayer for continued fertility in the village. Both at a funeral,
when a member of the community has left a gap to be filled, and especially
at the *chinamwali* the *Nyau* dance has the intention of obtaining fertility. One
informant said:

> *Nyau* is an integral part of the *chinamwali* ritual to ensure that the young
> woman will have children. It is a prayer to the *mizimu* that they may in-
> tercede with *Chauta* that the young woman will have many children and

---

[6] This statement was written down in a copybook and given to Fr. D. Roy. A. Hovington
mentions this copybook and copies much of its content. Subsequently, the copybook itself
was unfortunately lost.

healthy children. If the *Nyau* were not to come, perhaps the young woman might die, perhaps she might be barren *(Nyau ndi chigawo chenicheni cha mwambo wa chinamwali wakutsimikizira kuti adzabereka ana. Ndi pemphero kwa mizimu kuti anenere kwa Chauta kuti namwaliyo akhale ndi ana ambiri ndi moyo wamphamvu. Ngati Nyau sibwera kapena namwaliyo adzafa kapena adzakhala wopanda ana).*

The songs of the *Nyau* have often been branded as obscene. These songs and the things shouted during the dance are called *zolaula* by the people themselves. This has often been translated as "dirty", "obscene", "filthy". But the meaning of the verb *kulaula* is: to utter words hidden.[7] *Zolaula* indicates that those songs or expressions mention the male or female private parts. The reason why they use these *zolaula* is stated by many informants as follows: "If people mention these organs it is in order to be proud of them, they want to praise the power which *Chiuta* has given them" *(ngati amatchula ziwalo'zo amanyadira, akufuna kutamanda mphamvu, Chiuta anawapatsa).* The dances and songs are in some way a celebration of the powers of life, a eulogy of the generative powers of man, and of the Creator.

I have gone through almost 300 different *Nyau* songs and many *maliro* songs and in most of them there is some mention of male or female organs. Some gestures of the dance are called "provocative" by some. Are they not rather a crude mime of fertility? The "obscenity" appears to be a "down-to-earth ritual of fertility". We suggest therefore that basically *Nyau* is a ritual petition for fertility on the occasion of a burial and at the female initiation rites. The dance is referred to as "our great prayer" *(pemphero lathu lalikulu).* Prayer for what? Surely this is to be found in the songs and the occasion on which the dance is performed. These seem to indicate that the prayer is to obtain fertility.

Another important aspect of these *Nyau* songs is that many contain some moral teaching. Informants insisted on this point again and again. They said that these songs reminded the people of the ancestral customs concerning conjugal relations and *mdulo*-taboos.[8]

---

[7] D.C. Scott, *Cyclopaedic Dictionary of the Mang'anja Language,* p. 273.

[8] Cf. the respective section in chapter six on *mdulo.*

The following are a few examples:

1. *Iwe maliro akuti m'nyumba.*
   Listen, they say that there is a dead person in the house (meaning: re-member, when there is a death in the village, nobody may have conju-gal relations).
2. *Mwana iwe, mwana iwe, wamtengera mbolo yanga, maye, wapachika pa thandala patalitali, mbolo yanga maye.*
   Oh child, you have taken my penis, alas, and put it on the shelf high up, Alas, my penis (meaning: the child has caused his parents a taboo on conjugal relations.)
3. *Ana inu, ndapita ku maliro, koma musati mukwatane.*
   Children I am going to a funeral, remember don't have conjugal rela-tions (meaning: while the mother is away, her grown up children are not allowed to have conjugal relations until she has come back to the village).
4. *Sindikudya chiwala, nyama yopanda mchere.*
   I do not eat grasshoppers, that is meat without any taste. (Meaning: it is wrong to have any sexual relations with a child).

During the day of the *Nyau* dance, members are forbidden to have sexual relations. At their close they must take a ritual bath in water mixed with medicine. Only after that may they resume marital life without danger of *mdulo*. While dancing they are "in close relationship with the *mizimu*". As mentioned earlier we find here the "cool" and "hot" notions. The allegation that on the occasion of the nocturnal dances sexual orgies took place, does not seem to agree with this taboo.[9] People usually are very frightened of breaking the *mdulo* taboos.

We could sum up by suggesting that the *Nyau* appears to be a ritual fertility dance in an atmosphere of mystery and proximity to the *mizimu*, and in de-pendence on the local chief who is the link between the living and the dead. Old people say that in the past there were no schools, they knew only *Nyau*.

---

[9] Cf. I. Linden, *Catholics, Peasants, and Chewa Resistance in Nyasaland*, pp. 119, 124.

They believed that *Chiuta* gave them rain and children *(amatipatsa mvula ndi ana)* because they knew how to ask for them by means of *mfunde* and *Nyau*.

d) Other Attempts of Explanation

First there is a partial explanation of the *zolaula* at the dances. I was told that when that women began to get tired and stopped singing with gusto, a dancer would shout some *zolaula* at them and the women would answer back. This was a way of reviving their attention. It is to be remembered that the participation of the women is essential. Nobody would dance if there were no women present. They are necessary as a chorus, and without them there would be no animation.

M.G. Marwick explains many of the things that happen at the *Nyau* as the setting up of behaviour patterns which call for detestation.[10] At the *Nyau*, normal rules of respectful and decent behaviour are suspended in order to show people the necessity of law and order and good manners. This is the way he explains in particular all the excesses during the *Nyau* initiation.

J.M. Schoffeleers explains the obscenities as a reversal of normal positions.[11] Husbands have no authority in their wives' village (uxorilocality). *Nyau* emphasizes social reversal by the constant use of obscene language in which most of the things are expressed in terms of male or female organs, and by the perfomance of acts which go against normal behaviour and would provoke sharp reactions in ordinary circumstances. It is a way of taking revenge in a system of uxorilocality without any danger of prosecution.

One can also say that the *gule wamkulu* is an occasion for people to relax, a kind of carnival which helps people to maintain their psychological balance. Their daily life is so permeated by rules dealing with politeness, submission to the elders, and many other restrictions, that they need a short period of complete freedom. It is a "big show" which helps everybody to feel happy

---

[10] Cf. M.G. Marwick, *Sorcery in its Social Setting*, Manchester: University Press, 1965, pp. 235-236.

[11] Cf. J.M. Schoffeleers, "Symbolic and Social Aspects of Spirit Worship ", p. 400.

(food, beer, songs, excitement). These physiological and sociological explanations are helpful in understanding the phenomenon of *Nyau*, but they are
not complete without the religious meaning which alone can explain the
deeper significance of the *Nyau*. J.M. Schoffeleers, in his study of the *Nyau*
among the Mang'anja, has developed a theory with which he explains the
Nyau dance in terms of the creation myth.[12] According to this myth the invention of fire by men ended the peaceful living together of *Chiuta,* men
and the animals. Paradise is destroyed by the fault of men. After inventing
fire and setting fire to the bush, they even made weapons with which to kill
animals. They also made use of fire to roast the animals they had killed for
food. Animals ran away from men and became furious with them. *Chiuta*
Himself had to climb up to heaven by means of the thread which Spider
had spun for Him. *Chiuta* then decreed [and this is an addition to the myths
which J.M. Schoffeleers alone gives] that men had to die and go to Him in
heaven in order to make rainclouds with which to extinguish the fires they
had started on earth.[13]

J.M. Schoffeleers suggests that the *Nyau* symbolically re-enacts a temporary
reconciliation. The masked dancers represent the spirits and the structures
represent the wild animals from the bush who agree to come to the village
to associate with men. All are united around pots of beer, an essential feature of the *Nyau* feast, as they were at first united around the waters which
came from the sky. But the reconciliation is only temporary. When the performance is finished, the animal structures are burnt and man symbolically
repeats what happened at the time of the first cataclysm. The *Nyau* are to be
seen, then, says J.M. Schoffeleers, as a mystery play which relates the story

---

[12] Cf. J.M. Schoffeleers, "Symbolic and Social Aspects of Spirit Worship", pp. 307-415, especially the conclusion pp. 412-415. J.M. Schoffeleers published this theory as well in "The
Religious Significance of Bush fires in Malawi", in: *Cahiers des Religious Africanes* 10 (1971),
pp. 271-281, reprint in: J.M. Schoffeleers, *Religion and the Dramatisation of Life. Spirit Beliefs and
Rituals in Southern and Central Malawi,* Kachere Monograph, no. 5, Blantyre: CLAIM, 1997,
pp. 22-33.
[13] The versions given by A. Werner, *The Natives of British Central Africa,* London: Constable,
1906, p. 73, and by D. MacDonald, *Africana,* 1882 (new edit. 1969), vol. 1, pp. 296-297,
merely state: *Mulungu* then went with the Spider on high. And He said: 'When they die, let
them come on high here'. Cf. our comments on pp. 35ff.

of the beginning of the world. It is also a cosmic ritual, because it symbolizes at the same time the movement of the two seasons with the intention
of influencing them. One season during which the rains fall, the other during which men make bush-fires. Black smoke goes up from these fires and
is transformed into clouds. These come down again as rain during the following season. It is not without reason, J.M. Schoffeleers argues, that the
Nyau founding myths stress that the *Nyau* originated at the time of a famine
(referring to the one according to which a certain Nyanda invented the *Nyau*
dance in order to obtain food in a period of famine).[14] The way to counteract a famine is to kill animals or to make rain fall from the sky, and both
elements are symbolically represented in the burning of the animals structures.

It seems to us however, that this interpretation makes too much of a symbolism based on the "primal myth", as J.M. Schoffeleers calls it. There are
no references to such symbolism in the 300 *Nyau* songs which I have ana-
lysed. This interpretation seems to disregard the more obvious reference to
fertility which can be found in the songs and the gestures of the dancers.
Finally it takes no account of the various "characters" which the dancers
purport to portray. We shall consider now how these various dancers express Chewa beliefs in the spirits and the after-life.

5. Selected Animal Structures and Masked Dancers

a) Animal Structures

All the animal structures represent wild animals *(nyama za ku tchire)*. These
are the animals that kill men. People are afraid of them. They are the symbolic representation of something powerful and frightening. The people say
that these animal structures represent powerful spirits. There is some sort of

---

[14] This is one of several traditions, cf p. 136ff.

hierarchy among them: some are classed as "big" ones, others have lesser importance.[15]

1. *Njobvu* (the elephant). This is the most important structure of all. It takes four men inside, one in each leg. The outside is covered with sacks, painted dark grey with mud. The *Njobvu* represent the *mzimu* of important chiefs. It is considered the king of the animals because of its massiveness. The *Njobvu* has a *liunde* all to itself, which is a sign of its importance. It is treated as a chief. No youngsters are allowed to go to its *liunde*, only the older members of the *Nyau*, who also accompany it wherever it goes. Women have to stay far away from it. It comes only at the *maliro* of a chief. It does not shout anything but dances with dignity. The *Njobvu* conveys the belief that an important chief after his death will be more important and influential than other *mizimu*.

The following four represent other important and benevolent *mizimu*: *Kalulu, Chimkoko, Mdondo, Kasiya maliro*. They are the *mizimu* of honoured elders.

2. *Kalulu* (the hare) is much smaller than *Njobvu* and is carried by only one man. It is covered with grass painted dark grey with mud. It is the representation of an important ancestor who commands respect. While it dances other members of the *Nyau* make a lot of dust to prevent people from seeing the *Kalulu* very well. Women have to stay at a certain distance. All this in order to preserve a certain mystery. It is a way of showing respect to such an important ancestor. The *Kalulu* does not sing anything and dances only a short while. It is usually the first one of the animal structures to dance. It is interesting to note that the hare is the symbol of a wise and clever man. In all the stories the *Kalulu* is like the fox in the fables of La Fontaine.

3. *Chimkoko:* It also represents the *mzimu* of a respected ancestor. It is covered with husks from the maize-cob. Five to ten men are inside the

---

[15] W.H.J. Rangeley has described how some of these animals structures are made, in: "Nyau in the Kotakota District", pp. 19-33.

Chimkoko. It comes to dance at a funeral and dances around the house where the deceased is lying to show that the *mzimu* want to give him rest and feel sympathy with the bereaved *(kusonyetsa chisoni).* During this dance the women relatives of the deceased wail loudly *(kubuma maliro).* The *Chimkoko* symbolizes the solidarity between the ancestors and the living and their sympathy for the mourners.

4. *Ndondo* (snake) is the second in importance after the *Njobvu.* It is covered with grass and husks from the maize-cob and is painted with mud. It is carried by 5 to 12 men. The *Ndondo* symbolizes a mighty and powerful *mzimu* who can be exacting and who often trouble people with his demands. Important members of the *Nyau* want a *Ndondo* to dance at their *maliro.* It marks the importance of a deceased himself.

Kasiya maliro - night version

5. *Kasiya maliro* (antelope) is a symbol of *mizimu* who will be leading the *mzimu* of the deceased into the world of the *mizimu.* They come as it were to receive him *(kulandira).* It is a symbol of the mercy *(chifundo)* of the *mizimu.* It walks ahead of the corpse in the funeral procession. Before that, it comes to the house of the deceased to weep *(kulira)* in sympathy with the bereaved. It is covered with sacks and painted dark grey. Three people carry it.

So far we have seen benevolent and sympathetic *mizimu.* The following two, *Chilembwe* and *Mkango,* represent powerful, but bad and angry *mizimu.*

6. *Chilembwe* is covered with sacks and is painted black. Two men carry it. It represents a *mzimu* who makes people suffer because he is angry. It erupts all of a sudden into a group of watchers to symbolize that such an angry spirit comes without warning. When it comes women run far away. The people fear it because they fear an angry spirit. It dances only at the *maliro* of important people.

7. *Mkango* (lion) represents a bad spirit who terrifies people. This spirit is like a lion who attacks people without distinction and does not let go. It really wants to kill and has no mercy. When it comes the women run far away. It is covered with sacks and sisal is used as hair. This *chirombo* symbolizes the terrible power of the *mizimu*. Such a *mzimu*, once he is angry, knows no mercy. On the other hand man has only himself to blame because he has roused the anger of the *mizimu*, like someone who has roused the anger of a lion.

The following animal structures represent less important *mizimu*.

8. *Thunga* (snake) is covered with husks from the maize-cob, and is carried by one man. It symbolizes the suddenness with which a *mzimu* can erupt into one's life and reminds people that a *mzimu* is always something to be feared. One sees a snake only when it is already too near.

9. *Mkala* is carried by one man and is covered with grass and husks. It represents a spirit who is in the retinue of a more important one (the *Chimkoko*). It often dances with the *Chimkoko*. It takes the place of the *Chimkoko* at a *maliro* of a less important person or if people cannot afford to pay for a *Chimkoko*. The meaning is the same as that of the *Chimkoko*. It is, as it were, a representative of the *Chimkoko*. It is the animal structure found most at a *maliro*.

10. *Ng'ombe* (bull) is covered with sacks and is painted dark grey with mud. It represents a male spirit. It is interesting to note how in the Chewa matrilineal society the *Ng'ombe* symbolizes the spirits of the husband or

father *(mizimu yakuchimuna)* who come to sympathize with the family of the deceased. The typical role of the *Ng'ombe* is also to cheer up the people by its dance and by the coarse songs sung at its dance.

11. *Gandali* represent the *mzimu* of wise men, former counsellors of a chief. The animal has a white spot on top of its head which symbolizes the baldness of an old man.

12. *Fisi* (hyena) is a structure covered with husks of the maize-cob and is carried by two men. It represents the *mzimu* of a thief who is eaten up by greed. Like a *fisi* he only howls and seeks to satisfy its greed. It teaches how greed punishes itself in the life hereafter. Here we have one dancer (like later on, the *mfiti)*, who has a distinctive lesson of morality.

b) Masked Dancers

What is most striking is the variety of the masked dancers. This is already true of the animal structures, but in the number and variety of the masked dancers it comes out even more. This cannot possibly be mere coincidence, it must have some deeper meaning. The whole range of dancers appears on the one hand to present the various aspects of the traditional beliefs in the role of the *mizimu* with regard to the living, and on the other hand to give a moral teaching showing that the condition of a *mzimu* in the life hereafter is connected with his way of life on earth. We shall present 31 characters whom we found in the area under survey. There are many more in other areas. The variety proves a lively popular imagination and interest in the subject. There is no particular sequence in the way we present the different dancers.

1. *Maliya* is dressed like a woman, with a scarf around the head and beads around the waist. She represents a *mzimu* that is tenderhearted like a woman. There is no cruelty in this *mzimu*, only goodness. While dancing the dancer shows the string of beads around the waist. He dances well and his dance is meant to make people happy. It is said that this

figure and its name has been copied from Christianity (Maliya - Maria, mother of Christ).

2. *Chabwera kumanda* wears a black mask and has a goat skin or a leopard skin around the waist, with strips of cloth hanging all around. He represents a *mzimu* who comes to annoy people by asking: "I want *Nyau* dances, I want beer, I want meat, etc." That is why they call him "The one who comes back from the grave" *(chabwera kumanda)*. While dancing he pursues people who try to run away. This is to show his insistence on getting what he wants. He enters the house of the deceased and may even jump right on top of the roof. This is to indicate that he represents the *mzimu* of this particular deceased person and will not desist until his desires are satisfied.

3. *Chadzunda* looks very much like *Chabwera kumanda*. He behaves like an old man who is bent double. He does not assault people. But the general meaning is the same as that of *Chabwera kumanda*: to represent a *mzimu* who comes to ask for beer or something similar.

4. *Kachipapa* or *Mdzalira* is a kindhearted spirit who does not attack people but shows sympathy with the bereaved. Hence he is called "the one who comes here to weep" *(mdzalira)*. While dancing he shields part of his face with his hand as mourners do. He dances together with the women the *chisamba* dance (a women's dance) and sings with them. He has rags all around his waist and human hair, glued together with the sap of the wild fig, is fixed to his face right down to his neck.

5. *Kamkhwindi* or *Kambumbunde* represents a wicked spirit who attacks people doing them a lot of harm. He wears a black mask with sisal as hair and has leaves around waist and shoulders. He looks and behaves like a madman and he attacks people who have done nothing wrong. The purpose is to portray a cruel and savage spirit who wants to appear so. He has a spear and a bludgeon in his hands. He does not sing but only shouts. The women shout obscenities at him to show their disap-

proval of his cruelty. Because of this he runs after them to beat them
Then they shout: "We will not do it any more".

6. *Mbiyazodooka* represents a spirit in the marginal state, on his way to the
    spirit world, who needs help. He asks: "Give me a goat, beer, a chicken
    dance *Nyau* for me". He just repeats this over and over again. He car-
    ries on his head, supported by one hand, a fragment of a broken earth-
    enware pot. People throw small coins into it. People sing: "Go back to
    your home at the grave". He has a bundle of leaves in his hand and
    wipes himself with it. He wears a black cloth mask and some rags
    around the waist.

7. *Gutende* is a cruel spirit. He has huge horns to symbolize his cruelty. In
    his lifetime he was one who had killed people. He is clothed in old
    sacks, has a red wooden mask and two long horns. He sings: "Who
    wants my horns" (i.e. who wants to continue my deeds?). The people
    answer: "Keep them yourself" (i.e. we don't want to do so).

8. *Simoni* has a red mask, usually looking very English with sideburns, and
    he is dressed in a suit made of sacks. This is obviously a mask that is in-
    spired by the colonial officials and may also have been copied from
    Christianity (Simon Peter). It is difficult to pinpoint his exact signifi-
    cance. Some say that he is a mere parody of a colonial official or Chris-
    tianity. During his dance he chases the women who retreat.

9. *Makanja* or *Namkhwanya* represents a spirit who comes to punish peo-
    ple. He walks on stilts and looks very threatening. Because of his long
    stilts he looks "superhuman"; in fact the stilts symbolize his wicked su-
    perhuman power. He is actually the spirit of a deceased *mfiti* who after
    his death continues to perpetrate his evil deeds. The women are scared
    of him and run away. The body, with the long legs, is covered with
    sacks, he has a mask of any colour, red, white or black and rags are
    fixed here and there to his clothing. He comes to the *chinamwali* cere-
    mony because he is the *chirombo* most feared and most impressive.

10. *Kasinja* or *Kamchacha* is the messenger of more important spirits. During a dance he announces what is coming next. Sisal is fixed to his shoulders, elbows, wrists and around his waist. He has a face made of grass which is pointed on top.

11. *Pedegu* represent the spirit who is kind-hearted although he looks very rough and dirty. He is draped in sacks. His head is hanging to one side and is covered with a red wooden mask. He teaches that appearances are deceptive, and that a poor man all clothed in rags or an invalid abandoned by everybody may have a kind heart.

12. *Nyolonyo* dances with the women at a funeral and comes to cheer the mourners. He wears strips of cloth or of sisal around the waist and has a square mask, black or grey, with feathers on the corners. He carries an axe, but this does not add any fierceness to his character.

13. *Akusacha* or *Kwinimbira* or *Pirimindila* come in gangs of 15 to 20 representing evil spirits who come to attack any person. They dance at night to frighten people, but they can also be seen during the day running through the villages. They carry sacks in which they put the things they find on their way, like chickens. They are clothed only in leaves around their waist.

14. *Demu* is clothed in sacks and rags and has a black or grey wooden mask. He sings women's songs. There are men who like to be with the women to dance the *chisamba* (a woman's dance) with them. When they dance they take a cloth and bind it around their waist like a skirt. People laugh at them and say: he is not a man, he is a woman, he likes to be with women. Such a person is despised by men. *Demu* represents such a person and is the object of much laughter and "dirty" songs.

15. *Chimbano* is a spirit who is "stupid" and attacks any person, relative or not. As we have seen, a *mzimu* is supposed to punish his own relatives only, like a man who during his lifetime is only interested and responsible for his own lineage *(khola)*. He is clothed in rags, looks very fright-

ening and has the face of a beast (wooden mask with big teeth). Everybody shows fear of him.

16. *Chaudza* is the spirit of a person who died long ago. He has a small loincloth and a black face-mask. He has a frightening appearance.

17. *Nanyikwi* represents again a spirit who may attack anybody without distinction. He beats anybody and everybody. He has a long stick and bludgeon in his hands. Long banana leaves hang from shoulders to feet. He wears a small sack-cloth mask. He does not dance but runs around in the village. He makes a sound like he, he. People flee from him.

18. *Kapoli* represents the spirit of a young man. He shouts with a very high pitched voice. He wears sisal around waist, wrists and shoulders, and has a pointed grass mask on his head. He sings very dirty songs, like a young man who wants to show-off and who is proud of his sexual prowess.

19. *Nkhandwe* is not really a dancer, but someone who at night comes to frighten people with his cries: ke-ke-ke. He represents evil spirits who like mad men run around in the bush and are not social. These evil spirits are loners like wild beasts in the bush. They may attack a member of any lineage. These are the *ziwanda*, evil spirits who wander around trying to harm people.

20. *Kabvisanza* with *Njoka*. This dancer has with him a live snake (usually the *chapota misampha*) which is here the symbol of an evil spirit ready to kill people without mercy. The dancer himself is clothed in rags with some sisal around his waist.

21. *Kadyankhadze* is an ugly and frightening figure who dances far from the crowd. He represents *ziwanda*, spirits of wicked people who had no heart for their fellowmen and who themselves have no peace. He wears

a very small loin cloth and a huge pointed mask of grass. His body and face are spotted with different colours.

22. *Ndatola* represents a spirit who asks people to help him in his needs. He wears leaves around waist and shoulders and a red mask. He steals things like a chicken, an axe, etc, which the people then have to redeem with coins.

23. *Ngangande* again represents a spirit who is cruel. He wears sacks and a wooden mask with huge protruding teeth.

24. *Ajere* represents the spirit of wicked people who killed with evil medicines *(m'pheranjiru)*. *Ajere* dancers appear in a group, they wear black loin cloths and masks of straw and small whitish cloths fixed with some strings on their shoulders and they carry axes. They accompany the *Njobvu*, this indicating that powerful chiefs often use evil sorcerers to reach their aims.

25. *Chabebe* represents the spirit of a *mfiti*. He is tied up like a bundle with bamboo sticks and rope. He has a sack-cloth mask. His appearance is intended to show his evil deeds and also his punishment to be meted out in the after-life because of the evil deeds done during his life on earth.

26. *Lekakundipenya* (stop looking at me) represents very nasty, ugly spirits. He has an appearance which inspires awe. Pregnant women refuse to look at him because they are afraid that their child may have an ugly face like his.

27. *Kamatuwa* goes practically naked with ashes all over his body. He represents a spirit who is in extreme need. Dancers who represent *mizimu* in need, as *Kumatuwa, Mbiyazodooka, Ndatola*, remind the relatives of the deceased that he is in a period of transition. People believe that such *mizimu* come back to the village for help.

28. *Bwana wokwera pa ndege (pa galimoto)* (a white man in an aeroplane or a car). A person who was rich and powerful on earth will be a powerful spirit in the hereafter. People believe that he could only become rich and powerful because he had access to important medicines. The white man is believed to be rich because he has more powerful medicines than the people in Africa.

29. *Kanambulunje* is a small animal structure of only about 1 m high representing the spirits of a dead child. The spirit of a child will go to the world of the *mizimu* but will be only a small one.

30. *Mfiti* (witch) has an ugly face and is ragged and dirty. His ugly and cruel appearance is in keeping with the evil character of a *mfiti*. In the hereafter the spirit of a *mfiti* will continue his ugly and cruel exploits.

31. *Chitsiru* (the mad woman) has the pitiful appearance of an old woman in rags who does all sorts of unbecoming thing, like appearing to relieve herself, etc. She is an object of great hilarity among the audience. What her exact significance is with regard to the spirit-world was not clear to me. She rather seemed to be some sort of clown.

6. Conclusion

However much the *Nyau* may have "degenerated" and may look, when seen superficially, as mere amusement, it is fundamentally a way of placating the *mizimu (pemphero lathu lalikulu la mizimu)* that they do not come to make people suffer. *Nyau* is a way of ensuring the intercession of the *mizimu* with *Chiuta*. Moreover, the *gule wamkulu* is a symbolic representation of the invisible spirit world. The dancers who represent the *mizimu* identify themselves with the *mizimu* to such an extent that they have to undergo, symbolically, a transformation like that of a deceased person before he can enter into the spirit world. They enter into a marginal state which is characterized by "reversals", a behaviour which is the opposite of normal behaviour in the village. This is a symbolic way of asserting that representing the *mizimu* they are indeed "different" from normal.

The *mizimu* are approached as intercessors and protectors, but they are also feared as guardians of the ancestral customs who can bring havoc when they are angered by the living. Just so the *Nyau* appear at a funeral to comfort and console the bereaved, they are also threatening and violent, representing spirits bringing disaster and suffering. At the initiation they are the teachers of ancestral customs and of accepted behaviour, but at the same time they are savage in meting out punishment so that the initiates are left with fear of the spirits for the rest of their lives.

A *Nyau* dance can be likened to a mystery play in which each actor portrays a particular aspect of their belief in the *mizimu* and the afterlife. The *Nyau* ritual can be called a prayer because it is intended to please and placate the *mizimu* so that they do not come to the village to make people suffer. It also ensures that the deceased will be accepted by the *mizimu* as a true member of the tribe who was faithful to the ancestral customs and above all to the *Nyau*. *Nyau* is also a prayer for fertility at the funeral ceremonies and especially at the initiation of girls. The repeated mentioning of the life-giving organs of men and women is a way of praising the power which God has given and of showing that they are proud of being able to hand on life.

Other partial explanations insist on the *Nyau* being a display of behaviour to be detested, or a reversal of normal social positions in an uxorilocal society, or an occasion to relax, to maintain one's psychological balance. However much these explanations help to understand certain side-aspects of the *Nyau*, we suggest that the religious meaning provides the only real answer to the *Nyau*.

The *mfunde*, the *Nyau*, and the *maliro* ceremonies appear to be the most popular religious rites in which reference is made to the invisible spiritual world, man's dependence is acknowledged and help is sought.

The *Nyau* is the vehicle of much of the religious thinking and aspirations of the Chewa and is also the means by which he becomes a true member of the tribe. The *Nyau* embodies tradition and has proven to be also the mainspring of resistance to outside interference throughout the centuries. It is into this tradition that a young man has to be initiated if he wants to be a real man, a real Chewa. The role of the *Nyau* in the girls' initiation will be seen in the following chapter. After all that has been written it will not come as a surprise to hear that the *Nyau* has been for the missions the greatest "obstacle" and in the eyes of the Colonial Administration "the cause of backwardness". The *Nyau* is the embodiment of tradition and resistance and, by definition, is not open to change. If one day *Nyau* becomes no more than a "folkloric dance", as some would like to see it, then it would cease to be *Nyau*.

Chapter 6
Mdulo

In village life, frequent allusion is made to *mdulo*. In fact, people's lives are to a great extent subjected to *mdulo* taboos. The word *mdulo* comes from the same root as the verb *kudula* (to cut). A person, by disregarding such a taboo, causes death or some other disaster to a third person. In some rare cases, a person can inflict *mdulo* on himself. *Mdulo* taboos are always related to sexual activity. In our survey on the alleged causes of death we have found that out of 451 cases 44 were said to be caused by *mdulo*, 33 children and 11 adults.

1. Definition

Mdulo had been mentioned by various authors, among them A.G.O. Hodgson,[1] W.H.J. Rangeley,[2] and M.G. Marwick.[3] Other authors hardly mentioned it at all, as for example D.C. Scott who discusses the phenomenon of *mdulo* under the name of *tsempho*.[4] Among the authors who have dealt with *mdulo*, W.H.J. Rangeley is the most comprehensive. He gave an alternative explanation of the word. According to him, *kudula* refers to the symbolic act performed by the mother of a culprit, breaking the string of beads *(mkuzi)* she wears around her waist, indicating by this that the family does not want

---

[1] A.G.O. Hodgson, "Notes on the Achewa and Angoni of the Dowa District of the Nyasaland Protectorate", in: *Journal of the Royal Anthropological Institute* 63 (1933), pp. 129-135.

[2] Cf. W.H.J. Rangeley, "Notes on Chewa Law", in: *The Nyasaland Journal* 1 (1948), no. 3, pp. 34-44.

[3] Cf. M.G. Marwick, *Sorcery in its Social Setting*, Manchester: University Press, 1965.

[4] Cf. entry "tsempho", in: D.C. Scott, *Cyclopaedic Dictionary of the Mang'anja Language*, Edinburgh: Foreign Mission Committee of the Church of Scotland, 1892. The author merely mentions: "A sickness supposed to arise from a mother's putting salt into food when sick; or if she or the husband puts salt into the food when guilty of adultery".

to have anything more to do with this person, who by his misbehaviour has heaped shame on his family.[5] However, this explanation does not take into account that the subject of *mdulo* is in most cases an "innocent party" and not the culprit himself. Therefore I think that this explanation is less likely. M.G. Marwick points out that the categories of "hot" and "cold" are a key to the understanding of the *mdulo* beliefs. With the help of new material gained during my research I hope not only to complete the enumeration of the *mdulo* taboos given by W.H.J. Rangeley, but also to make a step forward towards a better understanding of the beliefs themselves underlying the *mdulo* taboos.

The above mentioned authors have not made the connection with the forms of *kudula* in the context of a *mfunde* (rain sacrifice), *maliro* (funeral) or *Nyau*. We have already mentioned these forms of the *mdulo* taboo in previous chapters. The following explanation of the beliefs on which *mdulo* is based is equally valid for these other forms of *kudula*. In connection with family life *mdulo* appears to be the supernatural sanction enforcing the two main duties of husband and wife, namely: the obligation to avoid adultery *(chigololo)* and the obligation to favour procreation and to care for their children *(kusamala)*. In a negative form *mdulo* presents the basic law governing family morality.

M.G. Marwick was of the opinion that *mdulo* cannot be classified as religious, because the Chewa conceive not of supernatural beings who have to be persuaded to soften their hearts when angry and to provide help when needed, but of supernatural impersonal forces that determine automatic and invariable consequences of certain human actions."[6] I would like, respectfully, to disagree with this opinion. When asked, informants answered in every single case that *mdulo* is a punishment inflicted by the ancestral spirits. Although it is true that *mdulo* is thought of as an automatic consequence of certain misbehaviour, it is believed to be inflicted by the *mizimu*, and not caused by impersonal forces. As one informant commented: "In order to

---

[5] W.H.J. Rangeley, "Notes on Chewa Tribal Law", p. 35.

[6] M.G. Marwick, *Sorcery in its Social Setting*, pp. 66.

make us follow this law, our ancestors threatened us with this dreadful thing. If you commit adultery, your child will die, a pregnant woman will die in child-birth, moreover *Chauta* will be angry, your cattle will die, wild animals and diseases will not leave the village. All this they said to make us follow the law forbidding adultery. This is the most important law in the customs of the Chewa" *(chifukwa chakusungitsa lamulo limeneli anayambitsa chiwopsezo chakuti Chauta atikwiyira, ng'ombe zikutha, ndi zirombo, matenda sachoka m'mudzi. zonsezi akazinena chifukwa chofuna kusungitsa lamulo loti: usachite chigololo. Lamulo limeneli linali lalikulu pa miyambo ya Achewa).* Mdulo is therefore believed to be a supernatural sanction established by the ancestral spirits in the case of failure to observe certain rules. As such the consideration of *mdulo* definitely comes within the field of a religious study. *Mdulo* has some similarity with the spiritual sanctions *thek* and *nueer* described by E.E. Evans-Pritchard in his study of the Nuer religion.[7]

The belief in *mdulo* is deeply rooted in Chewa culture. W.H.J. Rangeley wrote that "it is probable that not a single Chewa, whether he be an ordained priest, a teacher or a primitive pagan, does not believe in *mdulo*".[8] M.G. Marwick added that "the dangers of *mdulo* dog the Chewa from the womb to the grave".[9]

2. Different Aspects of the *mdulo* - Complex

a) Symptoms

The symptoms of *mdulo* are said to be a swelling of the cheeks *(kutupa masaya),* and of the legs *(kutupa miyendo),* the swelling and becoming hard of the abdomen *(kuuma mimba),* pain in the chest *(chifukwa),* and the vomiting of blood *(kusanza magazi).* W.H.J. Rangeley reported that medical officers examining a person said to be suffering from *mdulo* almost invariably diagnosed anaemia due to debilitating diseases such as hookworm, malaria, dys-

---

[7] Cf. E.E. Evans-Pritchard, *Nuer Religion,* London: OUP, 1956 p. 177.

[8] W.H.J. Rangeley, "Notes on Chewa Tribal Law", p. 34.

[9] M.G. Marwick, *Sorcery in its Social Setting,* p. 66.

entery, bilharzia, and chronic malnutrition.[10] Some cases of tuberculosis are also called *mdulo*. One thing seems to be clear: *mdulo* cannot be equated with any one illness known to western medical science, it covers a number of illnesses.

Allegations of *mdulo* are very frequent, which is in keeping with the fact that anaemia caused by debilitating diseases is extremely common. There is also a high level of child mortality. The Chewa believe firmly in their explanation of the disease and do not easily accept European explanations or their medicines in the case of a *mdulo* patient. They believe that the only way to deal with it is to find out who caused it, if necessary by having recourse to the diviner *(woombeza ula)*, and to use the traditional way of treating it. *Mdulo* is defined in relation to specific Chewa beliefs and not in relation to specific symptoms. As such *mdulo* is a specific "cultural disease", definable only by reference to a specific Chewa cultural background. This is not to say that some of the symptoms are not recognizable as those for instance of bilharzia or tuberculosis. But when we speak of *mdulo* we do not speak in terms of a modern medical diagnosis, but of a complex cultural diagnosis: this child has *mdulo* - therefore its father must have committed adultery - the father has to confess his fault - the proper medicines have to be obtained from the medicine man *(sing'anga)* and the proper way of applying them has to be followed strictly.

b) Underlying Beliefs

As many have said before, in societies which have to maintain themselves in the face of diseases and a high mortality rate, fertility is one of the most important values. This fertility is believed to depend on the right use of sex according to the traditions laid down by the ancestors. Anything which is thought to harm the fertility of a couple is seen as a crime against the whole group and against the ancestors who are believed to be the guardians of the traditions in the tribe. They protect and guarantee fertility and survival of the group as long as the members of the group follow the traditions. They punish and withdraw fertility if traditions are not followed. There exists a

---

[10] Cf. W.H.J. Rangeley, "Notes on Chewa Tribal Law", p. 36.

great number of detailed regulations concerning the sexual activities. These are believed to ensure the optimum conditions for human reproduction, and, when faithfully adhered to, they also ensure the benevolence of the ancestral spirits. The Chewa believe that *Chiuta* has given man the possibility to reproduce himself. But He has given this to the group, not to each individual person. Ancestral spirits are the channel through which fertility comes to men. This explains why some people have children, while others have none. Fertility depends first and foremost on one's standing with the ancestral spirits. And this depends on the faithful observance of the traditions concerning sexual activity. Among the Chewa these regulations have taken the form of *mdulo* taboos.

c) *Hot* and *Cold* [11]

What is mysterious and potent is often thought of as something dangerous. Sexual activity, sexual fluids and especially menstruation, are highly mysterious and powerful and therefore dangerous. This is expressed by classifying them as "hot". People who are not engaged in sexual activity, such as old people, people who have abstained for some time and above all small children are on the contrary "cool". Moreover, it is believed that what is powerful can be mutually dangerous. "Hot" can be dangerous to "hot" when different categories of "hot" are brought together. "Hot" then stands for dangerous, while "cool" stands for vulnerable. There are different degrees of being vulnerable. The most vulnerable are new-born children. To be "cool" is also a prerequisite for any person taking part in major rituals, such as *mfunde* (rain sacrifice), and the vigil before a burial. The ancestral spirits, the dead, are thought of as "cool". Any person who would on such occasions be "hot" would *kudula* (cut i.e. spoil) the ritual. The ancestral spirits will not fail to punish.[12]

That is the reason why the night before a *mfunde* all the people have to sleep out in the open to ensure that none have conjugal relations. At a funeral

[11] The Chewa speak of a person who is 'cool' or 'hot' (*munthu wozizira, munthu wotentha*).

[12] It is interesting to note that the Chewa status of "coolness" corresponds with what many other religions call "purity" in relation to a sacrifice. Cf. the various conditions of purity required of a Jewish priest in the book of Leviticus.

people sleep out in the open for the same reason. To be "cool" is also required of the women who brew beer which is to be offered as sacrifice. The women who go with the chiefs and the children to the *kachisi* at the Bunda rain shrine, in order to help with the preparation of the sacrifice, have to be older women beyond child-bearing. The *Nyau* dancers have to abstain during the days of the dances, because they too have to be "cool" since they are thought to be in close contact with the spirits. The reason why women cannot be members of the *Nyau* is said to be because they are frequently "impure" because of their monthly periods which render them "hot". The only women allowed near the *dambwe* to bring food are older women beyond child-bearing. At Bunda the chiefs who are closely connected with the *mfunde* (the chiefs *Chadza, Mwenda,* and *Chilowa*) have to remain "cool" during all the time the rain might fall. The *Makewana* was identified with the rain shrine and so was never allowed to be married or to have sexual relations, unless with the "python" *Kamundi,* as we have seen. Her servants, the *Matsano,* were young girls before the age of sexual activity.

In all these cases "coolness" is required of any person coming into contact with the spirits, because the spirits are thought of as "cool". The rains are also thought of as "cool". The "coolness" required on the occasion of a *mfunde* or even for visiting the rain shrine, goes so far as to preclude anyone from wearing red clothing, when going near the *kachisi,* since red is the colour associated with "hotness". Nor is a *mfunde* or any other sacrifice ever offered during the hours when the sun is high and very hot. The sacrifice is offered during the cool hours of the early morning or else during the late afternoon.

Returning to the subject of *mdulo* with reference to the family, we see for example that a new-born child is considered extremely vulnerable and can be handled only by people who are definitely "cool". For a "hot" person to touch the child would surely result in the death of the baby. Parents are said to "have cut" their child *(anadula mwana wawo),* resp. the child is said "to have been cut" *(anadulidwa).*
Many, if not most of the *mdulo* taboos, come down to the idea that the "hotness" in one person can cause the death of a person who is particularly

vulnerable because of certain circumstances. "Hotness" is always caused by recent sexual relations or by menstruation. Not every person who is "cool" is necessarily vulnerable but only in certain particular circumstances. In a number of cases, however, a "hot" person can be dangerous to another "hot" person. Parents, for example, have to abstain from relations while their daughter is having her first menstruation or when she is pregnant. Sexual activities of successive generations are thought to interfere with one another. The older generation has to give way to the younger generation in this respect. A girl who is having her first menstruation can cause *mdulo* to the village chief should he have relations with his wife during the time the girl is indisposed.

The notions of "hot" *(wotentha)* and "cool" *(woziziro)* are everyday concepts in Chewa village life. It is important to note that the conditions of being "hot" or "cool" are not thought of as moral categories, as something good or bad. What is wrong is to disregard the rules determining one's behaviour with respect to these conditions and so to risk causing *mdulo* to someone.

d) The Medium Salt

The Chewa believe that salt is a medium by which the mysterious power emanating from someone who is "hot" can reach out to other people and cause *mdulo*. A menstruating woman, for example, is not allowed to put salt in the food she is preparing for her family. To do so during the days of her periods would cause *mdulo*.

I tried to find out why salt, of all substances, has become such a medium through which "hotness" can pass. Some informants thought that salt was chosen to act as a deterrent because it was such an everyday and indispensable commodity. People don't like *ndiwo* that is not salted. The prohibition for an adulterous woman to salt the food, under pain of causing *mdulo*, was intended as a deterrent against adultery. The husband might want to know why he was being given unsalted food. The ancestors would have chosen salt precisely because of this everyday use people make of it. In this way the taboo became an effective deterrent. In other cases the absence of salt in the food is a warning to the husband that his wife is having her monthly periods.

It is true that the women, in all these cases, can call a small girl and tell her to put the salt in the food. But this is something the husband can observe. One informant gave another explanation as to why salt became connected with the *mdulo* taboos. His reflexion may well give us the key to the understanding of the role of salt in this respect. Speaking about a woman during her monthly period he said:

> The blood of a woman during her periods is like poison, it can kill people. While a woman has her periods she is bad, she can harm people. Salt is like the life or the blood of the *ndiwo* (side dish eaten together with *nsima* the main dish of stiff maize porridge). When such a woman puts salt in the food, it is as if she puts her bad blood in the food and so she kills people. Salt is like blood, and in these circumstances, it is like her bad blood. In a remedy against *mdulo* people add some salt in order to give back to the child its life. Because, they think, perhaps the mother has given to the child bad salt in its food, i.e salt that the mother has made bad because of disregarding the important law concerning her monthly periods *(Pa mwezi magazi aja ndi poison, mpaka kupha anthu. Munthu wamkazi pamene ali kusamba ali woipa, angathe kuononga. Mchere umafanizira moyo kapena mphamvu ya ndiwo. Pamene ali kusamba kuthira mchere ndi monga kuipitsa anthu ena ndi magazi ake. Mchere ndi wolingana ndi magazi aja, magazi a moyo. Pa mankhwala a mdulo anthu amaonjeza mchere kubwezera moyo wa mwana. Chifukwa kapena anapatsa mwanayo mchere woipa m'ndiwo, mchere umene mayi anaipitsa chifukwa cha kusatsata lamulo lalikulu lija la masiku a kusamba).*

In this case, then, the idea that things that are similar will also bring about results that are similar is the key to the understanding of the connection between salt and *mdulo*. The salt, which is like the blood of the food, is associated with the "bad blood" of the woman during her periods. The menstrual flow is called "blood" by the Chewa. If the woman is issuing bad blood, the salt also turns bad and has the same effect as the bad blood of the woman. In other cases the salt is associated with the blood of the woman which has become "hot" (i.e. dangerous, i.e. bad), because of the adultery she has committed.

Among the Bemba in Zambia similar taboos are connected with fire instead of salt.[13] Salt, then, is thought of as a way in which blood or the "badness of an act" can reach out to other people and kill them. One can give the following principle: whenever relations are not allowed, food may not be salted. To put salt in food in such circumstances would have the same effect as intercourse itself would have, i.e. *mdulo*.

The Chewa use three kinds of salt: 1) European salt *(mchere)* which can be bought in the shops; 2) water made salty by being filtered through the ashes of burnt grasses; 3) water made salty by being filtered through salty soil. The last two kinds of salt are called *chidulo* (that which cuts). It is very bitter and it serves only to salt certain vegetables. It is to be noted that the name *chidulo* (the type of salt used before the European salt became available) comes from the same root as *kudula* and *mdulo*. This salt "cuts" the vegetables (in French: *hacher),* and in the same way the *mdulo* disease will "cut" the intestines of the person.

3. Spectrum of *mdulo* Taboos

To appreciate fully the importance and the wide spectrum of the *mdulo* taboos, it is good to present a list of them. We shall try to group them under a number of headings. Several of these taboos can be found in W.H.J. Rangeley.[14] Some of the taboos are no longer observed by younger people while older people still appear to stick to them. Other taboos are observed by the quasi-totality of the Chewa. Each time we shall indicate by the words "in the past" the taboos which are no longer observed by the younger generation. However, I thought it right to present them as well, because some people still observe them, and they can help us to appreciate the wide spectrum of these *mdulo* beliefs. Together with the *mdulo* taboos, we shall also describe certain rituals, such as the *kutenga mwana* rite and parts of the girls' initiation rites, because of their close connection with the *mdulo* beliefs.

---

[13] Cf. A.I. Richards, *Chisungu*, London: Faber & Faber, p. 33.

[14] Cf. W.H.J. Rangeley. "Notes on Chewa Tribal Law", pp. 34-44.

a) A New-born Child

Pregnancy

If during a pregnancy the husband or the woman herself commit adultery, *mdulo* will be the consequence. In the case of the woman herself having committed adultery, she is said to have "mixed different bloods" *(wasakaniza magazi osiyanasiyana)*. In this case she will lose the child *(kuchoka mimba)*, or she herself will die in child-birth. If the father has committed adultery, his wife will faint repeatedly or often become indisposed and vomit blood during her pregnancy, and finally she may die while giving birth. The child itself will either be stillborn or will die soon after birth. If it does survive it will remain very weak.

In all these cases, if there is any suspicion that either has misbehaved, the appropriate medicine must be used at once. A number of different roots must be gathered and made into a bundle *(chikunje)* and boiled in water, to which some salt has been added. Both husband and wife have to put in some salt because both may have done wrong. They will take another pot, as big as the one in which they are boiling the *chikunje,* and put it upside down on top of the first pot. With mud they have to close any space left between the two brims. The husband plasters one side, his wife the other. Once the water has boiled for some time, they take the pots from the fire. While covering the whole with a blanket, they lift off the pot which is on top. Then the woman will bend over the pot and inhale the fumes, with the blanket covering her head to prevent any of the precious fumes from escaping. This method will also be used if later it is feared that a child has *mdulo.* The father will take the child in his arms and both will inhale the fumes. These are cases where the father has caused the *mdulo.* If the mother is responsible, she will hold the child over the fumes.

Birth

Among the people in the villages there is a general mistrust to deliver the baby in hospital, because they are not sure that the midwife and the nurses are *ozizira* (cool). In fact, all those who touch the child have to be "cool", or they may cause *mdulo* to the child. Moreover it is completely against the customs for young women who themselves have not had at least one child to assist at the birth of a child. This is the work of the older women *(azamba)*. When the delivery has to take place in hospital they try to obtain medicine from a *sing'anga* (medicine man) so as to protect the child.

Kuturutsa Chikuta
Washing the new-born with medicated water

If the young woman has difficulty in giving birth, the old women assisting her *(azamba)* will try to make her confess that she had adulterous relations during her pregnancy. They believe that such adulterous relations will result in the death of the child and even of the mother, because she has mixed different bloods *(kusakaniza magazi osiyanasiyana)*. This fear will make her tense and make the delivery difficult. If she confesses that she has slept with such-and-such a man *(ndagona ndi uje),* and the right medicines are used immediately, all may go well. Such a confession will help her to relax. E.E. Evans-Pritchard noted the same belief among the Nuer: "The sin and its consequences become less by being confessed".[15] If, after repeated efforts to make her confess, the woman maintains that she has done nothing wrong, the husband will be approached and made to confess his adulterous relations during the time of the pregnancy of his wife. If his wife dies or the child, either at birth or immediately afterwards, the husband is simply declared to have committed adultery. He will be found guilty without any possibility of defence and will be fined heavily (a cow or more), payable to the brothers of his wife. I have known several cases in which the brothers were absolutely ruthless and made the husband pay exorbitant fines.

---

[15] E.E. Evans-Pritchard, *Nuer Religion,* 1956, p. 187.

When a child is born, it is said to be *woziᵶira* (cool), *wa nthete* (unripe), *wa ka* *mphepo* (of the wind), *ngosatha mlandu* (the case is not yet settled), *ngosapita ka* *malo* (has not gone yet to the place). Such a child is not yet considered fully a human person and is in a particularly vulnerable condition. The child will remain like that until it is "taken" *(kutenga mwana)*. If such a child, before it is "taken", dies, it will not be buried in the normal fashion. Only a few women will go to put it in a very shallow grave (not more than a foot deep). To bury it in a deeper grave would be tantamount to making its mother sterile. The child is still thought of as part of the mother *(chiwalo cha mayi)* and to bury it in a deep grave would be the same as to bury the womb of its mother, making it imposible for her to have another child.

Until the umbilical cord has dried off, the child is kept inside the house where it is born *(chikuta)* with the doors shut for fear of evil (hot) influences, which can even be carried by the wind or the rays of a fire. After the umbilical cord has dried off (after 5 to 7 days), a string with *mphinjiri* (medicine) is tied around the child's waist to protect it against evil influences, and it is brought out of the house for the first time *(kutuluka chikuta)*. While the child is kept in the house, only its grandmother and the *aᵶamba,* who have helped at the delivery, are allowed to enter. Its own father may not enter the *chikuta*. After the child is been "brought out" and until it is "taken" *(kutenga)* no married person or grown-up girl is allowed near the child, let alone touch it. These people are possibly "hot" and could give *mdulo* to the child. Only its mother, father, old women, and young girls may hold the child. During all the time before the *kutenga* the parents of the child are not allowed to resume relations, they would become "hot" and give *mdulo* to the child. The following have also to abstain from relations until the child is "taken" *(kutenga)*: all grandparents *(agogo),* i.e. the parents of both, the father and the mother, plus the other wives of a grandfather if he is polygamous, similarly the other wives of the father of the child if he is polygamous. All the sisters of the mother of the child, and also those of the father of the child, if he has moved with his family to his own village *(chitengwa)*. All the sisters of the child itself, if any. All the *aᵶamba* who assisted at the birth of the child. Even if any of these persons were to have adulterous relations during this time, they would give *mdulo* to the child.

In order to protect the child against *mdulo*, if it is accidentally touched by a "hot" person, it is given medicine mixed into thin maize porridge. To this is added medicine made from the stomach of a rat and a civet cat so that the child may eat much and as often as these animals and grow fast. As an additional protection a *mphinjiri* (medicine) is also fixed to its *mkuzi* (string around its waist).

Christians are not to use these *mphinjiri;* when under pressure from their mother and the *azamba*, they bathe the child in water mixed with medicine.[16] As long as the child is not "taken" its mother should not go to a burial, neither should its father help to fill in a grave. During this time the mother of the child is not allowed to put salt in the food for the family. Salt may not even be kept in the house. If such a child should die before being "taken" *(kutenga)* it is immediately assumed that its father has had adulterous relations, or that the child has been touched by a "hot" person. Even today practically all people including Christians observe these taboos with respect to the new-born child.

The *kutenga mwana* ritual

When the child is 4 to 6 weeks old (some people wait up to 3 months), it is time for the *kutenga*. A chicken is offered to the tutor *(phungu)* of the child's mother as an invitation to come and explain once more the ritual to the parents. The essential part of the ritual is everywhere the same. Additional secondary rites may differ from place to place.

The essential rite is the following: The father must have relations with his wife while the child is lying in between them. The parents lie on their side, facing one another, and both hold the child. The woman must remain immobile. The man must effect intercourse all alone without any cooperation on the part of the wife. He is not allowed to hold her with his hands or in any other way. Failure to effect intercourse under these conditions is relatively frequent, and it causes great embarrassment to the husband. If he fails during the first night, he can try again the following night. If he fails again,

---

[16] P. Braire, "Coutumes Indigènes", Rome: Archives of the Missionaries of Africa (White Fathers), Ms, 44 pages, 1927, p. 1.

he is said to have "missed" *(kusempha)* the child. This gives the child *tsempho* (to be missed) which is another name for *mdulo*. To avoid *tsempho* they can then take the child to another family where the husband is known to be strong *(wa mphamvu)* and to ask them to perform the *kutenga* in the name of the child's parents. To have relations once during that night is not enough, it must be three times. The essential condition, i.e. that the husband must effect intercourse alone, holds good for each intercourse. The usual time is about 8-9 p.m., 12.00, and 4-5 a.m.

The rite of *kutenga mwana* intends to give strength to the child. Until then, the child is not yet fully born, not yet fully a human person. The role of the father, they believe, is to give his strength to the child. Already during pregnancy sexual intercourse is considered important because this is the way the father "feeds" *(kulera)* the child, adds strength to the child. During the *kutenga* he gives his strength to the child and it is not until then that the child is considered safe. The rite is also known as *kusonyeza mphamvu* (to prove one's strength), *kupatsa mphamvu* (to give one's strength). It is considered a real test of strength for the man.

M.G. Marwick, writing about the Chewa in the eastern province of Zambia, mentioned a different rite.[17] The father has to have coitus interruptus and mixed seminal and vaginal fluid is rubbed on the child. He further continues: "A strong mystical tie between father and child is assumed to exist, for if the father does not "make firm his heart" *(kulimbika mtima)* sufficiently to break off intercourse at the right moment, the child will not receive from him any strength of character". This quotation by itself would show a profound difference not only in the rite itself, but also in its effect. M.G. Marwick mentions "strength of character", while all our informants insisted on something much more fundamental: the quality of life itself. However, M.G. Marwick also mentions that the "coldness" of the child is taken away by this rite. Presumably this means that the child is made safe.

---

[17] Cf. M.G. Marwick, *Sorcery in its Social Setting*, p. 67.

The secondary rites differ from place to place. In some places there are no secondary rites at all. The following two examples were mentioned by informants.

After having effected intercourse the first time, the husband has to withdraw in time so that his wife can take some semen and anoint with it the face and the body of the child, and to put some on the *mkuzi* of the child. Finally she has to anoint her own breasts with it as well, so that they might grow full. This has to be done only once. The second and third intercourse that night have to be complete. It is obvious that this secondary rite symbolizes the same as the essential rite: the father strengthens his child.

Kufunditsa mwana
Warming up the child

Another additional rite is that the father has to take the child, if it is a boy, and the mother, if it is a girl, and jump across the fire which is burning in the house. This seems to symbolize that the child is now warmed *(kufunditsa mwana)*. Until then it was "cold". It is interesting to note here that the word used is *kufunda* (to warm), which means that the condition of "coldness" is removed. The child was vulnerable. The child is not said to become "hot". "Hot" means dangerous and is the condition of someone who has had recent sexual intercourse, or the condition of a woman having her monthly periods. Such a person is "hot" i.e. dangerous. The child is "warmed", its condition of extreme vulnerability is removed, but it does not become "hot" *(wotentha)*.

From now on the mother of the child can salt the food for the family. The morning following the *kutenga* she prepares some salted *ndiwo* and brings it to all the persons who had to abstain from relations because of her child. This is to let them know that the child has been "taken" and that from now on everybody can resume conjugal relations. The child is given a string with white beads to wear around its waist, because it is now made right *(woyeretsedwa)*. It is a day of rejoicing. The child is now *wofunda* (warm), *munthu weniweni* (a real human being), *ali wamkulu* (grown), *ali wolimba tsopano* (is now strong), *watha mlandu* (the case is settled). The rite itself is also called *kufunditsa mwana* (to warm the child), *kulimbitsa mwana* (to strengthen the child), *kulera mwana* (to feed the child), *kutola mwana* (to take up the child), *kuika mwana pa mphasa* (to put the child on the mat), *kupita naye ku malo* (to take it to the place), and *kutha mlandu* (to settle the case).

Alternative ways of *kutenga mwana*

If the father of the child is far away and it would be too long to wait for his return, or when the father has not been able to do the *kutenga* himself, one of the following alternatives canbe employed.

1. The relatives may choose another family, preferably related but not necessarily, who will be asked to do the *kutenga*. At night the child is taken to that family and they perform the rite exactly as if they were the parents of the child. They will be given 3 to 5 Kwacha for this service, or 3 to 5 chicken (1 Kwacha is 50 pence). The child will be known as *mwana wotumiza* (a child that has been sent elsewhere), and the women will be called *mayi wake wa chibwenzi* (his mother in friendship).
2. Alternatively the relatives may arrange for a young man to come to the mother of the child at night (*kulowetsa fisi*, i.e. to make a hyena come in), and do the *kutenga* instead of the father. This *fisi* will be paid for his service as above.
3. A third method is to buy from the *sing'anga* (medicine man) two special *mphinjiri* (medicine hidden in two little pieces of reed). These are fixed to the legs of a cock. They watch the cock. As soon as he has mounted a hen, they remove the two *mphinjiri* and fix them to the *mkuzi* (string around the waist) of the child.

4. It may also happen that the mother wants to wait till her husband comes back and then do the *kutenga*. In the meantime she gets some medicine from the *sing'anga* which she fixes to the *mkuzi* of the child. This will protect the child if any of the persons who were supposed to *kudika* (abstain from relations because of this child) would get tired of waiting and have relations, or if any other "hot" person would touch it.

It is sometimes said that the custom of *kutenga mwana* is dying out, but the fact is that all the informants insisted that all non-Christians are faithful to the rite in one way or another, and that many Christians too, out of fear for possible consequences and under pressure from their non-Christian relatives (especially their mother and *azamba*), still perform this rite. All these non-Christian relatives cannot resume their conjugal relations as long as the child is not taken. They can put considerable pressure on a young woman to conform.[18] It is finally to be noted that the *kutenga* has to be done in the case of all the children, and not only in the case of a first child. In the section "various *mdulo* taboos" of this chapter, the obligations of the parents with regard to a child that has been "taken" can be found. It has to be noted that if the child lives with an elderly relative, e.g. its grandmother, this person must follow all the regulations which bind its parents, because the child is, as it were, her child. It is quite regular that some of the children, once they have reached the age of about 6 or 7 years, are sent to live with their grandmother or another elderly relative.

b) The First Menstruation of a Young Woman

In this section and the following we shall describe some of the rites of the initiation of girls *(chinamwali)*, as they are closely connected with *mdulo*.

A young girl is instructed to give warning as soon as she experiences her first menstruation. She will tell her grandmother, her elder sister, or some friend. The person in whom the girl confides has to tell the mother of the girl that her daughter has "grown-up" *(kukula, kutha msinkhu)*, has "fallen down" *(kugwa pansi)*, or has "broken the reed " *(kuthyola bano)*. The daughter

---

[18] Cf. W.H.J. Rangeley, "Notes on Chewa Tribal Law", p. 38.

will not tell her mother directly, since these things are not mentioned between mother and daughter. The mother then tells her husband "our daughter has done wrong to us" *(mwana wathu watichimwira)*. From now on, the
parents have to abstain from conjugal relations till after the seclusion of the
girl. This obligation rests also on the grandparents, all the sisters of the girl
and her maternal aunts. They could give *mdulo* to the girl if they disregarded
this obligation. She has entered upon a state of transition and is vulnerable
till she has been made strong again.

She is taken to a house where she has to stay till the end of her period. If
already married she is not allowed to have any relations with her husband.
She is not allowed to do anything or to speak to anybody other than to
those who are in charge of her: the *namkungwi* (the elderly woman in charge
of the girls' initiation) and her *phungu* (tutor). All that she uses during these
days must be old: her clothes, the mat on which she sleeps, and the utensils
used for cooking. Afterwards all the items will be burnt and thrown away
because they will have become impure.

Her mother gives a chicken to the *namkungwi* who takes it to the chief and
tells him that such-and-such a girl has grown-up. From now on the chief
has to abstain from all relations with his wife. If the chief of the village is
not a *mwini mzinda* (a chief who has the right to have initiation in his area),
the obligation to abstain falls also on the chief *mwini mzinda* where the girl
will be initiated. If he should not abstain, he would contract *mdulo* himself.
This would happen for instance if the girl kept secret that she had her first
period, and the chief, unaware, were to have relations with his wife. The girl
is said to have killed the chief in such a case. This is the only case in which a
person other than the girl herself contracts *mdulo* because of her. In all other
cases it is the other people who, by disregarding the taboo, would cause
mdulo to the girl.

The reason is the following. The chief is mysteriously a link between his
subjects and the spirits of the dead. Fertility is granted by *Chiuta* upon the
intercession by the spirits and passes down a mystical chain of which the
chief is an essential link. This is symbolically expressed by the fact that the

villagers may only have conjugal relations when the chief is in the village. If he is absent, they have to abstain. The chief has also the mystical task of "opening the womb of the girl". He does so by having intercourse with his own wife on the last day of the seclusion of the girl. The chief's wife is a symbol of all his female subjects. It is by having intercourse with her, that he mysteriously assures fertility for his subjects, and symbolically "opens the womb of the girl".

The wife is identified to such an extent with the girl, that the chief would contract *mdulo* by having relations with his wife, as long as the girl is having her first period. It is as if his own wife had her periods. A person having relations with a woman during her periods, "cuts himself" *(mdulo)*. This is the reason why the chief has to be informed immediately of the fact that a girl in his village has "grown-up". If the chief were not informed, his authority and sacred function would be disregarded. This might even result in "killing the chief" were he to have relations with his wife unaware that there is a grown-up girl in the village. Once he is warned, the chief *mwini mzinda* prepares with the roots of a *chibwezo* or a *kabzerebzere* a medicine called *khundabwi* or *phundabwi*. The chicken which the *namkungwi* gives him, is cooked together with this medicine and the chief eats it as a protection for himself. The rest of the roots are burnt and the ashes are mixed with salt. This mixture is used for salting the food of the chief. He also sends some of it to the *namkungwi* who will salt with it the food of the girl during the time of her seclusion. From now on the girl is a *namwali* and belongs to the chief *mwini mzinda*. She will be initiated at a *chinamwali* ceremony which will take place during the hot season. Until then she remains in a state of transition.

During the days of her seclusion the *namkungwi* and her tutors give her instructions dealing with the days that a woman is not allowed to have relations with her husband (the *mdulo* taboos), how she has to behave with regard to men other than her husband, the respect she has to show to older people, and especially the chief, and finally the days that she may not put salt in the food which she is preparing.

On the last day the girl's head is shaven. That night her husband, if she is already married, comes to the house. Once more the *namkungwi* makes sure that they are well instructed. The girl has prepared some *ndiwo,* part of which is given to her various relatives. They may not eat this *ndiwo* because it is still impure. They have to stamp on it *(kuponda)* so as to stamp out the impurity of the girl. That night her husband must have relations with her. He imparts his strength to her and she becomes strong again. This is called *kutha namwali* (to end the puberty). The next morning the rest of the *ndiwo* is warmed and brought to the *namkungwi,* the tutors, and all the other relatives who had to abstain on account of the girl. They may eat it because it has now been purified by the act of ritual intercourse. Everybody can now resume conjugal relations, except the girl and her husband. She is still in a marginal state until after the *chinamwali* ritual. If ever she should become pregnant during this time, she would be accused of having "killed the chief". The single act of intercourse at the end of her seclusion would not cause a pregnancy, for according to their way of thinking repeated acts are necessary, a single one would not suffice. The period during which she is not allowed to have relations with her husband is known as *kulanda namwali* (to take away the puberty).

If the girl is not yet married, or if her husband is away, another young man is chosen to act as her husband on the last night of her seclusion. The parents of the girl bring a cock which will be eaten by this young man so as to give him strength. The young man is called *fisi* (hyena) because he comes secretly. Nowadays such a young man will be given 4 Kwacha (2 Pounds). Many still follow this way in the villages because, as we were told, it is cheaper than buying protective medicine from the *sing'anga* (medicine man). If they do not want to use a *fisi,* medicine can be bought from the *sing'anga* which will be fixed to the *mkuzi* of the girl as a precaution against pregnancy and *mdulo.* Without this her relatives cannot resume relations.

Girls who are at school, will remain home for a few days while they are secluded and given instructions. Those who are in boarding schools receive medicine from their parents which will prevent them from becoming pregnant and enable the relatives to resume relations. The instructions will be postponed till the holidays. Sometimes a girl does not inform that she has had her first menstruation, because she fears the initiation, or she feels that she does not need any advice from the older women. If such a girl becomes pregnant, she will be accused of "having killed the chief". There will be a big case *(mlandu)*, and her parents will have to pay a heavy fine to the chief: a cow or the equivalent in money (about 70 Kwacha i.e. 35 Pounds). She herself will be severely punished and put to shame on the day of her *chinamwali*. She is called a *chimbwinda* (stupid girl).

The act of ritual intercourse with her husband on the last night of her seclusion makes the girl strong. There is a parallel with the act of ritual intercourse at the *kutenga mwana* ritual. In both cases we find that the man imparts his strength to those who are weak. This will be repeated again at the end of the *chinamwali* ritual.

c) The Solemn Initiation of a Young Woman (chinamwali chaching'ono)

Some months after the first instruction the solemn initiation will take place, usually during the season after the harvest (June till November), when there is plenty of leisure and food. This initiation is called *chinamwali chaching'ono* (small *chinamwali*). The *chinamwali chachikulu* (big *chinamwali*) is the ceremony marking the first pregnancy.

As often as possible the initiation of several girls will be held at one ceremony, because of the high costs involved. The *chinamwali* lasts normally 5 days and is a time of great rejoicing in the village. At the *chinamwali* a tribute has to be paid to the chief for each girl. This tribute is called *mtula ngala* and amounts to 11.50 to 12.50 Kwacha (about 6 Pounds). The *Nyau* is normally an integral part of the *chinamwali* ceremony. However, on account of the expenses, it may happen that the masked dancers do not come if there are not enough girls. We can distinguish three cases:

1. *Mkangali,* this is the normal case. The *Nyau* dancers come.
2. *Chimbwinda,* the case of a *namwali* who is pregnant. If it is not combined with a normal *chinamwali-mkangali,* there will be no *Nyau*.

3. *Chikudzukudzu* is the case when there are not enough girls and the people cannot afford the expenses of a *mkangali*. The *Nyau* dancers do not come.

During the *chinamwali* ceremonies the chief, the parents and other relatives mentioned above, the *namkungwi* and the tutors, have to abstain from conjugal relations for fear of causing *mdulo* to the *namwali*. It seems that originally they had to abstain from the moment of the first seclusion of the *namwali* till after the *chinamwali*, as the *namwali* herself and her husband still have to do today.

Chinamwali - Instruction of the maiden

The *chinamwali* lasts five days. We shall proceed day by day and indicate the rites which appear to have a particular connection with our subject-matter. Since the *chinamwali* is to a great extent purely a women's affair which men are not allowed to attend, apart from the public ceremonies at the *bwalo*, we had to find some women ready to talk. We consulted three different groups. Each one came from a different area. One group consisted of three older women who besides remembering their own initiation remarkably well, had also been several times *phungu* (tutors) to other younger women. The other two groups consisted of younger women. This permitted us to check whether particular rites were still performed today. The only real differences were in the *namwali* songs, which although identical as to meaning, had local variations.

The first day: *tsiku logwira anamwali*

Tsiku logwira anamwali means "the day that the young girls are captured". In the afternoon of the first day, the *namkungwi* and the tutors fetch the girls and conduct them to the *tsimba* (the house where the initiation will take place). If a girl runs away, she is followed and brought back. The girls are afraid and neither laugh nor talk. Together the *namkungwi*, the tutors and the girls enter the *tsimba*. Each girl sits between her two tutors, who undress her, leaving her with only a small cloth *(thewera)*. This symbolizes that her girlhood, the things she was familiar with, is taken away from her. Her girlhood is over and she passes into a transition state symbolized by wearing no clothes. The girls are given instructions, the *miyambo* as it is called and are taught the secret *chinamwali* songs that contain this *miyambo* so called because the uninitiated are not supposed to know them, at least not to understand them. In these songs symbolic language is used, which is difficult to translate. We have collected about one hundred of these songs. They all contain some teaching, which reminds the women of the *miyambo* (instructions) of their *chinamwali*. In this way the instructions are being kept alive throughout the life of the woman.

The girls are taught the *chinamwali* dances, some of which they will have to execute during the public meetings on the *bwalo*. Other dances are meant for the more intimate moments when husband and wife are together in their homes. The *namkungwi* initiates the instructions and then leaves it to the tutors to see to it that the girls learn them. This teaching is called *kulanga anamwali* (to punish the *namwali)*, or *kudula mutu* (to make them submissive). At the *tsimba* they are not beaten or punished in any way. They just have to learn these things, hour after hour. Other women already initiated are allowed to enter the *tsimba* and to join in the singing of the songs. But no uninitiated person is allowed in there.

While they are being taught the songs they are instructed to perform those duties that will be theirs later on when they sing the same songs. The idea is that every time a woman is with her husband in their house at night, she has to sing these songs which will remind her of what she has to do and what she should not do, according to the customs laid down by the ancestors. Since relations between husband and wife are not something which concerns them alone, but also the group, they may not do what they fancy themselves. They have to follow the ancestral customs. The ancestral spirits will not cease to watch whether they are faithful to these customs. If they neglect the customs a fortiori, if they refuse even to be initiated into them their union will remain sterile, or worse, they may kill each other. They believe that life comes from *Chiuta,* but through the intermediary of the spirits These spirits will intercede for them and obtain fertility.

The customs *(miyambo)* surrounding the conjugal relations, are laid down by the ancestors. The songs are a constant reminder of these *miyambo.* One of the most important items of these *miyambo* concerns the days when they are not supposed to have relations. If they do not follow these *miyambo,* they cause *mdulo.* The main idea, then, of these songs is to remind them constantly and throughout their lives of the *miyambo* laid down by the ancestors, many of which are enforced by the threat of *mdulo.* The teaching of these songs continues till late in the night, and is continued throughout the following days.

Late at night the girls are given some time for sleep. But even then they will not sleep much because the *Nyau* dancers come round the *tsimba,* and even push the door open, in order to frighten the girls. Even the most intrepid of the girls will be scared. This enhances the idea of the mysterious character and importance of the instructions. The memory of the threatening behaviour of the *Nyau* dancers, representing the *mizimu,* will remain with them for the rest of their lives. The following is one of the most important *chinamwali* songs, containing the *miyambo* concerning the taboo on relations during the menstrual periods. This song is supposed to be sung each night before sexual relations. The following is the version used around the Bunda area.

1. Mnzako akati ndaima ndaimandaima	When your companion says: I am standing
Pholokoto wa mtengo wa pa dambo	Standing like a tree upright at the *dambo* (brook)
Kubala akuti wirira,	The woman says: it is rough with long grass,
Kugwa akuti lakata	The woman during her periods says: it fell

	down,
Tandiuza chidalakata	Tell me why it fell down
Idalakata ndi nkhole	What fell down is menstrual blood

Refrain:

Nkhole ikana ukulu	Menstrual blood refuses pregnancy (here intercourse)
Phungu ndati miyambo tsiling'inthu	My tutor told us the *miyambo* of intercourse
Kafunde-kafunde miyambo	Remember, remember the *miyambo*

2. Mnzako akati tsegula	When your companion says: Open.
Kodi nditsegule bwanji?	How can I open?
uku kwalenga dera	There is a gap here
Tandiuze chalenga dera	Tell me the reason of the gap.
Yalenga dera ndi nkhole	The reason of the gap is the menstrual blood.

Refrain

3. Mnzako akati madzi wanga, madzi wanga.	When your companion says: Where is my water?
Ndimatunga ndimatunga a	I draw water from inside me
Mkango amayenda nalilima	The lion goes about roaring
Tandiuza chidalilima.	Tell me the reason why it is roaring.
Idaliluma ndi nkhole	What is roaring is my periods.

Refrain

4. Mnzako akati mtengo wanga, Mtengo wanga.	When your companion says: my tree, My tree (symbol of penis).
Ndimadula ndimadula, nufiyirira	I cut it, I cut it. It is red with blood.
Tandiuza chafiyirira.	Tell me the reason why it is red.
Yafiyirira ndi nkhole	The reason why it is red is menstruation.

Refrain
The second day: *tsiku la chiwuluwulu*

Tsiku la chiwuluwulu means "the day of the big fear".[19] When it gets light the tutors go with the *namwali* to the *dambo* (brook) to wash. After that they go together to the *mtengo* (a big tree chosen for its shade). It is the assembly place of the women during the *chinamwali*. It is away from the village some-where in the bush. During the *chinamwali* the men are not allowed to ap-proach it. The *namkungwi* first examines the girls to see whether they have learnt what they were taught the day before. If she is content with the result, she continues with her instructions.

On this second day the *namkungwi* examines the girls to find out whether some are already pregnant. If she finds that one is pregnant, she reports her to the chief. The parents of the girl will have a big case *(mlandu)* and the girl herself will be severely punished. At about 3 p.m. all go together to the *bwalo*. There the women dance, and during the dance the girls have to lie flat on their stomachs. They are covered with a cloth which is spread length-wise, as is done only for a corpse. This rite symbolizes that the girl has now died and that she will rise as a woman. The women dance around her and sing:

> Mwana thunga e e e e e.
> Mwana thunga e e e e e.
> Mwana thunga e e e e e.

That is: daughter of the *thunga* (a snake). The snake here is a symbol of the male, and the whole ceremony symbolizes intercourse. The girl has grown up, she is now a woman and can bear children. There are many other songs, all with the same meaning. This dance lasts for about an hour. In the eve-ning the *namkungwi* takes the girls to the place where the *Nyau* structures are hidden, as explained earlier in the chapter on *Nyau*. After that they retire to the *tsimba,* where the teaching continues. At night the *Nyau* dancers again

---

[19] The entry *Uluwulu* in D.C. Scott & A. Hetherwick, *Dictionary of the Nyanja Language*, London: The Religious Tract Society, 1929, reads: "Uluwulu, hair standing up over the body; especially of the hair of head and shoulders, as in illness *(tsempho);* munthu wodwala tsempho tsitsi lache lichita uluwulu monga nthenga za ana a mbalame" (p. 581). *Tsiku la chiwuluwulu* is then the day when hair is standing up of fear.

roam round the *tsimba*. The objective of the pedagogics of this day is to ritually teach the girls fear as being the case when the hair is standing up over the body (*uluwulu*). This would happen whenever they violated the taboos and the customs.

The third day: *tsiku la mchezo wa akazi*

Tsiku la mchezo wa akazi means "the day of the women's (nocturnal) dance". The whole day is spent at the *mtengo* where the girls are taught. In the evening the *namkungwi* together with the *aphungu*, the girls and all the other initiated women of the village, go to the house of the chief for the *mchezo wa akazi* (nocturnal dance of the women). The women dance naked in front of the chief who is the only man present at this ceremony. The dance lasts for many hours till deep in the night. It symbolizes that the women expect fertility to come from the spirits through the intermediary of the chief.

The women are very secretive about this dance. A.G.O. Hodgson already reported it mentioning that the women dance naked in front of the chief.[20] He thought that the dance meant that the women were symbolically the children of the chief. He added that the chief was not supposed to be aroused by the sight of these women dancing naked in front of him. We have pointed out already that the chief is, as it were, symbolically, the husband of all the women in the village. He brings them fertility. The people of the village are not supposed to have conjugal relations while the chief is absent, because a woman cannot have relations while her husband is away. During the ceremony the women dance an erotic dance, the one which the girls are taught to perform in front of their husbands as a prelude to their conjugal relations. Other erotic dances are also performed. As the *chinamwali* ceremony is meant to obtain fertility for the young women who are being initiated, this dance of the women in front of the village chief is to be understood as an erotic dance in front of their "symbolic husband" in order to gain fertility.

---

[20] Cf. A.G.O. Hodgson, "Notes on the Achewa and Angoni", p. 134.

The fourth day: *tsiku la chingondo*

A young woman with chingondo

Tsiku la chingondo means "the day of the clay helmet". At the *mtengo* early in the morning, the *phungus* prepare the *chingondo:* They put a piece of cloth tight around the top half of the girl's head and then model with clay some sort of helmet around her head. On top of the helmet they model some animal figure. It is whitened with flour and painted with red and black spots. The *phungu* put all their skill and pride into its fashioning. Its exact meaning is not clear. The women say that it is a festive head-dress. The girls are dressed with many strings of colourful beads and their body is dotted with numerous white spots. On the other hand the small animal figure leads us to think that there is some symbolic meaning here. While the girls are on their way to the *bwalo* they are stopped by the *namkungwi*, who carries a small bow and arrows. She stands on one side of the path, and the girls on the other. While she aims at one girl after another, she sings: *Nyama yanga ma e. Nyama yanga ma e* (my animal). After that each girl jumps to the other side of the path. Then they proceed together to the *bwalo*. This appears to be a symbolic hunting ritual. It may be interesting to note that on the final day the husband also carries a bow and a spear and makes threatening gestures towards the on-lookers symbolically defending his bride. While they do so the girls themselves have to follow their husbands

While they do so the girls themselves have to follow their husbands and each time he stops they have to kneel down. This seems to indicate that the girls, who were free so far, have been caught and are no longer free.

In their advance towards the *bwalo* the girls are carried on the shoulders of their *phungu*. The dance on the *bwalo* also is performed by the tutors still carrying the girls on their shoulders. After this dance they carry them from house to house, where small presents are given to the girls. When at last they reach the *tsimba*, the girls themselves break the *chingondo* by rubbing and knocking their heads on the ground. The fragments are collected by the mother of the girl and her *phungu* and thrown away at a secret place.

The fifth day: *tsiku lomaliza*

Tsiku lomaliza means "the last day". In the afternoon the girls go to the *bwalo* where they are told to lie on their stomach. Again they are covered with a cloth that is spread lengthwise symbolizing that they are like corpses. *Nyau* dancers come and cover the girls with earth. Then *Nyau* dancers take branches which the girls have to clasp firmly without letting go. The dancers drag them around and around on the *bwalo*. Finally the *namkungwi* redeems each girl with some money. She begs them to stop and to let the girls go. I was told this was a punishment for past bad behaviour. Finally the husbands of the girls come to the *bwalo* and each girl is handed over to her respective husband. There follows the rite, referred to already, of the husband brandishing his weapon. Then all retire to the *tsimba*. Later towards the evening the *namkungwi* once more instructs the *namwali* joined now by their husbands. Each couple is reminded that they must have relations that night. This ritual intercourse ends the *chinamwali* ceremony. The chief also has intercourse with his wife by which he symbolically "opens the womb of the *namwali*".

On the next morning, the *phungu* comes to find out whether everything went well. If the answer is that intercourse has taken place, the *phungu* does the *nthungululu* (shrill cry of joy made by the women) and informs everybody concerned. All those who had to abstain from conjugal relations on account of the *namwali* may now resume them. If the young man did not succeed, he has to put a piece of wood at the door early in the morning. By this the *phungu* understands that "things did not go well" *(muno zinthu zakanika)* Next evening the husband tries again. If he fails again, he is sent away and a *fisi* is called in. From now on the *namwali* will be known by a new name. The former one will never be used again. She belongs now to the group of the grown-up women.

In a context in which fertility is very much desired, and sterility considered as one of the greatest evils, the *chinamwali* ceremony takes on a very important significance. If a girl is not initiated, and consequently does not know the *miyambo* (customs relating to *mdulo* and concerning her relations with her husband) people have no doubt about the result: this woman will have no children, or the children will die soon.

The Christians have obtained for their girls that they will be initiated by Christian women, without going through the *chinamwali* ritual. They pay the same tribute *(mtula ngala)* to the chief as the other non-Christian girls.

d) The Ceremony at the First Pregnancy (chinamwali chachikulu)

When the young woman becomes pregnant her husband has immediately to warn his parents and those of his wife. These have to abstain from conjugal relations from now on till after the *kutenga mwana*-ritual. The *namkungwi*, the tutor of the young woman *(phungu)*, and the women of the village who have already had a child *(achembere)* take the young woman to the bush, where they will perform a ritual called *chisamba* or *chinamwali chachikulu*. This ritual lasts for three days and is reserved for *achembere*. Other women and men are not allowed near the place where they perform the ritual. During the night all sleep together in the home of the young woman. The husband has to sleep elsewhere. During these days they teach her the customs and songs related to her pregnancy, the birth of the child, and the care she has to take of the child. In these songs often symbolic language is used to describe the male and female organs. At other times, however, a crude and down-to earth language is used. During these songs the male is often laughed at. Many of the instructions *(miyambo)* given during the *chinamwali* are repeated.

e) A Boy Reaching Puberty

The following is reported by Rangeley,[21] but informants denied that people in the area we investigated know about this custom. When a boy notices the first sign of having reached puberty (nocturnal emission) he has to report it immediately. He is in a dangerous state (transition) which must be terminated by a ritual act of intercourse. If he is already betrothed, he must have intercourse with his betrothed wife during three consecutive nights. If he is not yet married, one of his female cousins will be chosen to have intercourse with him during three consecutive nights. Until he has had such intercourse he may not eat salted food for fear of contracting *mdulo*.

f) Adultery

Another major law is sanctioned by the *mdulo* taboos: the prohibition of *chigololo* (adultery). If a woman has committed adultery, she cannot salt her family's food. If a wife gives unsalted food to her husband while at the same time not refusing him sexual relations (thus showing that it is not the time of her period) she gives her husband reason to suspect that she has been having adulterous relations. It is to be noted that when a husband returns from a journey he watches his wife while she is preparing the food. If she does not put salt in the food herself (but gets a small girl to do it) this suggests that something might have happened during his absence. An adulterous husband cannot eat salted food together with his sons (a father eats with his sons who are old enough to feed themselves). He has to finish all the food, so that nobody else eats what is left over. He might give the remains to a dog. The fact that he refuses to eat with his sons is an indication for the woman that something has happened. To avoid this, the husband may say that he does not want to eat because he has eaten already with some friends and is no longer hungry. If, at night, they have relations, all is well again. The effect of the adultery is taken away by the subsequent relations between husband and wife. After having had relations the wife may again salt the food and the husband may again eat salted food with his sons. An adulterous woman may obtain some medicine and put it in the food with the salt.

---

[21] Cf. W.H.J. Rangeley, "Notes of Chewa Tribal Law", p. 41.

An adulterous husband may also try to get some medicine and throw it on the fire on which his wife is cooking the family food. He will pretend to be blowing up the fire, or to be lighting his cigarette at the fire. That medicine will burn and the fumes from it will be inhaled by the wife and children and so immunize them against *mdulo*. Again, other men take some leaves of the *Mbwazi* tree and rub them in their hands. The smell of these leaves is believed to produce the same effect. These medicines are ways of "hiding their adultery" *(kubisa za chigololo)*. A woman may also have prepared food and salted it before the adultery took place. Such food can be given to the family without risk. If a husband commits adultery during the pregnancy of his wife, or after the birth but before the *kutenga* of the child, he is believed to kill the child because of *mdulo*.

If a husband commits adultery in his own house, while his small child is in the house, he kills it with *mdulo*. The reason is that the child, while small, sleeps in between its parents for safety's sake (danger of rats, etc.). This does not mean that it lies there even during the relations of its parents, but it lies very near even then. When a father commits adultery he is said "to leave the child aside". On the contrary, if a woman commits adultery while her child is not with her in the house, she kills the child, because she "puts the child aside". These regulations enhance the importance of the law forbidding adultery. However, people have found ways to circumvent the taboo by means of medicines.

g) The Case of a Polygamous Husband

Nowadays, if someone has two wives, he normally builds a house for each, often at some distance from one another. But if all live in the same house, he is not allowed to have relations with one of his wives while the other is absent with her child. When one of these wives becomes pregnant, the husband may not resume relations with the other wife till after the *kutenga* of the child. They are considered "one family". However, some informants mention that not all people go so far. According to them it all depends on whether or not they think they do wrong by doing so. If they think they do wrong, their action causes *mdulo*. If they are convinced that they do no wrong, they do not cause *mdulo* (*Ngati amaganiza kuti alakwa pa kutere, amaopa koma ngati saopa, angathe kupitiriza ndi mkazi wina).* This is an interesting statement because it underlines the conviction that *mdulo* is a punishment for wrongdoing. If a person is convinced that he is doing no wrong, he does not cause *mdulo. Mdulo,* therefore, is something they fear as consequence of wrong-doing. A husband is not allowed to marry a second wife while his first wife is pregnant. He would cause *mdulo* to the unborn child.

b) Various other Cases of kudula

The following cases we have put together, because they all express the fear that the mysterious power emanating from the sexual act is believed to destroy or to damage the effect of another "creative" activity. However, these taboos are no longer observed by most of the Chewa. Some older people may still observe them.

A woman may not have relations with her husband in the following cases:

* when one of her chickens begins to lay eggs,
* when her goat or pig has young,
* when they plant or harvest,
* when she herself or one of her sisters is brewing beer,
* when her husband goes hunting or fishing,
* when she is making earthenware pots,
* when her husband melts iron-ore in a furnace *(ng'anjo),*
* when her husband is making a drum,
* when she is preparing *chidulo* (native salt),
* when the village is being moved to a new place *(masasa),* until the chief has a new house built.

In the case of certain medicines, the medicineman *(sing'anga)* warns that conjugal relations might destroy the effect of the medicine. When people go to buy salt, they first give a pinch of salt to their wives and children, before having relations with their wives. This goes back to the time that people had to go far to get salt and had first to share some salt with their companions before having relations with their wives. If they broke this rule, they gave *mdulo* to their companions.

i) 3.9 Mfunde, Maliro, and Nyau

The following is just a summary of what we have already discussed and seen in previous chapters. The evening before a *mfunde* all the people have to sleep outdoors and observe the taboo on sexual relations. To disregard this taboo is called *kudula kachisi*. The chiefs, closely connected with the rain shrine, have to observe a much longer period of abstinence (cf. p. 42f).

When there is a funeral in the village, the people have to abstain from relations during the night before the burial. Those who do not belong to the family may go home once the burial itself is over. The members of the family have to abstain till after the first *kumeta*. A wife mourning her husband has to wait till after the "second *kumeta*". During the "vigil" people have to sleep out in the open. Anybody going into a house for the night is suspected of breaking the taboo. If someone falls ill soon afterwards, that person will be accused of having caused *mdulo*. To break the taboo is known as *kutaya manda* (to throw away, to disregard the grave). People attending the funeral have to be "cool" because the dead are "cool" (cf. p. 111).

The *Nyau* dancers have to observe a taboo on sexual relations throughout the period of their dance. Should any of them break this taboo, he is believed to cause *mdulo* to his companions. They have to remain "cool" because they are in such close contact with the *mizimu*.

k) Various mdulo Taboos during Initiation

The following list covers various *mdulo* taboos as they are taught to the young women and men in the initiation instructions.

During the monthly periods of the woman

Each time a woman has her periods she must "sleep on a separate mat" and is not allowed to have relations with her husband, as intercourse would give *mdulo* to her husband. On the first day of her periods she has to remove her *mkuzi* (string of beads around her waist) and hang them on a nail on the wall, so that her husband will understand. When her periods are over, she has to clean the house, replace the floor with mud *(kuzira)*, wash all her clothes, and put back her *mkuzi* around her waist. During the days of her periods she may not put salt in the food which she prepares for the family. In the past, she was told not to close the door of the house herself during these days, letting someone else do it for her. If she were to close the door, she would render her husband sterile *(udzatsekera nguwo ya mwamuna)*. The reason for this and other prohibitions was that the woman in such conditions was dangerous *(woipa i.e. bad)*, and because of a lack of hygiene she could pass her "hotness" to her husband.

During pregnancy

From the 6th or 7th month a woman is forbidden to have further conjugal relations. Before that, intercourse was believed important (but not more often than once a day) because this was the way the father fed the child *(ku-lera mwana)*.

From the birth of a child till the *kutenga mwana* rite

No relations are allowed under pain of causing *mdulo* to the child.

When something belonging to the child is left outside at night

As long as the child is not weaned (about two years) the mother may not have relations with her husband when she has left something outside the house, which is used for the child, such as its carrying - cloth *(mbereko)*, its *mkuzi*, or the baskets in which she prepares its food. She would give *mdulo* to the child if she did. If, inadvertently, she had intercourse, she may never use these objects again, but has to give or throw them away. In case any of the things used in the house are lent to another family, they have to abstain from relations until they are returned.

In the case of illness

When one of the children is ill, the parents have to abstain from relations. If not, they would give *mdulo* to the child. If measles *(chikuku)* or small-pox *(nthomba)* have been reported in the area, all the parents of young children have to abstain from conjugal relations. When the parents of either the husband or the wife are ill, they have to abstain from relations. When the woman herself is afflicted by some disease such as leprosy, or when she has

an infected wound (tropical ulcer for instance), she should not have relations, according to some informants. In the past, as soon as a contagious
disease had been reported in an area, all the people there had to abstain
from relations. This was not observed when an epidemic of cholera plagued
the area in 1974.

A girl in the lineage has her first periods or passes through the *chi-namwali*

All her close relatives have to abstain, i.e. her parents, grand-parents, the
sisters of her mother, and her own sisters. Moreover, if the family lives in
the village of the father *(chitengwa),* all his sisters who live in the same village
have to abstain as well.

Daughter or daughter-in-law is pregnant

The parents have to abstain until the time of the child is taken *(kutenga).*

Till the child is weaned

In the past it was said that a woman had to refuse relations till her child was
weaned. This explains why, even now, so many young men go to work in
the mines of South Africa soon after the birth of their child and stay there
till they can resume relations with their wife.

When a small child is absent

As long as a child sleeps in the house of its parents (until about the age of 7)
and is absent for one reason or other, the parents may not have relations.

Case of a boy coming to the house to take some food

At about the age of 7 a boy goes to sleep with the other boys of the village
at the *bwalo* or *mphala* (boys house), or in the kitchen house. He is told that
when he comes to the house of his parents in their absence and takes some
food from one of the cooking pots, he will get *masaya,* a swelling of the
cheeks. This they tell him in order to frighten him and deter him from tak-

ing food. This is not a case of *mdulo*, contrary to what W.H.J. Rangeley seems to have understood.[22]

The initiation of a boy who has reached puberty

When such a boy (or a younger one, as is now often the case) goes to the *Nyau* to be initiated, his parents have to abstain till he comes back from the initiation. Such a boy is told never to go to the place where his parents sleep. Neither should he ever touch the clothes of his parents (this is, they say, like "undressing his parents"). He might get *mdulo* if he disregards this taboo.

Son is absent

As long as a son was not married, his parents had, in the past, to abstain from conjugal relations during his absence from the village. *Sing'anga* now sell medicine permitting the parents to have relations in such a case. But when he returns, even today, they have to give him some food in which they have put some medicine *(phundabwi)*, before they give him any other food.

Unmarried daughter

Some say that parents of a grown-up daughter have to abstain from relations as long as they have not found a husband for their daughter. If against the wishes of her parents a daughter gets married or goes to live with her husband in his village the parents have to observe the following ritual upon her return. The daughter cooks some *ndiwo* and salts it. Her mother does the same. (This is called *za mchere*, i.e. the ritual of the salt). Each hands at the same moment to the other the *ndiwo* thus prepared *(mphambano manja,* i.e. crossing their hands). After that they can eat together and have relations with their husbands. This is a sign of reunion, reconciliation *(kufungatira, kulumikizana)*. Another way is to cook *ndiwo* and both mother and daughter pour some salt into the food at the same time.

---

[22] Cf. W.H.J. Rangeley, "Notes on Chewa Tribal Law", p. 40.

Parents are absent

When the mother is away from the village, all the grown-up children who are married and living in the same village, have to abstain until her return. According to some informants the same holds good when the father is away, but other informants do not know this last custom. Again some informants noted that younger people no longer observe this taboo while others say it persists.

The chief is absent from his village

Formerly when the chief was absent from his village, and even today according to some informants in some areas, all the people in the village had to abstain from relations.

Most of the above regulations stress the duty on the part of the parents to care for *(kusamala)* their children. If they do not care for them *(kusamala)*, they kill their children *(mdulo)*. The taboos also stress the fear that sexual activity of succeeding generations interfere with one another. The parents have to give way. Some taboos stress the belief that there is a chain of fertility which comes down through the chief, the parents, to the actual husband and wife. If one of these links in the chain is absent, there should be no intercourse. Another idea is the importance of reconciliation.

l) Sanctions on Violations of mdulo Taboos

Although *mdulo* is believed to be a punishment inflicted by the spirits of the dead, and as such it is a "supernatural punishment". There is often a fine imposed when a person is accused of having violated *mdulo* taboo. For instance, if a woman dies in child-birth, the husband is accused of having caused *mdulo* and is found guilty without any possibility of defence. He is made to pay a heavy fine to the brothers of his deceased wife. Belief in *mdulo* is so strong that an accused person, who might previously have solemnly declared his innocence, will often admit his guilt once a person has died. It takes, says N. Salaun, a very courageous man to maintain his plea of innocence.[23] Rangeley notes that there is hardly any Chewa who does not at

---

[23] Cf. N. Salaun, "Notes on the Achewa", polycopied, Lilongwe: Language Centre, p. 67.

some time or other have to pay damage for *mdulo*. The amount of money, he says, changing hands because of *mdulo* is considerable.[24] The fear of *mdulo* causes many a man to spend a lot of money to find protective medicine for himself and his family. Modern *sing'anga* specialize in these preventive medicines. In the market of Lilongwe there are rows of stalls where *sing'anga* offer their merchandise.

4. Conclusion

To be "hot" or to be "cold" are not moral categories but conditions. Not to observe the rules concerning these conditions is wrong and *mdulo* may be the consequence. The *mdulo* taboos constitute, as it were, in a negative way, ideals to be striven after and social values to be maintained. They stress a sense of personal responsibility. Each person has to observe these taboos and by doing so contributes to the welfare of the community. The *mdulo* beliefs act as a check on sexual misconduct and as a stimulant for parental care for children. The various customs and *mdulo* taboos are spelled out and repeated over and over again in the initiation instructions. It is therefore understandable that great importance is attached by the older generations to these initiations and that any slackening of the discipline concerning these initiations is resented as an effort to undermine the tribal customs and ultimately the welfare and the moral fibre of the community.

Mdulo beliefs state that illness and death can be a consequence of bad behaviour, and that they can be prevented to some extent by good behaviour. They instill a sense of responsibility towards one's fellow men and the community. Sexual misconduct *(chigololo)* and lack of parental care *(kusasamala)*, as defined by the *mdulo* taboos, are to be a crime against the family and the community as a whole. *Mdulo* beliefs refer to the all important goods: health and life, and threaten with illness and death. They refer to a concept of life based on right conduct, and to death as being caused by bad conduct.

---

[24] Cf. W.H.J. Rangeley, "Notes on Chewa Tribal Law", p. 35.

Prevention of illness and death consists above all in the faithful observance of the ancestral customs. Prevention of illness and death can also be obtained by the judicious use of the right medicines. However, medicines have often become a substitute for good conduct. *Sing'anga* offer medicines for sale which allow sexual freedom without consequence.

The *mdulo* beliefs inculcate in particular the value of *kusamala* (caring for the children). The Chewa attach much value to this obligation. Parents who neglect their duty are severely criticized. The family holds the mother responsible for the care of the young child. It is striking to see how a mother always keeps her child near her, never letting him out of her sight. This care for her child is further explicitated by the *mdulo* belief that insists on sexual abstinence in many circumstances because of the mysterious influence sexual activity is thought to have in those circumstances.

Infidelity is also understood as a lack of care for the mother and her child who is seen as the source of much evil and suffering. *Mdulo* beliefs offer an explanation of the cause of illness and death. They stress that it can be prevented by good behaviour. In this way, *mdulo* beliefs have instilled a sense of responsibility with regard to other persons, and have closed the door to selfish individualism.

Even if today a section of the population lives less under the threat of disease and death because of improved medical and hygienic conditions, one cannot underestimate the weight of centuries' old beliefs. M.G. Marwick noted that "the whole complex of beliefs concerning *mdulo* exerts a strong influence on every Chewa, and appears to have withstood the onslaught of modern changes far better, for instance, than the cult of lineage spirits".[25] The importance of the *mdulo* beliefs should not be minimised. It can be assessed from the frequency of references to *mdulo* in everyday family and village life, and from the repeated insistence on initiation. As A.I. Richards noted for the Bemba, we can say for the Chewa, without any exaggeration,

---

[25] M.G. Marwick, *Sorcery in its Social Setting*, p. 68.

that there is a constant pre-occupation with fear for *mdulo*.[26] Although the *mdulo* taboo highlight the importance of fertility and the horror of sterility, it has, as a matter of fact, acted as a system of birth control which proves too effective. People complain that if they observe all the taboos, they would have hardly any children at all.

---

[26] Cf. A.I. Richards, *Chisungu*, p. 35. It must be noted, however, that the *mdulo* beliefs of the Chewa are similar, but not identical to those of the Bemba.

Chapter 7
Witchcraft *(ufiti)*

According to our survey made 296 out of 451 cases death were believed to have been caused by witchcraft *(ufiti)*. This high percentage indicates a tremendous pre-occupation with belief in witchcraft. M.G. Marwick thought that close to 100% of all Chewa believe in witchcraft, be they educated or not, Christians or not, old or young.[1] There is no doubt that belief in witchcraft is deeply rooted in the mentality of the Chewa and that it continues to influence their behaviour. Even Christians, in time of stress, frequently revert to behaviour inspired by fear of witchcraft. M.G. Marwick, conducting a survey among the Chewa of Zambia in 1948-49 and 1952-53, noted that 55% of the deaths were said to have been caused by witchcraft.[2] The significantly higher percentage (close to 65%) reached in our survey could be an indication that belief in witchcraft has increased as a result of upheavals brought about by factors of social change in the last 20 years. This is a pattern that has been observed in many parts of Africa. On the other hand it could be true, as J.M. Schoffeleers declares, that the centre of interest is shifting from the traditional religious practices (such as offerings to the ancestral spirits) towards a type of pseudo-religion dominated by magic and belief in witchcraft.[3]

One could discuss whether or not witchcraft as such ought to figure in a study of Traditional Religions. However, not only does belief in witchcraft refer to supposedly supra-human powers *(mphamvu yopambana mphamvu ya anthu)*, but it also has an indirect function in maintaining the moral norms laid down by the ancestors. Those serve to correct anti-social behaviour,

---

[1] Cf. M.G. Marwick, *Sorcery in its Social Setting*, Manchester: University Press, 1965, p. 72.

[2] Cf. M.G. Marwick, *Sorcery in its Social Setting*, pp. 14-17.

[3] Personal conversation with J.M. Schoffeleers in 1975.

such as greed and uncontrolled anger. Moral norms are closely tied to Traditional Religion in so far as they originated from and are sanctioned by the ancestral spirits. As such we believe that belief in witchcraft has to be considered in a study of Chewa Traditional Religion.

M.G. Marwick made a study of sorcery and witchcraft with reference to the particular social setting of the Chewa matrilineal society.[4] He pointed out how witchcraft is related to social conflicts inherent in that particular system. In our study we consider these same beliefs from the point of view of their religious implications. Since M.G. Marwick has made such an extensive study of witchcraft and sorcery among the Chewa, we do not think it necessary to present the same material again in detail. In the following pages we shall limit ourselves to the description of some facets of contemporary Chewa belief in witchcraft.

The difference between a "true" witch and a sorcerer

M.G. Marwick preferred to translate *mfiti* as "sorcerer", though he noted that this word does not quite cover the nuances of the word *mfiti*.[5] I believe that it is better to distinguish clearly between the two different meanings of the word *mfiti*. Although the Chewa use the same general term, they clearly distinguish between two categories. The first category is sometimes called *mfiti yeniyeni* (a true witch), while the other is called *m'pheranjiru* (killer by malice). It is important to see the difference between the two meanings of *mfiti*. The *mfiti yeniyeni* is a personification of something which is believed somehow to exist and is certainly feared but which is essentially a product of the mind, a rationalization by which people explain suffering and which points to evil in men as the cause of such suffering. The other, the *mfiti m'pheranjiru* refers to people who exist in flesh and blood, who practise their evil trade. They belong to the world in which things really do happen. A *mfiti yeniyeni* does not really eat human flesh, he is merely believed to do so. Poisoning and other such evil practices indulged in by a *mfiti m'pheranjiru* really do take place. We shall from now on call the first category *mfiti* and the second

---

[4] Cf. M.G. Marwick, *Sorcery in its Social Setting*, 1965, passim.

[5] Cf. M.G. Marwick, *Sorcery in its Social Setting*, 1965, pp. 81-82.

"sorcerer". The reason why we refer the term *mfiti* to witch is that the Chewa belief has its own particularities, somehow different from the notion given of a witch by E.E. Evans-Pritchard.[6]

M.G. Marwick noted that "the anthropologist can usually believe that sorcery is attempted (even though he may not accept allegations regarding its prevalence or its effectiveness); whereas he can only dismiss as fantastic the idea that witchcraft is ever practised, let alone that it is effective."[7] However, it should not be dismissed too easily for, as we shall see, *ufiti* stands for evil, and as such it is a belief with deep roots in reality. Dealing with the second category, the "sorcerer" *(m'pheranjiru)*, we want to point out that many cases, in which a sorcerer is said to have killed a person, are probably mere allegations without any proof. However, these allegations have some foundation since in fact some people are indeed killed by sorcerers out of malice or upon demand by another person. Some people, as we shall see, are also killed in order that sorcerers can prepare *chizimba* (activating agent made from human bodies and used to prepare particularly powerful medicines).

1. The "true" Witch *(mfiti yeniyeni)*

The *mfiti yeniyeni* are said to eat human flesh. They kill in order to have human flesh to eat. They are also called *a maliseche* (the one who is naked) because they are said to go about naked at night. The following is the standard description of a *mfiti yeniyeni* by informants.

When a person is being buried, the *mfiti* throws into the open grave some magic medicine *(mankhwala)*. This remains invisible to non-*mfiti*. This *mankhwala* will help the *mfiti* to raise the corpse more easily. In the evening the *mfiti* of the surrounding areas gather at the graveside. They have a way of informing one another (a lizard is said to beat a drum) that human flesh is available and they respond to the invitation with great avidity. One of the *mfiti* throws some *mankhwala* on the grave and calls the deceased by name:

---

[6] Cf. E.E. Evans-Pritchard, *Witchcraft, Oracle and Magic among the Azande*, London: OUP, 1937, pp. 21, 387.

[7] M.G. Marwick, *Sorcery in its Social Setting*, p. 81.

"N.N. rise up, come out, your father is calling you" *(uje, dzuka, tuluka, bambo wako akuitana)*. If the deceased does not answer the first call, some more *mankhwala* is thrown until he arises from the grave. When he does so he is still drowsy with sleep. The *mfiti* use a different *mankhwala* to wake him up and to make him strong and fat. With a third *mankhwala,* they kill him. To raise a corpse from the grave is called *kufukula mtembo.* Some *mfiti* have *mankhwala* with which they can remove the body from the house before it is buried. What the people bury is then only some shade *(chithunzi).*

The *mfiti* then skin the corpse, starting with the feet. They leave no traces on the ground, because they do not put the flesh down. With their *mankhwala* they bend some trees down and hang the strips of flesh on the branches. As soon as they are ready, they release the trees and no traces at all are left behind. The flesh is divided into equal shares. When a *mfiti* wants to eat some of the flesh he just adds it to a pot in which a woman is cooking some *ndiwo* (side-dish) and takes it out again when it is cooked. He then eats it as *ndiwo* (side-dish) with his *nsima* (maize porridge which is the staple food). All this is invisible to other people. The *mfiti* are said to kill people in order to replenish their supply of human flesh. Each *mfiti* of a group has to furnish a corpse in turn. Usually they kill only their close relatives. In answer to the question why they do this, I was told: "When you want to slaughter a cow or a goat, you take them from your own fold *(khola)"*. M.G. Marwick received a similar answer.[8] There is here a parallel with the belief that a *mzimu* interferes normally in the lives of his own *khola* (fold i.e. lineage group) only, as we have seen (cf. p. 74).

E.G. Parrinder pointed out that the idea of witches eating human flesh is fairly widespread in Africa, but added that it is clear that what is meant is some sort of spiritual eating.[9] They are said to devour the soul of the flesh, or the spiritual body with the result that the person wastes away. Pains and paralysis appear in different limbs. When the centre of blood, the heart or the liver is reached, the victim dies. One of the main tasks of the witchdoc-

---

[8] M.G. Marwick, *Sorcery in its Social Setting,* p. 3.

[9] Cf. E.G. Parrinder, *African Traditional Religion,* London, 1954, new edit., London: Sheldon Press, 1974, p. 126.

tors is to discover what witches have done with the soul of the victim. However, among the Chewa, there seems to be the idea that corpses are actually eaten. W.H.J. Rangeley appeared to have thought that it actually happened but that it occured more rarely in his time. He added: "Long ago, in some areas, it was necessary to guard new graves for fear these *mfiti* would dig up corpses to eat portions of the flesh. Even now it is very occasionally necessary to guard graves."[10]

The Chewa say that tropical ulcers are signs that *mfiti* are gradually eating a body away while the person is still alive *(munthu wa zironda anthu amaganiza kuti mfiti zimadya munthuyo)*. We have pointed out already that it seems to us that the *mfiti yeniyeni* is believed to exist but does not really exist in fact. People who actually eat human flesh are not to be found. But there is a definite belief that people do so, that they really and physically do eat human corpses. The guarding of graves *(kulonda manda)* of which W.H.J. Rangeley spoke, occurs more frequently than he seemed to think. I have several cases on record, the last as late as November 1975.

We have to distinguish between the belief that people eat human corpses and the fact that there are cases in which corpses are used in order to provide *chizimba*. *Chizimba* is an activating agent in particularly powerful *mankhwala*. We shall return to this later. Such cases do happen. I have several of them on record, one of which dates from May 1975. A husband killed his wife and cut out certain parts and organs from the corpse in order to sell them for money to a sorcerer. It was found that certain parts were missing from the body: one breast, the heart, the lungs, and the genitals *(ndiye anapezeka kuti ziwalo zina palibe. Anamuchotsa bere limodzi, ndi mtima, ndi mapapu, ndi maliseche)*. It is a fact that corpses are sometimes mutilated in order to make *chizimba*, but this should not be confused with the belief that *mfiti* eat human flesh. People may speak in both cases of *mfiti*, but they make a distinction between the two. The first is a fact. The second is mere belief, however realistically it portrays the activities of a *mfiti*. An old woman told

---

[10] W.H.J. Rangeley, "Notes on Chewa Tribal Law", in: *The Nyasaland Journal* 1 (1948), no. 3, p. 59.

me that human flesh tasted very good, that is was as tender as that of a pig-
let.

a) What Makes a Person a mfiti?

E.E. Evans-Pritchard wrote that in the thought of the Azande people a
witch comes into being because of something physical, like a growth in the
intestines.[11] The Chewa discount any such physical cause. The various stories on the subject always relate that a person is given human flesh to eat
and some special *mankhwala* to drink, after which he is instructed in the arts
of *ufiti*. For example, grandparents may introduce their grandchildren into
ufiti. A person may be unaware that he is a *mfiti*, having been given human
flesh and *mankhwala* when he was young. Nevertheless an ordeal will show
him to be a *mfiti*. Although unaware of it, he must surely be a *mfiti*, for an
ordeal cannot be wrong. Some who want to become a *mfiti*, may approach a
known *mfiti* and ask to be given human flesh and the necessary *mankhwala*.
Sometimes, according to the tales, persons such as these will be ordered to
return home and kill any animal they may meet on the way. On his return to
the village people will tell him that a close relative has suddenly died. Unaware of it he has killed that person under the form of the animal he met on
the way. He will be unable to sleep at night for the *mankhwala* he has taken
will urge him to get up and go to the grave. The *mfiti* will be waiting for him
there and will give him a piece of flesh from the body of the relative he has
killed in such mysterious a fashion. By eating it he will become a *mfiti*.

L. Denis wrote down the following personal encounter, which is a good
example of the kind of story one can hear even today.[12]

> A young man came to see me one day trembling with fear. He said that
> he had passed through a village and had been invited into a house, where
> he found some men. The one who invited him said: "You look tired, eat
> with us, we have plenty of food." Then a dish was placed in front of him
> containing the hand of a child, cooked and ready to be eaten. He refused
> to eat from the dish. They threatened him. Finally they let him go, say-

---

[11] Cf. E.E. Evans-Pritchard, *Witchcraft, Oracle and Magic among the Azande*, pp. 21-22, 40.

[12] L. Denis, "Meurs et Coutumes Indigènes", Rome: MS, 7 Fascicles 1951-1958, Archives of
the Missionaries of Africa (White Fathers), vol. 7, no. 733.

ing: "You are lucky that other people saw you coming in here. Otherwise you would not leave this house alive. If you tell any person what you have witnessed here, you will die, your mother also, and your father and your brothers and sisters."

Whatever the value of this story, it illustrates that the people believe that it is by eating human flesh that one becomes a *mfiti*. According to our informants both men and women can be *mfiti*. Female *mfiti* are more ferocious, killing more people and showing no trace of mercy or compassion *(akazi akuluakulu, sakumva chisoni, ndi woipa kopambana, amapha kopambana)*.

b) The Powers of a mfiti yeniyeni

Mfiti are believed to be able to make themselves invisible. They can travel through the air in a *chipapa* (sort of flying basket) and cover almost instantaneously a distance of many hundreds of miles. We were told by someone who had finished his secondary studies how in his early years he was taken by his grandmother in her *chipapa* to South Africa to visit a relative. Another who had also completed his secondary studies, told us that some years previously a medicine man *(sing'anga)* had exhorted the people in his village to give up their witchcraft and to destroy their *mankhwala* and that he had seen several people coming with their *chipapa* on that occasion. *Mfiti* can also change themselves into animals such as lions, hyenas, foxes and owls. They are also said to change themselves into crocodiles. When someone is killed by a crocodile, people say that a *mfiti* has taken him. They may sometimes take the form of rats or small black ants in order to enter a house.

Anyone who dances at night at the door of another person's house is definitely a *mfiti*. He is actually performing the *kutamba* dance which is a means of bewitching *(kulodza)* the person inside the house, who will surely die soon afterwards. The *mfiti* is said to be already rejoicing in advance. He always performs his dance naked. To walk about naked at night is another characteristic of *mfiti*. One of the names for *mfiti* is actually *a maliseche* (the one who is naked). I was told by one informant how he returned to his village late at night from the Independence celebrations in Lilongwe in May 1975. He was walking with others in a group. Suddenly the village chief, who was leading the group, stopped dead. In front of them stood two naked men. Everybody saw them and all were terrified. The chief asked the two men permission to proceed. The two stepped aside and let the people pass. All were scared to death and ran back to the village without uttering a word. There is no doubt that they had met with two *mfiti*. These stories of *mfiti* going about their sinister business naked are extremely common. In December 1975 a young man was stopped by two men, beaten and forced to eat from a maize-cob on which they had put *mankhwala*. Again these two men were naked. The young man fell ill afterwards and lost his speech which he recovered only after many weeks in hospital. A person who is found at the graveyard, especially at night, is surely a *mfiti*. He cannot have any other business there than *kufukula* (raise a corpse). Nobody will ever go alone to the graveyard for fear of being accused of being a *mfiti*.

c) The Unmasking and the Punishment of a mfiti

The people believe that there are some former *mfiti* who have abandoned their ghoulish past and now make use of their knowledge of the secret *mankhwala* of a *mfiti* to unmask *mfiti*. They are called *mlondola (kulondola,* i.e. discover). These former *mfiti* have become famous medicine men *(sing'anga)* because they even have the power of curing illnesses caused by a *mfiti*. A *mfiti* can also be discovered by the diviner with his lots *(ula)*. A person, indicated by the *ula* of having caused death or illness, can clear himself by submitting to the poison ordeal. He is told: "Go and maintain your plea of not guilty at the *nthando* (place where the ordeal takes place)" *(mukakanira ku nthando)*. This ordeal also had to be undergone by a group in the case of an epidemic or a witch hunt. Nowadays it is forbidden by the anti-witchcraft legislation and has in fact been suppressed to a great extent. W.H.J. Rangeley noted that it is sometimes practised in a modified way, so that for instance a dog or a chicken is given the poison.[13] The person is considered guilty or innocent according to whether as death follows or not. W.H.J. Rangeley's findings are confirmed by the stories that are still current today, though it is very difficult to know exactly what happens, for people are obviously extremely reticent about the whole matter.

---

[13] W.H.J. Rangeley, "Notes on Chewa Tribal Law", p. 62.

Whenever a *mfiti* was unmasked, and especially if he was caught red-handed (digging in the graveyard) he was killed without any form of judgment. The way to execute a *mfiti* was to impale him on a pointed piece of bamboo (with or without poison). Even today people are found executed in this way. In March 1973 a person managed to escape and reach the hospital in Lilongwe with a piece of broomstick forced into his rectum. A crowd followed him and agitated against him for a time in front of the hospital. The case was related by the European doctor who treated the man. Apart from this case we have collected 7 other cases in which a person was said to have been in this way. This method of killing a *mfiti* is called *kukhoma chipasi* or *kumuchita chipasi* (to fix him a pointed stick). The seven cases reported were said to have happened within the period April 1975 to March 1976. Here we refer to what we already reported in speaking of burials, namely, that groups of young men have been known to offer to watch at a grave for a sum of money, and have

Mfiti ilaula

then gone at night to the house of some lonely old person and killed him. The following morning they announced that they killed a *mfiti* found around the grave *(kumuchita chipasi)*. They have then directed people to the house in question where they said the *mfiti* could be found.

It is also important to point out once more that I have simply reported what people say takes place, not what happened in fact. It was imposible for me to make any sort of investigation or examination of the facts themselves. However, it is the beliefs of the people that we are interested in, and their way of explaining things. The cases reported show that the belief in *mfiti* is still very much alive among the people. The community protects itself against *mfiti* through detection (by divination or ordeal) and punishment.

Even today the anger of the people may be uncontrolled. Although the ordeal is forbidden by the anti-witchcraft legislation, people think it is wiser to deal with it in their own way, and keep it well out of sight.

d) The mwabvi Ordeal

One of the most fundamental themes in Chewa Traditional Religion is the need to renounce *ufiti* and to purify oneself from anger and thirst for revenge, envy and inordinate ambition. The ordeal by poison consists in making the person drink a solution of *mwabvi,* a poison made from the bark of the *mwabvi* tree *(erythroplaeum guineense).* To drink the poison is called *kumwa mwabvi.* The place where a person is made to drink it *(kusangula)* is called *nthando.* It is in the bush far from water and the village, so that the victim cannot drink water and spoil the effect of the poison. The *mwambi* ordeal has been mentioned by most authors who have written about the Chewa, among others: D.C. Scott,[14] H.S. Stannus,[15] S.S. Murray,[16] W.H.J. Rangeley,[17] and M.G. Marwick.[18]

The following is an account of an ordeal by three persons who had to drink the poison ordeal themselves.[19] Because of an epidemic the chief ordered all the people of the village to take *mwabvi* so as to find out who was the *mfiti* causing the deaths. The *sing'anga* brought with him pieces of *mwabvi* bark, two gourds *(nsupa),* and the tooth of a hippo. Women carried his mortar, two pestles and water. He placed the men on one side and the women on the other. With the tooth of the hippo he started to break the bark. If a piece jumped to the men's side this was taken as a sign that there was a *mfiti*

---

[14] Scott, D.C., *Cyclopaedic Dictionary of the Mang'anja Language,* Edinburgh Foreign Mission Committee of the Church of Scotland, 1892, p. 407.

[15] H.S. Stannus, "Notes on some Tribes in British Central Africa", in: *Journal of the Royal Anthropological Institute* 40 (1910), p. 305.

[16] S.S. Murray, *A Handbook of Nyasaland,* London/Zomba: Government of Nyasaland, 1932, p. 90.

[17] W.H.J. Rangeley, "Notes on Chewa Tribal Law", p. 62.

[18] M.G. Marwick, *Sorcery in its Social Setting,* pp. 87-88.

[19] Reported by L. Denis, "Meurs et Coutumes Indigènes", vol. 7, no. 744. We have tried to summarize the story for it covers several pages and contains many repetitions.

among them. Similarly for the women if a piece jumped to their side. He then put the pieces of the bark in the mortar and started to pound them. He stopped at intervals and admonished the people: "You are going to take my *mankhwala*. It is very powerful and intelligent. If you have eaten no human flesh, if you have killed nobody with your *mankhwala*, it will do you no harm. But if you have eaten flesh, if you are a *mfiti*, you are going to die". A man and a woman had to help him with the pounding. When the powder was fine enough he mixed it with water and stirred it to make a solution which he poured into the two *nsupa*. He then called the people two by two, a man and a woman, and gave them the solution to drink making sure that nobody saw how much he gave to each one. Children and youngsters did not take part but watched the proceedings from a distance. After drinking the poison all went to sit down and wait for the effect. Two friends did not sit together, because if one did not succeed in vomiting, he might prevent the other from doing so.

Guilt was shown by the inability to vomit the poison. *Mwabvi* is a *mankhwala a nzeru* (intelligent medicine) which scrutinizes the whole body for signs of *ufiti* and remains of human flesh. If none is found the person regurgitates and vomits it. But if human flesh or *ufiti* is discovered, the *mwabvi* takes hold of it and refuses to let it go. Then the person cannot vomit but convulses with pain. The others insult him: "Surely you are a *mfiti*, the *mwabvi* has found *ufiti* in your body", and challenge him to confess. The dying person confesses that he is a *mfiti*. It must be true even if he did not know it, for the *mwabvi* cannot make a mistake. Perhaps he had been given human flesh to eat while he was still young. The people beat him with sticks and finally leave him to die in the bush a prey to hyenas.

Informants say that the death depended on the *sing'anga*. The person to whom he gave much *mwabvi* would vomit it and be saved. The one to whom he gave less would be unable to vomit and so would die. In fact, the chief often briefed the *sing'anga* and indicated the person who had to die. So convinced are the Chewa of the selective power of the *mwabvi*, that a person convinced of his own innocence does not hesitate to drink the *mwabvi*. A. Hetherwick described how he once met a person with whom he chatted and joked and who seemed to be perfectly happy and peaceful. Next morning Hetherwick learned that the man had been on his way to drink *mwabvi*. He wrote: "Faith in the never-failing accuracy of the ordeal kept the smile on his face. In this case his confidence was misplaced, for he died as a result of the test".[20]

This need to separate oneself from evil moves people voluntarily to drink *mwabvi* and to flock to a *mphulumutsi* or *chikanga*, leaders of purification movements. The diviner or witch-doctor is an important person in Chewa communities. He indicates those who have caused misfortune (who have evil in them) and he shows how this evil can be undone. It is said by some of the older Chewa that there is more evil and more witchcraft in the country today than in the past. This, they say, is because witch-doctors are forbidden to practice their art by the anti-witchcraft legislation. Their allegation is open to question, but we know it to be a fact that people believe that they have been left a prey to *mfiti* without the possibility of protecting themselves. It is difficult to reason with them because they identify the fact that evil exists (hate, greed, envy) with their belief in witchcraft. To deny the latter is the same for them as to deny the first.[21]

e) Protection against ufiti

People are keen to obtain *mankhwala* to protect themselves against *ufiti*, e.g. they will take the horn of an antelope or goat in which the *sing'anga* has sealed powerful *mankhwala* and hide it in the roof next to the door. This will prevent the *mfiti* from entering the house or it may perhaps warn the owner of the house that a *mfiti* is prowling around the house; sometimes it may render the house invisible to a *mfiti*. Other such protective *mankhwala* are sealed in a gourd or in the tail of an antelope. The one who has such protective *mankhwala* is a strong man *(munthu wokhwima)* with nothing to fear.

---

[20] A. Hetherwick, *The Gospel and the African*, Edinburgh: Clark, 1932, p. 73.

[21] M. Wilson has brought this out clearly, in: *Religion and the Transformation of Society*, Cambridge University Press, 1971, p. 36.

One of the greatest insults is to call someone a *mfiti*. So great is the fear of being called a *mfiti* that nobody will absent himself from a burial in his village or of his family. To go to a *maliro* is one of the most sacred duties for the Chewa to which everything else must give way. A person who could have gone and did not go is at once suspected of being a *mfiti*, since a *mfiti* fears to go to the funeral. The same applies to anybody who does not go to visit a sick person in the village. He is thought to be hiding something, to be afraid of going there. So he is suspected of having caused the illness. Anybody who is anti-social, who sets out to annoy other people and disturb the community, is thought to do so because he is a *mfiti*. A child whose teeth on the upper jaw appear before those on the lower jaw is also held to be a future *mfiti*. In the past such children were drowned in a river. Even now mothers will try to hide the fact.

f) Purification Movements

Literature exists about some of these movements in Malawi. The Mchape movement of 1935 was reported by, among others, A.I. Richards,[22] the Bwanali-Mphulumutsi movement of 1947 by M.G. Marwick.[23] The latter was truly a religious revival movement and its leaders were called *mpulumutsi (kupulumutsa,* i.e. to save), because they freed the people from the evil of *ufiti*. Emphasis was put on divine inspiration, confession of sins and frequent reference to moral precepts. Since then another movement has arisen. A certain Chikanga presented himself from 1957-1964 as being able to protect people against *ufiti* by making incisions in their skin and rubbing *mankhwala* into the cuts *(kutemera)*. Many people went to him from all over the Central Region. Even today some people who call themselves *chikanga*, operate in secret. To those explicit purification movements we have to add movements like the Watch Tower and the Lumpa Church in Zambia, 1953-

---

[22] Cf. A.I. Richards, "A Modern Movement of Witch-finders", in: *Africa* (1935), pp. 448-461. See also T.O. Ranger, "Mchape and the Study of Witchcraft Eradication", Paper read at the conference on the History of Central African Religious Systems, Lusaka, August 31 to September 8, 1972.

[23] M.G. Marwick, "Another Anti-witchcraft Movement in East Central Africa", in: *Africa* (1950), pp. 100-112.

1964,[24] that spilt over into Malawi. Lenshina insisted that people hand over all their witchcraft *mankhwala* and repent of their faults. We may also mention the independent African churches that emphasize purification from witchcraft. Fear of witchcraft is still very much alive among the Chewa, and even many Christians were anxious to join these movements, partly because of a deep desire to be purified and strengthened against witchcraft, partly because of outside social pressure. All who did not go to be purified were suspected of being *mfiti* themselves. A. Hovington who mentioned the purification movements, related that many of the Christians flocked to them and that at the time of his writing there were still witchfinders operating in Mozambique just across the frontier with Malawi.[25]

2. The Sorcerer *(mfiti m'pheranjiru)*

Magic has a morally neutral connotation. Its effects can be productive, curative or destructive. Here we speak of sorcery, i.e. all the forms of destructive magic socially unacceptable. In chapter eight we shall consider the forms of magic which are socially acceptable. Sorcerers are called *mfiti m'pheranjiru* (killers by malice). They are also called *sing'anga* (a term which also covers all the forms of socially acceptable magic).

A great number of cases in our survey refer to *mankhwala oipa* (evil medicines) as the cause of death. The medicines are put in beer *(kumwetsa mankhwala m'mowa)* or in food *(kudyetsa mankhwala)*. There can be little doubt that poison is used is some cases. But probably more often allegations are made because there are certain similarities with the effects of real poisoning, e.g. the suddenness of death of a healthy person. The reason why people are said to be killed by *mankhwala oipa* is usually vengeance or jealousy. One ex-

---

[24] Reported by J.P. Calmettes, "Lumpa Church, Genesis et Development", Dissertation, Institute Catholique de Paris, Juin 1969. See also by the same author, "The Lumpa Church and Witchcraft Eradication", Paper read at the Conference on the History of Central African Religious Systems, Lusaka, August 31 to September 8, 1972.

[25] Cf. A. Hovington, "The African Way of Life", Rome: 8 fascicles, MS, written over many years (last pages dated 1973), Archives, Missionaries of Africa (White Fathers) vol. 8, pp. 211-218; 282-285.

ample of vengeance is the following. A person consulted a diviner to find out why his child had died. After consulting his *ula*, the diviner answered that so and so had killed the child. He asked the father what he thought should be done. The father said: "Kill him, he killed my child, let him die as well" *(iphani basi, iyeyo anapha mwana wanga, iyeyo afenso)*. Jealousy often results from the fact that somebody is more enterprising or successful than his neighbours. The accepted norm is that people share. To fail to do so is to risk falling victim to *mankhwala*. The fear of arousing jealousy makes people ready to share all they have. It is considered very unwise to boast *(kudzi-tama)* about one's luck or to show off one's riches for this can easily lead to jealousies.

Sorcerers are also believed to have weapons with which they can kill at a distance. With this weapon called *ching'ani-ng'ani* (lightning) they never miss their objective and the person is killed as if by lighting. In my survey I collected 16 cases in which a person was believed to have been killed in this way. The services of the sorcerer are also enlisted to cause illness, insanity, sterility, paralysis and many other calamities. The sorcerers are said to use anything connected with the body (nail parings, excreta, hair, etc.) or a person's clothes and even his footprints. During the initiation instructions women are instructed to be very careful with the small cloth they wear during their monthly periods. For there is real danger that it could be used by a sorcerer against them. Someone can also cause death by a verbal spell *(ku-tukwana)*. He may say something like: "You, today before the sun has gone down" *(lero iwe sililowa dzuwali lero)*. This *kutukwana* is taken seriously and can easily lead to a case *(mlandu)*. If after *kutukwana* a person dies suddenly or falls ill, the person who casts the spell will be held responsible and accused of *ufiti*.

The person who gets rich is supposed to have very powerful *mankhwala* for how otherwise could one explain his success. The most powerful *mankhwala* are those to which *chizimba* has been added. *Chizimba* is an activating agent which, if made from a human body, makes the *mankhwala* really very powerful so that it is in a category all of its own. By using parts of the body as *chizimba* one uses, as it were, the life-force *(mphamvu)* of the dead person. In my survey I came across two cases in which a body was found seriously mutilated.

Kuika mu chigayo (to put somebody in a maize-mill)

In my survey I found that in 68 cases (44 adults and 24 children) out of the total of 451 it was alleged that someone had killed a person in order to put him in a maize-mill *(kuika mu chigayo)*. Sometimes there was a slight variant: in a shop *(kuika mu sitolo)*, in a lorry *(kuika mu galimoto)*, or simply to become rich *(anafuna kulemera)*. The belief that the owner of a maize-mill *(chigayo)* puts a person in the engine of the mill is explained, according to the popular version, in the following way. When a mill is running there is a sort of whining sound which suggests to simple folk that there is somebody inside the mill and in the past people who could not understand that a mill could work all by itself, believed that the owner of the mill had put a person inside it. When I asked the people whether they really believed this, they said "no", not the person himself but his life-force *(mphamvu)*. The owner of the mill has captured the life-force of that person and turned it into a powerful *mankhwala*. This points to their belief in *chizimba*. One informant said explicity: "They put him in the mill as *chizimba (anaika munthuyo mu chigayo ngati chizimba)*. If someone talks about buying a *chigayo*, his own family will be on the alert and will stay away from him for fear that he might kill them or one of their children to use in a *chigayo*. People tell some extremely realistic stories about those who are supposed to be inside the *chigayo*.

One such story was told to me by a man whom I considered more intelligent than many of his fellows. He said that some years ago, while he was walking along a road he came near a *chigayo* (he indicated the exact place) where he found a whole group of people gathered together. In the centre of the group he saw a young woman with a small child in her arms, both of whom were covered with engine oil. The lips of both the woman and the child were sewn together with metal wire. The woman looked terrified. She was said to have escaped from the *chigayo*. The people recognized her as a woman who had died some years earlier while pregnant. A person who is said to be put in a shop *(mu sitolo)* is often said to look after the money *(ku-*

sunga ndalama). This refers to the idea that the *mankhwala* which has been strengthened by *chizimba* will bring much money to the owner of the shop.

The majority of the cases are probably mere allegations without any proof. However, there surely exists a real preoccupation with the idea that a person who wants to become rich will stop at nothing and is ready even to kill in order to achieve his purpose. The extent of these beliefs in *ufiti* is an indication too that people are convinced of the existence of "evil".

3. The Deeper Roots of *ufiti* - Beliefs

It is undoubtedly a fact that *mankhwala oipa* are still being used today but it is impossible to say how often. In the majority of the cases in which people are alleged to have been killed by *ufiti* no real proof of the cause of death can be adduced. However the mere allegation that *ufiti* is involved in many cases indicates to what extent the people believe in "evil". Many authors have stressed that Africans do not easily accept natural causes of death (except of death in old age). For them death is believed to be caused by somebody. Even the educated find it difficult to believe in impersonal causes. The example given by M. Wilson is classic.[26] A Mponde teacher told her that he accepted that his brother died because of typhus, but: "Why did the infected louse bite my brother and not me? Who sent the louse?" I have found 16 cases of people killed by lightning *(ching'ani-ng'ani),* and in every single case the lightning was believed to have been sent by somebody. *Mfiti* or mysterious evil-doers are said to be responsible for many deaths. In my survey 296 out of 451 were said to have been caused by *ufiti.* If we break these down we get the following categories:

Mfiti yeniyeni	29
Kuika mu chigayo (sitolo, etc.)	68
Ching'ani-ng'ani	16
Kudyetsa - kumwetsa mankhwala oipa	40
Other forms of sorcery	143
Total	**296**

---

[26] Cf. M. Wilson, *Religion and Transformation of Society,* p. 17.

Why is it that such a proportion of deaths is attributed to *ufiti?* It is because the people are convinced that "evil" in people induces them to harm other people. This conviction is fundamental to the *mfiti* beliefs. In 114 cases of alleged *ufiti* I have been able to ascertain the supposed motivation (I do not include the passion for human flesh in the cases of *ufiti weniweni* nor of greed in the cases of *kuika mu chigayo).*

Motivation for witchcraft accusation

Hatred or revenge	12
Jealousy	55
Supposed adultery with wife of the one who killed	5
Jealousy between the wives of a polygamist	2
Chief killed by those jealous of his position	10
Difficulties because of money taken	5
Difficulties with in-laws	5
Revenge on *mfiti*	2
Husband killed wife because he wanted another one	1
Wife did not want the husband	1
After a fight	3
The victim did not pay his workers	1
Verbal spell *(kutukwana)*	1
Child died because the grandmother kept evil *mankhwala* in the house	3
Child died because its mother had refused to be initiated	2
Person was killed in order that "he could be buried at the *bwalo* of *Nyau*"	5
The victim revealed secrets of *Nyau*	1
Total	**114**

All these cases illustrate that the Chewa share the universal human experience that "evil in the heart of man" can move him to kill. For them death occurs because someone was determined on it, impelled precisely by that evil in his heart, by his greed, his anger or his jealousy. When a person dies, questions are always asked with a view to determining the cause of death. Did the dead man have an enemy who might have taken revenge? Was he rich and so likely to arouse jealousy? Were any spells cast? Does any one among his immediate associates show a desire to buy a *chigayo,* or a shop, or something similar? In this last case the motive for the killing might have been to obtain *chizimba*. Greed is believed to impel a man to go to any lengths to satisfy his passion for money. In the villages a person who wants to become richer than his fellows shows a greed which is socially unacceptable. If to all these questions the answer remains "no", then the people will think that a *mfiti yeniyeni* may have killed in order to satisfy his passion for human flesh. In any case they will consult a diviner in order to find out who the killer was. Evil in man is for them the explanation of many if not most of the misfortunes that befall them. For those who believe so strongly in personal causes, what other motive can move a man to kill or to inflict misfortune than the evil which is in his heart?

The *ufiti* allegations as to the cause of death indicate the degree and extent of fear which grips people and which is in direct proportion to the number of allegations. If, as M. Douglas believed, Africans are a happy people and if talk about fear is largely exaggerated by missionaries and travellers,[27] how can we explain this high number of *ufiti* allegations? Why do people so often explain death (and other misfortunes) in this way? To our mind, their explanations arise from a deep fear of mysterious evil-doers. Only this can account for the number of allegations, the resort to protective *mankhwala* and the rise of purification movements.

Many Christians share these fears of *ufiti* which in times of trouble often prove to be stronger than their Christian convictions. By their *ufiti* beliefs the Chewa attempt to explain suffering by referring to evil in man and projecting it on to a *mfiti*. The *mfiti* is the personification of evil in man. The experience of evil caused by men leads to a belief in mysterious evil-doers as the explanation of much of the suffering and misfortune. It makes people look for protection against and salvation from this power of evil. The so-called purification movements (often a syncretism of traditional beliefs and elements of Christianity) have a tremendous appeal because of their promise to rid their followers of evil. They undertake to cure the evil in the be-

---

[27] M. Douglas, *Purity and Danger*, London: Routledge and Kegan, 1966, pp. 1-2.

lievers themselves and to protect them from evil from outside (make them immune against *ufiti*).

Pombo Mulimire distributes medicine at the grave

Fear of evil makes people look for protection which they believe will be found in powers stronger than those of the *ufiti*. They hope to capture these powers in charms and *mphinjiri* (pieces of reed in which *mankhwala* has been inserted). One can only repeat here the understanding explanation of R.S. Rattray: "The labour and infinite pains, the prayers, the spells, the sacrifices, the abnegations, the heart-burning, the disappointments, the hopes that are inseparably bound up in each of these poor fetishes, we can only imagine in part, but they should never be quite lost sight of when we are considering such objects, or judging the makers of them."[28]

All these *ufiti* beliefs are but a reflexion of the profound human experience of evil, hatred, greed and envy, as the deepest causes of suffering. The Chewa do not believe in a Devil but they do believe in *mfiti* and *ziwanda* (the continuation of a *mfiti* in the life hereafter). For them *mfiti* and *ziwanda* are the incarnation, the personification of moral evil. As belief in the Devil often grows in importance in times of trouble, so among the Chewa belief in *ufiti* increases in times of social stress. The fear of being branded a *mfiti* has led the Chewa to cultivate the virtues of a "good man" *(munthu wabwino)* and to an almost exaggerated form of meekness and courtesy. Aggressiveness is foreign to the Chewa. In settling any case *(mlandu)* one has to try to recon-

---

[28] R.S. Rattray, *Religion and Art in Ashanti*, London: Oxford University Press, 1927 (reprint 1958), pp. 21-22, quoted in: E.G. Parrinder, *African Traditional Religion*, p. 116.

cile opponents without arousing anger or thirst for revenge in the heart of any of them.

The fear of evil which expresses itself in a feeling of solidarity with the suffering and sick may turn into a blind hatred for the *mfiti*. There is no other explanation for the fury against a suspected *mfiti*. In small-scale societies people believe in personal causes of misfortune. An example is the fury of the people against the unhappy driver who has caused an accident. Such a driver is believed to be a *mfiti*, an evil person who killed because he wanted to. I remember the case of a driver who drove too fast for the liking of his passengers. They said as follows: "He is a *mfiti*, he wants to kill us" *(ndi mfiti, akufuna kutipha)*.

Chapter 8
The Diviner and the Medicine Man

In the preceding chapter we spoke about *ufiti*, i.e. all use of magical power that is considered evil. In this present chapter we shall deal with the socially acceptable forms of magic. The general term for someone exercising such magical power is a *sing'anga*. This person can be at the same time a diviner *(woombeza ula)*.

We shall deal first with the diviner and then with the *sing'anga* (medicine man). In all cases, magical power is considered to be a participation in some higher form of power. The common human person has no access to this power, but the magician has for it is said to have been communicated to some men by the spirits of the dead. Such men are very possessive of their power which they communicate only to their chosen successor who will normally be a son or a sister's son.

1. The Diviner *(woombeza ula)*

a) The Person

For the Chewa, illness and death are rarely due to natural causes but to spirits or enemies. It is the task of the diviner to indicate who caused or "sent" illness or death. The diviner holds a very important position in Chewa society because he is the only man who can interpret by means of his lots *(ula)* the will of the spirits of the dead. These *mizimu* are believed to send misfortunes in order to warn or to punish their living descendants. The interpretation by the diviner is essential to ascertain what the *mizimu* want to convey. In such a society, ruled as it were by its *mzimu*, the diviner occupies a key position and is as it were the link with the world of the *mizimu*, their interpreter. The diviner can also tell whether an enemy or a *mfiti* has caused the misfortune and how his influence can be counteracted. In either case the diviner indicates what should be done to appease the *mizimu* or to fight back a *mfiti* and so avert the misfortune or prevent worse.

These days the diviner may be less prominent in public life than in the past. It is difficult to say exactly but it remains true that people continue to consult him and that his influence is profound. Within a ten miles' radius from where I was staying during my research I found ten practising diviners. There may have been more but those ten were well known and many people went to see them. Since the beliefs in the *mizimu* and in *ufiti* are deeply rooted in the mentality of the Chewa, the authority of the diviner is an important factor to be reckoned with in village life. Even Christians remain under the spell of his verdicts, although many may not consult him personally. Those who do not dare to see him personally allow other persons to do so for them. Those who refuse to have anything to do with him know that their relatives consult the diviner all the same behind their backs. They come under strong pressure to carry out what the diviner has asked, or, at least, not to prevent it being carried out by relatives. In particular the influence of the grandmother *(agogo)* and the mother-in-law *(mpongozi)* are very difficult to withstand.

Each diviner has his own method of consulting the *ula*. But what they all have in common is that they ask those who come to consult them to supply all necessary information, and to give the details of e.g. the illness and the relationships in the family and the village. In particular the diviner is interested to know whether there have been any disputes, whether the sick man has enemies, whether there are jealousies, whether any relative has recently died. It is only after obtaining this background information that the diviner will proceed with the invocation of his *ula*. In these village communities, where everybody knows everything about everybody else, the diviner may have an accurate insight into the relationships without having to ask many questions. The diviner is very astute in putting his questions. He is usually a master in weighing-up a situation with its strained relationships and suspicions. By his questions he usually guides and leads his client on till the client himself formulates his own suspicions.

The diviner usually dons an impressive apparel with many horns *(nyanga)* hanging around his neck. Often he uses a symbolic language. He may say for instance: "Has a lizard fallen into the fire"? "Has a snake entered into your house?" "Has a bird entered into your house?" These questions mean: "Has some misfortune happened in your family?" Or he may ask: "Have you set a trap and game has refused to be caught in it?" This means: "Has somebody cast a spell on you?" In some cases the diviner is an accomplished ventriloquist. The questions come from the *ula.* Or, at least, the people think they do.

Casting the lots

The consultation is usually done in the semi-darkness of a house. A diviner never consults his *ula* anywhere else but in his own house. His clients always have to go to him. His impressive apparel, the symbolic language used, the semi-darkness, and the fact that the *ula* seem to conduct the conversation, all contribute to the creation of a mysterious atmosphere in which the client feels the nearness of the *mizimu.* The *mizimu* are never directly invoked by the diviner, but they are believed to speak through the *ula.* The diviner invokes only his *ula.* He may say: "Axe, listen, these people have come to learn the truth. Don't mislead them". While consulting his *ula* the diviner continues to put leading questions to his client, inviting him tactfully to formulate his own suspicions and to reveal existing jealousies. From time to time, when an important point has been reached in the conversation, he will ask his *ula* to confirm it.

The following is one example of such a consultation reported to us. After the initial questions, the diviner started to probe into the relationships in the family. The client manifested that there was a difficulty between his maternal uncle and his mother. The diviner then asked: "Did the illness not start soon after your maternal uncle had a row with your mother?" "Yes, it started the day after they had a row". "Was it not your uncle who got angry?" "Yes, it was". "Did he do any *kutukwana* (cursing)?" "Yes, he did". "Well, your child is sick because of your uncle". The *ula* were then consulted to find out whether the maternal uncle sent the illness. The *ula* answered that the maternal uncle was indeed the cause of the illness. The diviner then pursued: "Did your first child not die some months ago?" "Were there no difficulties between your mother and your uncle already then?" "No doubt, your first child was killed by your uncle". "He now intends to kill your second child as well." "Don't be mistaken, he wants to kill you all. You did well to come here."

b) The "Master" of Kinship Tensions

The diviner is usually a master in appreciating the tensions and conflicts existing in a small-scale society. Since in the matrilineal societies there are always tensions between the husband *(mkamwini)* and his in-laws, between a young man and his maternal uncle *(mtsibweni)*, it is easy to guide the client towards the formulation of some suspicions. Suspicions constantly arise in these communities, dominated as they are by belief in witchcraft and by fears that even one's closest relative may be a *mfiti* motivated by hunger for human flesh or by a passion for money and thus ready to kill in order to have *chizimba*. As we have noted already, *mfiti* are believed to select their victims among their own relatives.

In my survey I found that 296 deaths were attributed to *ufiti*. In many of these cases the allegations concerned people in their own villages *(a kwao)*, or his enemies *(adani ake)*. Even so we have to keep in mind that people in a village are usually related to one another. In 96 cases the allegations were centred on a precise person. We can classify the cases as follows:

	Men	As chizimba	Women	As chizimba	Total	As chizimba
Maternal kin						
Mother killed child			3		3	
Grandmother killed child			1	1	1	1
Son killed mother	1	1			1	1
Material uncle killed child	20	7			20	7
Nephew killed maternal uncle	1	1			1	1
Brother killed brother	12	7			12	7
Sister killed sister			6	2	6	2
Sister killed brother			1		1	
Maternal aunt killed child			2		2	
Paternal kin						
Father killed child	18	14			18	14
Son killed father	4	2			4	2
Paternal uncle killed child	2				2	
Paternal aunt killed child			2		2	
Husband - wife						
Husband killed wife	4	2			4	2
Wife killed husband			3		3	
Co-wives						
Wife killed wife			4		4	
Co-wife killed child			2		2	
In-laws						
Mother-in-law killed son-in-law			1		1	
Son-in-law killed mother-in-law	2	1			2	1
Daughter-in-law killed mother-in-law			1		1	
Husband killed sister-in-law	2	1			2	1
Wife killed brother-in-law			1		1	
Sister-in-law killed child			1		1	
Total	**68**	**37**	**28**	**3**	**96**	**40**

From this table it would appear that the main areas of conflict are:

Maternal uncle versus sister's children	20
Father versus his own children	18
Brother versus brother	12
Total	**50**

It would also appear that men are thought much more prone to kill in order to make *chizimba* than women. 37 out of 40 cases are said to be done by men. Here the cases are divided as follows:

Father killed his own child	14
Maternal uncle killed his sister's child	7
Brother killed brother	7
Total	**28**

However, we think that the above can only serve as an indication, because the other 200 cases of death alleged to have been caused by *ufiti* are said to have been caused, by "people in his village" or "his enemies" without any further precision. There were a total of 68 cases of *chizimba* reported in our survey, of which 40 were alleged to have been perpetrated by precise persons. These we have indicated in our table. The above table gives some indication of what the people think, and of the fears and the suspicions that do exist within the family.

The allegations of witchcraft on the part of the maternal uncle, the father and of brothers among themselves, are indicative of the degree of rivalry which exists among them. The maternal uncle and the sister's son are rivals for the control of the young man's sisters and their children. The brothers themselves are rivals for the control of their sisters and the children of these sisters. The father - son relationship is strained because the son belongs to the group of his mother which regards the father as an outsider. The father has his own sorority group when he is at home *(kwathu kwenikweni)*. In the family group of his wife he is only a *tonde wobwereka* (borrowed he-goat). It

was M.G. Marwick who has extensively argued that the relationship between the *mfiti* allegations and the social tensions are inherent in a matrilineal system.[1]

c) Portrays of Diviners

I have collected information about the divining techniques of eight diviners
in whose vicinity I stayed during my fieldwork. Two other diviners lived in
the same vicinity, but I have been unable to collect enough precise information concerning their method of divining. I have collected evidence from
informants who had first hand experience since they assisted at seances of
divination. Unfortunately I was not able to visit a diviner myself.

1. Belifa, at Lumwira (T.A. Mazengera)

Belifa is a female diviner. She is also a healer. She is very famous and every
day crowds of people, some of them from afar, sit waiting round her house.
Belifa proceeds as follows. She asks her client to explain the complaint.
Then he/she has to strip and Belifa moves her hands over the body. She
then diagnoses the trouble and indicates its cause. "Your uncle has given
you this illness, he wants you to become mad" *(inu matenda anuwa amakupa-
tsani ndi amalume anu kuti muchite misala)*. Finally she gives medicine to drink
and other medicine to rub into cuts made in the skin *(kutemera mankhwala)*.
These are supposed not only to cure but also to protect against any further
attempt by his/her uncle to bewitch him. It is to be noted that Belifa does
not use *ula* as do other diviners. She moves her hands over the body, like a
doctor who touches with the hand the place where a person says he feels
pain. Her hands tell her exactly what illness the person is suffering from and
also who caused this illness.

2. Chematola, at Mpata Milonde (T.A. Kaphuka)

When a client comes to see Chematola, he is greeted by the *ula*. The *ula*
consist of a gourd *(nsupa)* hanging on a string from the main supporting
beam of the house. The *nsupa* continues the conversation. In the case reported, the person was ill because his elder brother had bewitched him. The

---

[1] M.G. Marwick, *Sorcery in its Social Setting*, Manchester: University Press, 1965.

latter was jealous of his cows and also of the fact that he had filled three grainstores *(nkhokwe)* with maize. The diviner gave the client medicine to drink, together with other medicine to bury near the door of his house so that his elder brother could not bewitch him again.

3. Chikokombe, at Phundu (T.A. Chadza)

When a client comes to see him, he is greeted in the usual manner and made to sit down. After putting some general questions to him the diviner gives him some medicines to drink. This medicine helps the diviner to make his diagnosis. In fact, he runs his hands over the body of the sick person. The combination of the power of the medicine and the power in his fingers gives the diviner insight into the condition of his client. In the case reported the diviner said: "People hate you because you work too much. That is why they bewitched you. But don't be afraid, you have come to me in time. Here are some medicines to drink and some other *otemera* (to be rubbed in cuts made in the skin of the patient)".

4. Chiwongola, at Chiseka (T.A. Chiseka)

This diviner did not seem to be using any *ula*. He merely put questions. In the case reported the person who visited him came on behalf of his father who was suffering from epilepsy *(linjiri-njiri)*. The diviner concluded that people had bewitched him because they were jealous of him. He would get better if he used the medicines provided. But, the diviner added, these medicines would make the father better only if the son who came to consult him abstained from marital relations for six months. If he broke this injunction, his father would relapse into epilepsy.

5. Nanyanga, at Mbewa (T.A. Chadza)

In the case reported the diviner put his initial questions and then started to explore the relationship between his client and his maternal uncle. The verdict was that the latter had bewitched him so as to make him mad. He gave the client medicine to drink as well as others to wash with.

6. Masoapatali, at Kachono (T.A. Chadza)

This diviner used two gourds *(nsupa)*, one of which he calls "the big one" and the other "the young one". In the case reported, the client arrived and said *zikomo* (please). This is the normal way of indicating that one has come to see a person. The diviner answered the normal *ee* of acknowledgement and then addressed the "young" *nsupa*: "A stranger has come to see us". The gourds were placed on a mat on the floor. The "young" *nsupa* passed on the information to the "big" one: "A stranger has come to see us". The "big" one answered: "You start". So the "young" *nsupa* addressed the client thus: *Moni, kodi muli bwanji?* (Good morning, how are you?), and continued: "I know that at your village there is that case of a woman who is six months pregnant". In fact the client had come to consult the diviner because he had come back from working at the mines in South Africa, and had found his wife pregnant. But the wife and her family denied it. So the husband challenged her: Let us go to the diviner. The *ula* confirmed that the woman was pregnant.

7. Chikhuti, at Chididi - Chiwamba (T.A. Chimutu)

His *ula* consist of a *nsupa* all covered with beads which talks to the client. In the case reported, the *nsupa* said that the child of the person who came to consult the *ula* had epilepsy because his uncle had bewitched it. The client had to return home and if the child should fall down again collect some soil from the precise spot of the fall. This soil he would have to take to the diviner to be mixed with medicine.

8. Gututu, at Kaphala Mtambo (T.A. Mazengera)

This diviner uses the steel of an axe and that of a hoe. He puts the axe down on the floor and draws a circle around it. The hoe he keeps in his hand, tapping the axe with it. If it produces a high tone, it denotes an affirmative answer; if a low note, a negative one. It is interesting to note that a number of the diviners do not seem to use the *ula* but have adopted a more modern approach. They imitate a doctor who puts questions and then touches the patient's body with his hand.

d) Methods of Divination

The following methods of divining were explained to us as in use by diviners up and down the country.

1. The diviner takes a small gourd *(nsupa)* and places inside it a horn *(nyanga)* filled with medicine. The diviner holds the gourd in his right hand and in his left a rattle made from an empty fruit with pebbles in it. When he puts questions to the *ula,* the horn will either remain straight or fall to one side and knock against the side of the gourd. It thus indicates the *ula's* affirmative or negative answer, according to the interpretation of the diviner.

2. The diviner uses a gourd with a long neck, in which he places some medicine. In his left hand he holds a rattle. The gourd is placed on a mat on the floor in an upright position. If the gourd falls over when a question is put, the answer is no. If it remains standing, the answer is yes. The diviner puts some castor-oil seeds in his nostrils to change his voice and make the proceedings appear all the more mysterious.

3. A rope is passed over a beam in the house and the two ends are held by the diviner. On one of the ends a horn *(nyanga)* is fixed. The people believe that this horn is free to move up and down the rope. Before each question the diviner replaces the horn high up on the rope. The horn will either stay there or will "slip down the rope". This is interpreted as the answer to the question.

4. The diviner holds five shells of the *nkhungwa* fruit in each hand. He shakes his hands at each question and lets the shells drop on the floor. The way they fall: right side up or upside down, is interpreted by the diviner as yes or no to the questions.

5. The diviner uses a gourd in which he has hidden all sorts of small objects, e.g. a small piece of white wood, of black wood, a piece of a mat, etc. Each object has its own particular meaning. The diviner puts a question, shakes the gourd, and slowly turns it over till one of the objects falls out of the gourd. This object with its precise meaning is the answer to the question.

6.   The diviner uses a gourd in which he has put some *mankhwala*. He places the gourd on top of a stalk of reed planted in the soil. He sits down about a yard away from the gourd facing it. When he puts a question the gourd gives the answer either by turning around on top of the stalk or by staying still. Diviners using this method are said to be very rare. They have particularly powerful *mankhwala*.

It is to be noted that some famous diviners asked their clients to come back the following morning. First the "*ula* have to be put to sleep", after which the seance continues. These diviners are called *a maloto* (of dreams). The *ula* are supposed to reveal the truth to the diviner in a dream during that night.

Consulting the diviner

The *ula* are never wrong. It may be that the diviner has stipulated that a sa-crifice be offered to a particular spirit. If after it the sick person does not recover, his relatives are free to consult another diviner. To him they will explain first that they have already consulted a diviner, that they have offered the sacrifice imposed by him, but that the sick person has not improved. The second diviner will not contradict the first one, he will merely say that besides the spirits who had to be appeased, there is also a *mfiti*. He will ask his *ula* which *mfiti* is preventing the sick man from getting better.

People will always follow the indications of the *ula*. In the case of an illness, the *ula* may say that the patient had a quarrel with someone and that the latter has a grudge against him which is the cause of the illness. The relatives of the sick man will then go to see the person with the grudge and let him know what the *ula* have indicated. They will beg him to be reconciled with the sick man. In such a case they will offer him a gourd with water from which he will drink, spitting the water out over the sick person. This will be the sign that he has forgiven the sick man and that the grudge has come out of his heart as the water from his mouth. Now the sick man will surely recover.

e) The Power of the Diviner

E.G. Parrinder wrote: "It is hard to believe that the chance throw of bones or nuts can reveal the past or uncover the future. From my own experience I would trace the true wisdom not to the divinatory system, but to the wide experience, the keen perceptiveness, and the deep intuition of the diviner himself. There is undoubtedly some degree of telepathy and extra-sensory perception at work at times."[2] W.H.J. Rangeley noted: "There is no doubt at all that the business was entirely fake, and that the *ula* gave information carefully ascertained beforehand by the *woombeza ula.*"[3] We believe that the diviner certainly has a vast practical knowledge of the psychology of his clients together with a deep understanding of the tensions and conflicts inherent in the matrilineal system. By means of his skillfully worded questions he coaxes the clients slowly to formulate his suspicions. Then with a show of mysterious power the *ula* confirm these suspicions which the client himself has expressed. This leaves the client all the more satisfied because the *ula* confirm his own deeper feelings. M.G. Marwick explains how the diviner whom he went to consult explained the case in terms of the tensions inherent in the matrilineal system.[4] These were the only terms of reference for the diviner, who could not see the case otherwise than in a context of uncle - sister's son rivalry (although he was clever enough to transpose it to a paternal uncle, knowing that the Europeans do not follow a matrilineal system).

---

[2] E.G. Parrinder, *African Traditional Religion*, London, 1954, new edit., London: Sheldon Press, 1974, p. 122.

[3] W.H.J. Rangeley, "Notes on Chewa Tribal Law", in: *The Nyasaland Journal* 1 (1948), no. 3, p. 58.

[4] Cf. M.G. Marwick, *Sorcery in its Social Setting*, pp. 5-8.

The role of the diviner in Chewa society is extremely important. He is the official interpreter of the will of the spirits of the dead. In modern psychological terms one may say that the diviner helps his clients to formulate their own deeper feelings of suspicion and of guilt towards the *mizimu* or their fellow men. He allocates responsibility and indicates the way to be followed to clear up the situation. As such he has a profound influence on his clients. He dispels the uncertainty and hopelessness of a given situation. As such he may be said to help his clients come to grips with it. On the other hand his influence is sinister. He keeps suspicions alive or rather accentuates them. In this way, instead of bringing about reconciliation, more often than not he creates greater tensions and gives rise to acts of revenge. Through his influence in village life he maintains the traditional beliefs and the corresponding climate of fear and hatred, confirms jealousies and so undermines attempts to promote genuine reform, frustrating the desire of those who would like to improve their situation and that of others. By his influence in confirming jealousies, feelings of hatred and in accentuating tensions, he helps directly to perpetuate the moral evil that beset family and village life.

f) The Interpreter of Dreams and Premonitions

The diviner is also the sole authoritative interpreter of dreams and premonitions which people believe the spirits of the deceased send to warn them of impending danger or to convey some other message. The following are samples of actual dreams and their interpretation.

1. A person who dreamt that he received what he asked for from someone was told that this was the promise of good fortune.
2. A person who dreamt that he was attacked by an animal without being hurt was told that this was a good omen.
3. A person who dreamt that he was crossing a river by means of a tree lying across the water and that he managed thus to keep his feet dry was told that it was a promise of good luck.
4. A person who dreamt that he was offered meat at a meal was told that this promised a good hunt.
5. A person who dreamt that a person in the village had died was told that something untoward was going to happen.

6. A woman who dreamt that she was helping another woman who gave birth to a still-born child was told that she herself would have a healthy baby.

7. A person who dreamt that his house was on fire was told that some misfortune would soon befall him.

8. A person who dreamt that the rain was leaking through the roof of his house was told that this foreboded some ominous happening.

9. A person who dreamt about someone else who was strong and healthy was told that he himself would fall ill.

10. A man who dreamt that he was bitten by his own dog was told not to go hunting as an animal would hurt him.

11. A person who dreamt that he was crossing a river that was swollen with dirty and muddy water was told that soon there would be a death in his family.

12. A person who dreamt that he was flying like a bird was told that this meant future good health.

13. A person who dreamt that he was catching plenty of fish was told that this was a promise that he would become rich.

14. A person who dreamt that he was drinking beer was warned that somebody was preparing to put poison in his beer.

15. A person who dreamt about leopards and other wild animals was warned that a *mfiti* was lying in wait for him.

16. A person who dreamt that a snake was following him was warned that somebody wanted to kill him.

It is interesting to note that most of these dreams were interpreted in a sense that has some similarity with the subject of the dream. However, some dreams were interpreted in a sense that was contrary to the subject of the dream, e.g. nos. 6 and 9.

2. The Medicine Man *(sing'anga)* or Magician

The term *sing'anga* is used for the medicine man who uses herbal medicines to cure diseases and also for the magician who prepares "magic medicines", called *mtsiliko* (or *chambu)*, *mphinjiri*, and *chithumwa*. On the whole people do not distinguish, as we do, between natural medicines and magic ones. All of them are supposed to possess the same value and efficacy. The general name for all such medicines is *mankhwala*.

At the *sing'anga's* house

Mtsiliko (verb: *kutsilika*), also called *chambu* in certain cases, is a magic intended to protect against sorcery or theft. It is used to protect houses, grainstores, gardens, villages, cattle-kraals, etc.

Mphinjiri is a piece of reed or wood hollowed out in which certain *mankhwala* has been inserted. Such a *mphinjiri* is usually fixed on a string, sometimes with beads, and worn around the neck, waist, or ankles. It is believed to ward off misfortunes.

Chithumwa is a small sachet made of cloth which contains some *mankhwala*. It is sown into the clothes or fixed around the neck with string and is believed to enable someone to obtain an object he desires.

There are innumerable kinds of *mankhwala*. Each *sing'anga* has his own preparations. We shall first give a number of examples of *mtsiliko* and then of *mphinjiri* and *chithumwa*. We shall leave aside "natural" herbal medicines which fall outside the scope of our present work.

Most of the *mankhwala* are made from roots of trees or plants, burnt and reduced to powder and mixed with oil. Other substances are added, like hairs of animals, insects (dead or alive), a quill from a hedgehog, or soil from the place where the person sat or fell down. We shall describe a few of the *mankhwala*. After the Chewa names in the samples we shall indicate the Latin names of those trees or plants that were found in the collection of J. Williamson.[5]

a) Examples of mtsiliko

To protect a house

To prevent *mfiti, ziwanda,* and thieves from entering, people ask a *sing'anga* to come to protect their house. If he is called before the work on the house is started, he comes at midnight and buries some of his *mankhwala* around the intended site of the house. The composition of one such *mankhwala* was a mixture of charcoal, castor-oil and a powder made from the roots of the following trees: *Mwabvi* (Erythrophleum guineense) and *Kakombwe* (Pistia stratiotes). The whole mixture was wrapped in the leaves of a maize-cob.

Another *sing'anga* used the following recipe. Some *nsima* (maize porridge) still simmering on the fire, but prepared for a visitor, some charcoal made from an old handle of an axe or hoe which has been discarded, twelve *msambi-msambi* (sort of water-insects), twelve tops of reed, a little sand from near a stream, twelve sharpened sticks made from the same wooden axe or hoe handle, some ashes taken from somewhere in the village and from other villages and twelve living frogs. When the preparations are started on the building a trench has first to be dug, into which the *sing'anga* puts the twelve frogs which have been coated with wet ashes, together with the twelve reed tops, the insects and the sticks. As he places them in the hole he says: "Let nobody come here at night, but only in the day-time. Those who come at night will find here only water". This he has to do while it is practically dark. The following day work on the house must be started. If the wife of the owner of the house has her period, she may not come near the place. The *sing'anga* then takes the *nsima* and charcoal and mixes them with eggs

---

[5] J. Williamson, *Useful Plants of Malawi*, Zomba: The Government Press, 1972

which have failed to hatch and adds castor-oil, which has been prepared by a barren person. This mixture is put in a gourd and buried under the doorway. A little is kept in another gourd for those who will live in the house. It will be rubbed in cuts made in the skin. The wife of the owner will not be treated in this way during her period.

It is interesting to note how the various ingredients have their own meaning. The frogs, the water-insects, the pieces of reed, the sand from near a stream evoke the idea of water. The belief is that if a *mfiti* comes near a house protected by these he will see only a pool of water. The charcoal which is black evokes the idea that the *mfiti* will be unable to see the house at night. The sharpened sticks evoke the traditional way of executing *mfiti* by impaling them. The fact that a woman having her period (being "hot") is kept at a distance evokes the idea that different powers can interfere with one another, so the power of the *mtsiliko* might be affected by the proximity of the woman.

If the *sing'anga* is called after the house has been built, he comes at midnight when everybody in the village is asleep and brings his *mankhwala* with him. This would consist of eight wooden sticks and eight smooth pebbles dipped in *mankhwala*. He digs two holes on either side of the doorway and two inside and to the rear of the house facing the doorway. This part of the house is called *kumiyendo* and together with the door-posts it has an important role to play in any *kutsilika* of a house. The sticks and the pebbles are buried in these holes. The wooden sticks evoke the killing of a *mfiti* and the pebbles, water. These pebbles in fact have to be collected at a place where two streams meet. Moreover the *sing'anga* must be naked while he collects them and has to keep his eyes closed. This refers to the *mfiti* who is supposed to walk about naked and will not now be able to see the house.

To protect the body

A person who suspects a neighbour of harbouring evil intentions against him and is afraid that he might be poisoned will ask the *sing'anga* for *mankhwala* to protect himself. This *mtsiliko* often takes the form of *mankhwala* which has to be rubbed into cuts in the skin *(otemera)*. Other *mankhwala* are supposed to protect a person against lightning thrown by an enemy.

To protect grainstores

In order to prevent thefts a horn *(nyanga)* containing *mankhwala* is placed at the bottom of a grainstore. The *sing'anga* will go sometimes to the graveyard to dig up the skull of a small child (preferably the skull of the child of the sister of the owner of the grainstore). This skull will be placed at the bottom of the grainstore and covered with an earthenware pot. This type of *mankhwala* is also believed to increase the maize in the grainstore and is called a *mfumba*. This *mfumba* should be considered as a *chizimba* (cf. p. 225f.). When people discover a child's skull at the bottom of a grainstore, they suspect the owner of having killed a child in order to obtain a *mfumba*.

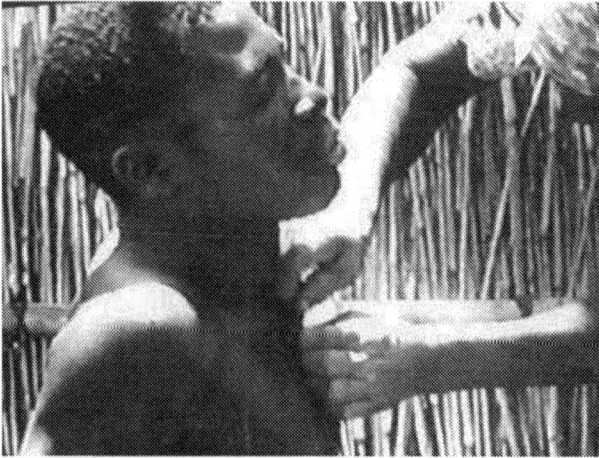

Incision at the sing'anga

To protect the fields

To protect a garden against thieves, spells and wild animals, a *chambu* is used. This *mankhwala* consists of roots dipped in castor-oil and covered with ashes. The owner of the field makes holes at each corner of the field and at the place where a path leads back to the village. In each hole the *sing'anga* puts some of his *mankhwala* and covers it over with soil except for the hole near the entrance which he covers with a small earthenware pot. He shows the owner how to lift this pot and put it back again. The owner may only enter his garden through this "entrance" and after lifting the pot. Anyone at all, even the owner himself or a member of his family, who enters the field in another way or without lifting the pot, would become lame or possibly even die. The *sing'anga* who prepared the *mtsiliko* is the only one able to intervene in any calamity arising from failure to abide by his injunctions. Against those who might want, with their magic, to diminish the maize in a field in order to increase the yield in their own field, people plant all around the field seeds which have previously been dipped in *mankhwala*. These will grow up as a magic enclosure protecting the maize in the field. Other people buy a small string from the *sing'anga* and hang it in a tree. This is a magic snake that will protect their crops against thieves. The *sing'anga* may also come and merely draw a line across the path. Any person crossing such a line would contract a mysterious disease.

To protect a cattle kraal

To protect cattle against thieves, wild beasts and diseases, people put *mankhwala* in holes around the kraal and on both sides of the entrance. The teeth of a hyena are believed to curl up while a thief is said to see only a pool of water and no kraal.

To protect a new village

Before building a new village the chief invites the *sing'anga* to come to protect it. The *sing'anga* walks around the confines of the new village and at the four points of the compass he buries some of his *mankhwala*, e.g. pieces of the roots of the *msolo* tree *(Pseudolachnostylis maprouneifolia)* and of the *mdima* shrub *(Royina lucida)* mixed with charcoal and castor oil. He also buries some *mankhwala* at the spot where the open space of the village (meeting place) is going to be. This will ensure protection for the village against *mfiti* and wild beasts. On the day the people settle in the new village the *sing'anga* comes again and instructs them to make a fire in which he puts some of his *mankhwala*. He then tells them to light their own fires from this fire. He also spreads some *mankhwala* on the trees surrounding the new village. On his return to the open space where the people are waiting for him, he proclaims the taboos which the people in that village will have to observe in the future. They may not commit any adultery in the village, they may not use the wood of a certain tree to cook their food or to warm themselves. They may not prepare eggs in hot ash but only boil them in water. Each *sing'anga* indicates the taboos that he wants. If later on some calamity befalls, e.g. wild beast devastate the village, the people will have only themselves to blame;

somebody will have violated one of those taboos and will have to be unmasked by the *ula*.

To protect a wife

To prevent their wives from committing adultery some husbands make them drink a *chambu* obtained from the *sing'anga*. Anyone committing adultery with such a woman would contract a disease which only that particular *sing'anga* can cure.

b) Examples of mphinjiri and chithumwa

These charms occupy a large place in the lives of the people. They are sought for many different purposes: to prevent or cure diseases, to obtain good luck, to protect against enemies and wild animals, to prevent conception, to cause abortion, to make oneself loved, to gain the favour of an employer, to be successful in business, exams, hunting, etc.

For small children

A *chilezi* (that which protects) is used for a newborn baby to protect it against *mdulo* in case a midwife or any other woman touches the baby who has had relations with her husband and so is "hot". It consists of a string made from the bark of a *msupani* tree *(Grevia mollis)* and four *mphinjiri* made from the roots of the plant *maso ang'ombe (Temnocalyx obovatus)*. The string is worn around the waist with two *mphinjiri* in front and two at the back. To prevent various types of diseases the child may be given a *njimiko* or a *mphingani njira* (that which lies across a path) to wear round its neck. This is a small sachet, decorated with beads, which contains three bits of the same shrub found at a crossroads (pieces from the stem and from branches on opposite sides of the stem). Against headaches it receives a *mphinjiri yothothoka* in which a piece of its dried up umbilical cord has been inserted. Against diseases sent by malevolent people the child receives a *mlungamlunga*, i.e. a piece of bark with eight holes made into it. This is placed on the spot where the child is suffering. The disease is supposed to enter into those holes. After use the *mlungamlunga* is burnt.

For girls and women

To make herself loved a girl wears a *chisomo* round her neck, a sachet containing a part of the root of a *mwiyo* plant or of the *cheseo (A. Subalata)*. She may also hide such a piece of root in her hair. This is also called *mankhwala a chikondi* (love medicine). To ensure fecundity and to give birth to a healthy baby, women wear a *njimiko* around the waist. They make six *mphinjiri* from the roots of the *maso ang'ombe (Temnocalyx obovatus)* and tie them on a string made from the fibres of the *bwazi (Cryptolepis oblonifolia)* in such a way that there are two *mphinjiri* in front and two on either side. This sort of charm is also often called *mlimbiko* (that which makes strong). There are many different ways of making such a charm.

For hunting

For protection hunters wear *mphinjiri* on their arms and rub their weapons with leaves of the *msolo (Pseudolachnostylis maprouneifolia)*. To ensure success they tie a piece of the root of a *mpetu (Boscia Sp.)* on their spears or insert the heart of the *suntche* mouse in the hollow shaft of the arrow. According to the people this mouse is very slow moving. So when wounded the game cannot run away fast. To attract game they take the heart of the first animal they kill and pierce it with the root of a *msolo (Pseudolachnostylis maprouneifolia)* or a *mdima (Royina lucida)*. They roast and eat it. The name of this *mankhwala* is *chikoka* (that which draws near). The game will not be afraid of the hunter and will approach him. To their nets they fix pieces of the branches of the *mpetu (Boscia sp.)* to prevent them from breaking.

To have a good harvest

Some people say that from the moment they plant they should abstain from cutting their hair or washing. They may not have any relations with their wives until after their maize is harvested. Some of the magic used to protect *(kutsilika)* their fields will also increase its yield.

To make oneself invisible

The tail of a hyena makes a thief invisible. He has to press the tail firmly with his hand. A. Werner reported that a *mankhwala* made from the *khombe (Strophanthus)* was used by chief *Msamara* to make himself invisible while escaping from the prison at Fort Johnston in 1892.[6] He had previously taken off his clothes, thinking that the drug would not make them invisible. Unfortunately the drug poisoned him.

To win a judicial process

Some people buy a *mphinjiri* from the *sing'anga* and keep it in their pocket pressing it lightly. This will ensure that the adversary is confused and so unable to put his case clearly enough to win it. Others take the leaves of the *tsophe (Scrofulacea),* squeeze the juice and rub their body with it.

In case of difficulties with the police

People carry in their pockets *mphinjiri* made from the roots of the *chipembere (Randia sp.).* Only those that grow in a *chizombwe* (a particular type of ant-hill) are used.

To keep the money safe

People boil a mixture of the dung of a *fututu* (sort of rat), the yellow flowers of the *katupe woyala (Lasiosiphon kraussianus),* and a coin, and encircle their money with it.

The above charms are only a few examples. Each *sing'anga* has his own remedies and the total number is quite immense. Many *sing'anga* will impose some sort of taboo while a person is using their charms. In the case of an illness almost invariably sexual continence is imposed until the patient is cured and the *sing'anga* has received his fee. On the day of the consultation, a chicken is given the *sing'anga* for his trouble in finding the right remedies *(chifukwa choponda mitengo).* The fee itself is given only after the patient is cured. If there is no cure there will be no fee.

3. Conclusion

---

[6] A. Werner, *The Natives of British Central Africa,* London: Constable, 1906, p. 83.

I remember vividly a conversation with two young men who had finished their secondary studies. They looked on magic as an African form of science and thought that, however advanced European technology was, it was definitely inferior to African magic. Western technology was terribly laborious, while magic, they said, was almost effortless and instantaneous. As examples they instanced several scientists, like Marconi, who had put up with tremendous privation in order to pursue their work. They said that they almost felt pity for such people. These young men were grieved by the fact that magic was dismissed as superstition. And yet, they said, one has only to look around in Africa to see its tremendous impact and achievements. While they agreed that many African magicians had not yet found the way to put their power to the best possible use, they believed that the power was there and that in modern Africa it would be put to a greater and more universal use for the good of all. It is a fact that the belief in magic is deeply rooted in Africa. It may be used for good and evil. Technology has helped western man to conquer matter. Magic will remain, for a long time yet, the alternative to which many in Africa will turn in their quest for a better life.

Chapter 9
Moral Beliefs

So far we have considered the religious beliefs and practices of the Chewa. In this last chapter we would like to consider more specifically their moral ideas on right and wrong, their notions of sin and of retribution. In this chapter much use will be made of previous chapters, especially those on *mdulo* and *ufiti*.

A. Hetherwick stated that the Chewa religious beliefs have no moral content because the Chewa lack all notion of sin and do not believe in a source of retribution. He must have used his own Christian notions of sin and retribution as terms of reference, without trying to appreciate the Chewa ethical notions from within their system of religious beliefs. Obviously, if one looks for a Christian notion of sin and retribution in the beliefs of the Chewa, none will be found. But this does not mean that there is no notion of sin or retribution at all. A. Hetherwick had been a missionary of the Blantyre Mission of the Church of Scotland for over 30 years when he made the following statements in the Croall Lectures of 1930-1931.

> In all I have said regarding the spirits world, I have said nothing of any ethical element in it. And that is because there is no ethical element in it at all. Morality does not enter into the native theosophy, nor in any measure at all into his conception of God or Spirit, or the spirit world, or the future life. The moral state of the living has no bearing on, or relation to, their condition or place in the other world.

> When any question of moral conduct is present, conscience at no time enters as a deciding factor in native life. The main determining factor in such matters is the fear of consequence which alone deters the Native from any course of moral misconduct, and keeps him in the right path. Consequences of the results of transgression, and not any voice of conscience, are the main deterrent factors in native conduct.

> Every crime in native law may be atoned for by payment of compensation according to a certain scale. Once he has paid the compensation demanded of him, he takes his place again in society, the case is finished.

> It is not surprising that we can find no conception of sin as a moral lapse or failure. Sin is just a crime to be compensated by payment.[1]

A. Hetherwick has been recognized as a man of great authority because of his learning, his many years of experience and his position as head of the Church of Scotland in Malawi. His ideas have been accepted uncritically by many missionaries. A. Hovington, another missionary, quotes Hetherwick with approval and after a lifetime spent in Malawi summarizes his own views as follows: "There is nothing in their belief in *Chiuta* which may influence their morality and makes them follow a way of life in conformity to their belief."[2]

1. Retribution

Despite what these authors have said, it is my opinion that the Chewa definitely have a notion of retribution included in the belief that a person, upon his death, will be accepted or rejected by the spirits of the dead. The expression used is *kulandilidwa* (to be received). Whether a person is accepted into the spirit world or not is believed to depend on his way of life before death. Those who are not received become *ziwanda* who wander about and find no repose.

One older person expressed in the following terms his belief that people who have done no evil will be received into the spirit world. "I will enter there because I have done no evil. The spirits will receive me. I did not kill. I did not steal. Therefore I cannot think of anything wrong because of which the spirits will punish me. I am in peace because I have nothing bad on my conscience" *(ine ndikalowa chifukwa ndilibe tchimo, ine Mulungu akandi-landira, kupha sindikupha, kuba sindikuba, tsono palibe chimene ine ndiganiza choipa*

---

[1] A. Hetherwick, *The Gospel and the African*, Edinburgh: Clark, 1932, pp. 110-114.

[2] A. Hovington, "The African Way of Life", Rome: 8 fascicles, Ms, written over many years (last pages dated 1973), Archives, Missionaries of Africa (White Fathers), vol. 7, p. 87.

choti Mulungu angandilange. Ine ndine dzungu m'gonera kumodzi (osadziwa chili chonse choipa). The expression *"dzungu m'gonera kumodzi"* means literally: a pumkin that lies only on one side. This refers to the fact that the person does not turn over and over in his sleep, while worry and fear make a person restless in his sleep. We have translated *Mulungu* by spirits, as in the expression *"kupita kwa Mulungu"* (to go to the spirit world).

A person was excluded from the family if he committed certain crimes and seriously offended family solidarity. This idea of someone being excluded from the family bond is projected onto the life after death. The people believe that the spirits refuse to receive someone who is a *mfiti*, who has killed or committed incest, or who has robbed a brother in need. A *chiwanda* is therefore like an exiled person, banned from the family community. He wanders about, utterly alone, with nowhere to settle and unable to find peace. A comparison is made between the family bond on earth and the bond believed to exist between the spirits of the dead in the hereafter, where the members of a family will be reunited in some way. Happiness can only be found in communion with one's brothers *(achibale),* both here below and hereafter.

The Chewa have the conviction that the evil a person commits will eventually catch up with him: *zoipa zitsata mwini* (evil follows its owner). Even if such a person manages to escape the consequences of his misdeeds for a long time, one day he will have to face them. However vague this idea of *kulandilidwa* in particular and of the spirit world in general may be, there is definitely a belief in some sort of retribution after death. A. Hetherwick noted that no mention can be found of God who rewards or punishes men for their moral behaviour. We should not forget that the Chewa believe that God has delegated the spirits of the deceased to look after their descendants in all matters. In virtue of that delegation the spirits punish not only by refusing to receive a person at his death, but also by sending misfortunes by which to punish and correct him during his lifetime. A number of expressions show that the Chewa do conceive somehow that God is the ultimate source of the moral order and of retribution. Thus for instance: if a person has been clever enough to escape punishment so far, people say: *"Chiuta* is more clever than the thief" *(Chiuta ndiye kalakambala)*, thereby expressing the belief that, in the end, the thief will not escape punishment from God. Another expression is: "What is visible is the harm done to other people, but the fear felt in one's heart is a sign that one has done wrong before *Chiuta" (chooneka panja ndicho chiipira anthu, koma nthumanzi yomveka mu mtima ndi chizindikiro cholakwira Chiuta)*.[3] Finally people currently say that if people commit e.g. adultery *Chiuta* will send them wild beasts and other misfortunes: *Chigololo chimakwiyitsa Chiuta ndi chifukwa chake angathe kuwatumizira zirombo ndi zovuta zina*. A. Hetherwick insisted that any crime could be paid for by making compensation *(lipo)*. Actually this is not correct, because other punishments were also imposed, like execution, mutilation, and banishment.[4]

2. Moral Evil

The main principle that one can hear again and again is that it is the duty of every Chewa to follow the customs laid down by the ancestors *(kutsata miyambo ya makolo)*. "If we do not follow them, we will fall ill or become mad", implying that the spirits of the deceased will not fail to punish them.

At the moment there is a current of ethnic re-awakening and the people are constantly being reminded that in order to preserve their ethnic identity they have to go back to the customs of the ancestors *(miyambo ya makolo)*. These customs contain the norms of what is good or evil. The welfare of the community depends on their observance. The spirits of the deceased are the channel through which fertility comes to the community. The survival of the community is dependent on the goodwill of the spirits and this is ensured by the exact observance of the traditions. It is interesting to note that in the eyes of the Chewa, what the ancestors themselves did, cannot be bad. When we asked them about the apparent immorality of certain acts, they calmly answered that their ancestors did so before them. "We did not start this, our ancestors started it. We cannot abandon what they started" *(si ife tidayamba zimenezi, ndi makolo, tsono ife sitingaleke za makolo athu)*. We can clas-

---

[3] *Nthumanzi* is connected with *nthuma*, blame.

[4] W.H.J. Rangeley, "Notes on Chewa Tribal Law", in: *The Nyasaland Journal* 1 (1948), no. 3, pp. 17-19.

sify the traditional norms of good or bad according to the two paramount social values in small scale societies: the need for solidarity within the group and the importance of fertility.

3. Solidarity

In a small-scale society there is a basic egalitarianism, nobody is supposed to want to have more than his fellows. If a person displays more drive and ambition than the other members of the group, he is suspected of wanting to be successful at other peoples' expense.

Preparing food together - Symbol of solidarity

The success of a person's work is believed to depend to some extent on the use of *mankhwala*. If a person is successful he must have used *chizimba* (medicine made out of human flesh). It implies that a victim is sacrificed in order that his "life-power" may be captured and made to serve the greed of somebody else.

There is also the belief that a person obtains power likened to *chizimba* by performing an act of incest. We know of the case of a man who made his own daughter pregnant "in order to become rich". Sexual intercourse with one's own daughter is regarded as such a heinous act that the father indulging in it would simply be considered as a *mfiti* who wants to obtain *chizimba*. It is important to note that at the root of *chizimba* there is always a particularly evil act, a defiance of the moral order. To believe that such defiance of the moral order yields power is, according to M. Wilson, who encountered some similar belief among the Nyakyusa, the "African equivalent of the myth of Faust selling his soul to the devil".[5] The 68 cases of *chizimba* reported in our survey show that the belief that such an evil act yields power, is still common among the Chewa. They regard greed and thirst for power as particularly evil in that it can push a man to defy all that should be sacred to him in order to achieve his evil purpose. They believe that a man would not hesitate to kill his child or to perpetrate incest with his daughter in order to obtain power. The strongest form of power is believed to reside in life itself. It could be said that such a belief is the typical reaction of conservatism in the face of change. It is true that a number of the cases referred to "maize mills, lorries, shops". But other forms of *chizimba* are much older, e.g. *mfumba* when a child is believed to be killed and it is placed at the bottom of a grain-store in order to increase the owner's maize. These are anterior to the introduction of modern economic changes.

4. Other Moral Obligations in the Context of Solidarity

It is important to note that these obligations apply only in respect of members of the same group and not in respect of people outside the group. The obligation to assist a brother *(mbale)* in need is not to be seen as the Chewa equivalent of the Christian obligation of charity. The Chewa *mbale* is strictly a member of the same family and nobody else. Within these limits people have to help one another *(kugwirizana, kuthandizana)*, especially when the other one is in need.

This solidarity is especially strong at a funeral *(maliro)*. Sympathy and comfort is given to the bereaved while the deceased himself is accompanied ritually on his journey towards the spirit-world. We have seen the importance attached to the obligation to assist at a funeral. This is a symbol of solidarity and is one of the most sacred duties for every Chewa. Peace is of paramount important for the community. Anybody willfully disturbing this peace is considered to be a *mfiti*. For a rain sacrifice it is required that all the people be at peace with one another. Anger disrupts this peace. Anger in a

---

[5] M. Wilson, *Religion and the Transformation of Society*, Cambridge: University Press, 1971, p. 88.

person's heart may push him to kill another person. Such anger is feared, since, unless it is removed, it is said never to be forgotten. A Chewa never forgets an insult. He will harbour a grievance in his heart which on a suitable occasion will be manifested in a violent fashion. *Mlandu suola* (literally: a case does not rot away, i.e. a grievance lasts till it is settled). In a judicial case *(mlandu)* great care is taken to allow all the parties involved to speak out, and every effort is made to come to a solution which is acceptable to all. A solution which is imposed without the aggrieved party agreeing to its fairness in fact solves nothing. Jealousies also disrupt peace in the community. A Chewa will take every possible care not to arouse jealousies. It is unwise to boast about one's success or even to speak about it. It is quite common to see people who are relatively rich in comparison with their neighbours going around dressed in torn and patched clothes. For the cohesion of the group it is important that proper respect *(ulemu)* be paid to the chiefs and elders *(akulu)*.

Drinking beer - Symbol of sharing and of community

At a time when vendettas between two families could lead to much bloodshed, it was considered a greater evil to kill a person of another family group than one's own brother. We were told that: "To kill a brother is not wrong, but to kill other people is wrong because they do not belong to the same family group, they are strangers" *(kupha achibale sikulakwa chifukwa wapha achibale ako. Koma ngati ukupha ena ndi kulakwa chifukwa si mtundu wako ndi alendo amenewo).* Notice the hyperbole here: "It is not wrong to kill a brother". The meaning is: "It is less wrong to kill a brother".

To steal from a brother in need is wrong, because it upsets the peace in the group, but to steal from a stranger is not particularly wrong. To steal from the government *(boma),* shops or employers is not wrong, they are rich anyway. If, however, somebody is caught repeatedly stealing and the family has to pay the fines, they may get tired of doing so and end up expelling such a thief from the family, because he has become a nuisance.

5. Fertility

Fertility is the other paramount value for the community. Fertility is believed to depend, inter alia, on the observance of the *mdulo* taboos as explained in chapter six. Great importance is attached to the right instruction in these *mdulo* taboos during the time of initiation. All youths have to be initiated into these traditions, lest they cause havoc in the community. Incest is considered one of the worst offences against the family. "To commit adultery with a stranger is not evil, but to do so with a person belonging to the same family group is evil" *(kuchita chigololo ndi munthu wina sikulakwa chifukwa ndi mlendo, koma kuchita chigololo ndi mbale wako ndi kulakwa).* Incest consists in having sexual relations with a person with whom one cannot contract marriage *(kulakwa ndi munthu amene sungathe kukwatira):* Thus: with one's sister (by the same mother) and half-sisters (by the same father but different mother), one's nieces (by one's brothers or sisters), one's cousins (by one's paternal aunts, paternal uncles or maternal aunts), one's maternal and paternal aunts, one's own daughters, the daughters of one's own children, the wives of one's father (and of course with one's own mother). One may marry a cross-cousin *(pa chisuweni),* i.e. the daughter of one's maternal uncle. To have sexual relations with one of these persons is called *kukashusha mbumba* (to destroy the family) and is looked upon as *ufiti.*

6. Moral Education

The Chewa attach great importance to restraint and reconciliation. Aggressive behaviour is interpreted by them as an indication of ill will, of an evil intention, and an accusation of witchcraft could follow. Fear of being accused of witchcraft has led to the particular characteristic in the Chewa of kindness and meekness, and even, one might say, of an exaggerated form of politeness. Misfortunes are mostly explained by evil in men. They are attributed either to the person's own sin which calls down the wrath of the spirits of the deceased or the anger of his fellow-men. On the occasion of a death we have heard people say: He died because of his own fault *(wafa ndi mtima wake,* literally: because of his heart). Even when misfortune is attributed to evil in other men *(m'pheranjiru)* it is considered in some way to be the victim's own fault. People will say he ought not to have quarrelled or to have aroused jealousies. If he had remained unassuming and peaceful, and had not shown ambition by working so hard, he would not have aroused anger or envy. It is therefore not recommended to be different from others or to give any occasion for other people to feel insulted and become angry. The only prudent behaviour is that of a polite and peaceful person who has no ambition to be more successful then his neighbours. If he happens to come into some money, he has to share it with other people, e.g. a worker coming back from the mines in South Africa is expected to share his money with relatives and friends. The point to be noted is that the Chewa do not attribute their misfortunes so much to outside spiritual powers as to evil in men, anger, jealousy, greed, lust, egoism, both in themselves and in their fellow-men.

A. Hetherwick wrote: "The African youth grew up with no moral discipline save his own superstitious fears, no teaching of self-restraint or high ideals of life".[6] This statement shows misunderstanding of those "superstitious fears". For these refer to the ancestral traditions handed down during initiation which, as we have tried to explain, are to be seen as a moral code. The songs learnt during initiation ceremonies continue to remind people throughout their lives of their obligations. Another point to be noted is that youths are instructed in the "wisdom of the tribe" *(nzeru za makolo)* by every possible means. Apart from the initiation itself, stories and many proverbs with a moral teaching are told during evening hours. Youths, too, remain under the supervision of their tutors *(phungu).* Life itself, with its hardships and the work in common, is the school in which their character is formed.

---

[6] A. Hetherwick, *The Gospel and the African,* p. 18.

If, of course, one sees no moral value in the ancestral customs *(miyambo ya makolo)*, then one will be inclined to repeat with A. Hetherwick, that the African youth grows up with no moral values at all.

Special mention should be made of proverbs. The Chewa are very fond of them for they are said to contain the wisdom of the ancestors *(nzeru za makolo)* especially in the field of moral beliefs. We have read close on one thousand proverbs.[7] E. Gray wrote that he had collected 400 proverbs in Malawi but that he had not come across one which mentioned the name of God.[8] However, although the proverbs make no direct mention of God or even of the spirits, they reflect a wisdom impregnated with the ethical values which were considered important and which were handed down by the ancestors. The proverbs we have studied are an expression of human wisdom, based on experience of life and an insight into human relationships. If in a discussion a proverb is quoted which is to the point, the business being dealt with is considered concluded and no more has to be said about it. Here are two examples:

Mdya makoko saiwala, aiwala ndi mdya nyemba
Literally: the one who eats beans forgets, but the one who eats husks does not forget. The meaning is: The one who insults someone forgets it easily, but the one who is insulted (who was been given husks to eat) will never forget it.

Kakonda mnzako lero mlekere, mawa kadzakonda iwe
Literally: the thing your friend likes, leave it to him. Tomorrow you may like the same thing. This is a Chewa version of: what you want people to do for you, do also for them, and what you do not want them to do to you, do not do to them.

---

[7] S.J. Ntara has collected 803 proverbs (Ntara, S.J., "Miyambo". A collection of 803 proverbs in Chichewa, Nkhoma: unpublished typescript, 1958). We have found another 200. Cf. the new collection of 2000 Nyanja (Chewa) proverbs in: J.C. Chakanza, *Wisdom of the People. 2000 Chinyanja Proverbs,* Blantyre: CLAIM, 2001.

[8] Quoted by E.W. Smith, *African Ideas of God,* London: Edinburgh House Press, 1950, (2nd ed. revised and edited by E.G. Parrinder, 3rd ed. 1966), p. 5.

Conclusion

In this book we have set out to examine and describe the Chewa religious beliefs and practices; not only those of the past, but also those of the present. The theme we chose to give unity to the whole is: religion is a support for man in suffering, for it offers an explanation for it and helps him to cope with it. The main reasons for suffering in the life of the Chewa are death, illness, drought and infertility. Our survey indicated that deaths were attributed in some cases to God (48), the spirits of the deceased (9) and natural diseases (38), but the majority by far were attributed to evil in man himself, witchcraft and sorcery in their various forms (296). God is believed to have created man and to nourish him by giving rain in due season. He is mighty and awe-inspiring, but is also the One who is thought to be kind and patient with man.

The Chewa have their myths concerning creation and the entrance of death into the world. These myths were already noted by D. MacDonald in 1882 when the first missionaries had barely entered the country.[1] The theory of J.M. Schoffeleers that death entered into the world because of the fault of man does not seem to give a really authentic Chewa version. We can give two reasons for saying this. First it cannot be found in the oldest collection of MacDonald. Secondly it does not accord with the Chewa beliefs about death. Death is seen as an evil, except in the case of old people, but that evil is attributed to men not to God, who is not thought to punish man for immoral conduct in this way. He has left the living in the care of the spirits of their deceased relatives. These punish men for their immoral conduct, but seldom if ever by inflicting death.

---

[1] Cf. D. MacDonald, *Africana, or the Heart of Heathen Africa*, 2 vols., Edinburgh: John Menzies & Co., 1881, vol. 1, pp. 279, 296-297.

Rain and fertility come from God, often through the intercession of the spirits of the dead. Drought is seen as one of the worst disasters in the life of the Chewa, dependent as they are on a single harvest a year, yet it does not appear to be as much a punishment for sin as the outcome of man's own disregard for the right performance of rain rituals, such as: the setting on fire of the bush on Bunda Hill by others than the officials of the shrine and at times when fire is thought to be incompatible with rain; disregard of the obligation to abide by the taboos on sexual relations in connection with the rain ritual; the cutting of the hair of the rain dignitary *(Chilowa);* or the killing of a rain snake. All this appears to be more connected with ancient rain making rituals and sympathetic magic than with the concept of God as patient and kind with His children. This contradiction inclines us to believe that the Chewa came to a sort of syncretism by combining two religious streams: the ancient rain cult and a belief in God who is good and gentle and who listens to His children's plea, a belief possibly influenced by Christianity.

The Chewa do not believe in the existence of spirits other than those of their deceased relatives. God is believed to have left the spirits in charge of the living, although He also listens to their prayers. It could be that here again is a syncretism of two religious streams: a belief in the spirits of the dead, and a belief in *Leza* and *Tate* (names indicating the goodness and kindness of God). The spirits are considered to be man's protectors and his intercessors with God, but they can be dangerous and devastating if angered. They are believed to interfere frequently in the lives of their living relatives by asking for sacrifices or *Nyau* dances. A spirit in the liminal state especially is believed to return to his relatives often since he has not yet settled in the hereafter.

The religious significance of the burial rites is to "send off the spirit" of the deceased person and to accompany him ritually through his liminal state to the final state of a *mzimu*. The aggregation into the spirit world will be celebrated in the final commemoration of the burial.

The *Nyau* has a profound religious significance. The dancers have to pass through a process of identification which highlights their difference from normal people and their function of representing the *mzimu*. Their dance at a funeral is believed to be a prayer to the *mizimu* interceding with them to accept the spirit of a deceased person as a faithful member of the clan. It is also a prayer to the spirit of the deceased himself beseeching him not to afflict the living. Yet another aspect of *Nyau* dances is that they are a ritual which seeks to obtain fertility for the community. The *Nyau* also assume the role of the *mizimu* as teachers of the customs and instil fear in those who do not observe the traditional customs. Finally their dance is a sort of mystery play in which individual dancers portray different facets of the belief in the spirits and in retribution in the after-life.

One of the deeper notions underlying much of Chewa thought is that of "hot" and "cold". Applications of the belief that mysterious powers can be mutually injurious can be found in many of the ritual prescriptions: it underlies much of the *mdulo* beliefs, the ritual behaviour at rain sacrifices, burial ceremonies, *Nyau*, initiation, and the role of chiefs.

The *mdulo* taboos constitute in a negative way ideals to be striven after. They stress a sense of personal responsibility for the well-being of others and for optimum conditions for procreation. The teaching of these *mdulo* during initiation is considered of major importance for the survival of the community. *Mdulo* beliefs state that illness, death and infertility can be consequences of bad behaviour, while life and fertility depend on right behaviour. What is right or bad is spelled out in the initiation instructions and is constantly recalled in the songs.

The Chewa have the conviction that there are hidden forces in men. Every man has moments when he experiences some such mysterious force to some degree as when instinctively he does something which afterwards proves to have been important. He ascribes this to his own *mzimu (ndayenda ndi mzimu wanga)*. When someone has been lucky he says: "I have a spirit" *(ndiri ndi mzimu)*.

People can put this mysterious force to use for good or for evil. The diviner and the medicine man use it to help their clients. The *mfiti* and the sorcerer, on the contrary, use it to kill and inflict suffering. The most specific example of the Chewa belief in such power is that one person can kill another in order to capture his "life-energy" and turn it to his own personal use *(chizimba)*.

The belief in this sort of mysterious force is the Chewa way of explaining causality. Things do not happen fortuitously, they are caused by someone. The cosmos of the Chewa is populated with spirits and people, wielding such mysterious spiritual force for good or bad. There is no clear dividing line between these mysterious spiritual powers and the spiritual proper. E.W. Smith called the former "magico-religious".[2]

In my survey I found that a total of 296 deaths were attributed to mysterious evildoers. The Chewa believe that these hidden forces are consciously or unconsciously operating when people are "possessed" by anger, greed, envy or ambition. These impel him to kill or cause suffering by means of these mysterious forces in him. This evil in man (anger, greed, envy or ambition) is the explanation of most misfortunes. These beliefs in personal causes of misfortune and in mysterious hidden forces create a climate of fear which leads the Chewa to use protective medicines.

A recurrent theme in Chewa Traditional Religion is purification from evil. People want to discover who are *mfiti*, but they also seek to clear themselves of all possible suspicion of *ufiti*. The fear of being suspected of being a *mfiti* results in a code of behaviour in which politeness and meekness are singularly valued and aggressive behaviour and ambition are actively discouraged. The Chewa notion of retribution is contained in the belief that the spirit of a deceased person will be received into the spirit world *(kulandilidwa)*. Some will not be received on account of their evil deeds on earth and will become *ziwanda,* haunting spirits who continue their evil exploits and are deprived of peace. Solidarity between brothers *(achibale)* is one of the conditions for a

---

[2] E.W. Smith, *African Ideas of God*, London: Edinburgh House Press, 1950, (2nd ed. revised and edited by E.G. Parrinder, 3rd ed. 1966), p. 16.

happy life. The same belief is transferred to the afterlife. To be exiled, ex-pelled from the community is the punishment meted out to evildoers not only on earth, but also in the hereafter.

In the present prevailing conditions of social change, it seems possible that there will be a shift from corporate religious practice to a more individual one. One indication of such a shift is that in Lilongwe town a burial society has been founded to guarantee that each burial will be attended by some people. In village life such need for a burial society is totally unthinkable. It is also possible that there is a greater recourse to protective medicines, since the traditional defence against mysterious evildoers (ordeal and purification movements) are against the law. People can rely only on protective medi-cine to ward off danger.

In the years to come cultural dynamics will change the landscape of Chewa Traditional Culture and Religion quite extensively. Against a kind of mis-leading conservatism it has to be noted that Chewa religion was and is in a permanen state of transformation. I. Linden for example has shown how in the past the *Nyau* societies were more aggressive. Accordingly, as pressure mounted to change the customs, the *Nyau* was the defender of the tradi-tions against the tide of change.[3] Today, however, things are changing fast, not only in the towns but in the villages as well. Even the *Nyau* will be un-able to halt it. The small communities in the villages which are less and less self-sufficient enter increasingly into contact with outsiders and with mod-ern ideas. They are more and more pressed to work for self-improvement and to co-operate with the larger community in nation-building. At a time when the emphasis was on the small community, the spirits of the deceased were looked upon as the protectors and guardians. People believed that they depended on these spirits of the deceased. Now that the emphasis is shift-ing from the community to the individual and that people are urged to take their own responsibilities and work as self-employed, it could well be that solidarity in the group will no longer be stressed so strongly. To the weak-ening of the importance of the group may correspond a feeling of being less

---

[3] Cf. L. Linden, *Catholics, Peasants and Chewa Resistance in Nyasaland 1889-1939*, London: Heinemann, 1974, chapter on *Nyau*, passim.

dependent on the spirits of the deceased. Individual may turn increasingly to *mankhwala* to protect themselves and to achieve their aims. It could be that magic will come to play the role of a pseudo-religion. There is yet no evidence to support such a hypothesis because we lack the necessary statistical material. However, one gets the impression that, especially in the towns, there is a trend towards a greater use of *mankhwala* to which corresponds a definite falling away of the various public religious practices by which formerly the help of the spirits of the deceased was sought.

How social change is unavoidable has been described by E.G. Parrinder in the epilogue to his book *African Traditional Religion*:

> Students of African society have felt deep concern at the rapidity of social and religious change in Africa. Some would have prohibited missions from doing their work, but the clock cannot be put back. Nationalism, trade and education are just as disturbing as the new religions and, unlike them, have little positive moral ideal to put in place of the old. The greatest danger in African religious life is that the old should disappear without some new religious force to take its place. The past has been so thoroughly impregnated with religion and its ethics that it is difficult to see how an ordered society can be established without them.[4]

Any new religion will then take the place of those traditional ones and truly inspire people only if it incorporates the Chewa religious convictions and responds to the people's deeper aspiration for purification and liberation from fear. It is our hope that the present work may contribute to a better understanding of the Chewa beliefs and religious aspirations.

---

[4] E.G. Parrinder, *African Traditional Religion*, London, 1954, new edit., London: Sheldon Press, 1974, p. 146.

Bibliography[*]

Anderson-Morshead, A.E.M. & A.G. Blood, *The History of the Universities' Mission to Central Africa*, London: UMCA, vol. 1 (1955), vol. 2 (1957), vol. 3 (1962)

Beattie, J., *Other Cultures*, London: Cohen and West, 1964

Blackman, B. & J.M. Schoffeleers, "Masks of Malawi", in: *African Arts* (1972), no. 4, pp. 36-41, 69, 88

Braire, P., "Coutumes Indigènes", Rome: Archives of the Missionaries of Africa (White Fathers), MS, 44 pages, 1927

Bruwer, J.P., "Notes on Maravi Origins and Migration", in: *African Studies* 9 (1950), pp. 32-34

Bruwer, J.P., "Remnants of a Rain Cult among the Achewa", in: *African Studies* 11 (1952), pp. 179-182

Bruwer, J.P., "Unkhoswe: the System of Guardianship in Chewa Matrilineal Society", in: *African Studies* 14 (1955), pp. 113-122

Calmettes, J.P., "The Lumpa Church and Witchcraft Eradication", Paper read at the Conference of the History of Central African Religious Systems, Lusaka, 31 August - 8 September 1972

Crawford, J.R., *Witchcraft and Sorcery in Rhodesia*, London: OUP, 1967

Denis, L., "Meurs et Coutumes Indigènes", Rome: MS, 7 Fascisles 1951-1958, Archives of the Missionaries of Africa (White Fathers)

Denis, L., "Coutumes des Achewa", Rome: MS (21 pages), not dated, Archives of the Missionaries of Africa (White Fathers)

Diary of the Catholic Mission of Mua, Rome: from 1902 onwards, MS. Archives of the Missionaries of Africa (White Fathers)

Diary of the Catholic Mission of Likuni, Rome: from 1903 onwards, MS. Archives of the Missionaries of Africa (White Fathers)

Doke, C.M. & G.G. Harrap, *The Lambas of Northern Rhodesia*, London, 1931

Douglas, M., *Purity and Danger*, London: Routledge and Kegan, 1966

Evans-Pritchard, E.E., *Witchcraft, Oracle and Magic among the Azande*, London: OUP, 1937

Evans-Pritchard, E.E., *Nuer Religion*, London: OUP, 1956

Foà, E., *La Traversée de l'Afrique du Zambèse au Congo Français*, Paris: Plon, 1900

Fortes, M. & G. Dieterlen (eds.), *African Systems of Thought*, London: OUP, 1965

Gelfand, M., *Lakeside Pioneers, a Social-medical Study of Nyasaland (1875-1920*, Oxford: Blackwell, 1964

---

[*] This bibliography contains the literature that Johann van Breugel used during his research. Fur further references see the updated bibliography that follows on p. 278.

274

Gwengwe, J.W., *Kukula ndi Mwambo*, Limbe: Malawi Publications and Literature Bureau, 1965

Scott, D.C. & A. Hetherwick, *Dictionary of the Nyanja Language*, London: The Religious Tract Society, 1929

Hetherwick, A., *The Gospel and the African*, Edinburgh: Clark, 1932

Hodgson, A.G.O. "Notes on the Achewa and Angoni of the Dowa District of the Nyasaland Protectorate", in: *Journal of the Royal Anthropological Institute* 63 (1933), pp. 123-166

Honoré, A., "Personal Diary 1902-1912", Rome: MS, Archives, Missionaries of Africa (White Fathers)

Hovington. A. (spp.: Bibi Minus Habens), An Essay of Encyclopedia: On the African Way of Life, around the South West Shores of Lake Malawi and Surroundings, typescript 1971-73, 8 Vols. & 1 Index, Archives, Missionaries of Africa (White Fathers)

Vol. I: Physiography, History, Agriculture, Tribes (413 pp.);

Vol. II: Angoni and Yao (305 pp.);

Vol. III: De la Conception d'un Enfant à sa Naissance et jusqu'à sa Puberté (279 pp.)

Vol. IV: From the Puberty till the Marriage (450 pp.);

Vol. V: Marriage Settlement and Married Life (402 pp.);

Vol. VI: The Four Elementary Necessities of the African Material Life: The Bodily Wants/Feeding/Dressing/Housing (390 pp.);

Vol. VII: Religion and Moral: Among the African People of Old with Reference to the Present Mentality (397 pp.);

Vol. VIII: The Worshipping of the Ancestors (303 pp.)

Langworthy, H.W., "A History of Undi's Kingdom to 1890", PhD Dissertation, Boston University, 1969

Langworthy, H.W., *Zambia before 1980, Aspects of Precolonial History*, London: Longman, 1972

Linden, I. & J.M. Schoffeleers, "The Resistance of the *Nyau* Societies to the Roman Catholic Missions in Colonial Malawi", in: T.O. Ranger & I. Kimambo (eds.), *The Historical Study of African Religion*, London: Heinemann, 1972, pp. 252-273

Linden, I., *Catholics, Peasants and Chewa Resistancce in Nyasaland 1889-1939*, London: Heinemann, 1974

Linden, I., "Chewa Initiation Rites and *Nyau* Societies: the Use of Religious Institutions in Local Politics at Mua", in: T.O. Ranger & J. Weller (eds.), *Themes in Christian History of Central Africa*, London, 1975, pp. 30-44

MacDonald, D., *Africana, or the Heart of Heathen Africa*, 2 vols., Edinburgh: John Menzies & Co., 1881; repr. New York: Negro Universities Press

Mair, L.M., "Marriage and Family in the Dedza District of Nyasaland", in: *Jour-*

nal of the Royal Anthropological Institute 81 (1951), pp. 103-119

Makumbi, A.J., *Maliro ndi Miyambo ya Achewa*, Blantyre/Cape Town 1955, new ed., Longman (Malawi), 1970

Malekebu, B., Chisunzi, A. Kambanga & J. Chipengule, *Makolo Athu*, Zomba: Nyasaland Education Department, 1949

Mangani, L., "The Notion of God in Old Malawi", MS (4 pages), not dated read by kind permission of the author

Marwick, M.G. "Another Anti-witchcraft Movement in East Central Africa", in: *Africa* (1950), pp. 100-112

Marwick, M.G., "History and Tradition in East Central Africa", in: *Journal of African History* 4 (1963), pp. 375-390

Marwick, M.G., *Sorcery in its Social Setting*, Manchester: University Press, 1965

Mbiti, J.S., *African Religion and Philosophy*, London: Heinemann, 1969

Mbiti, J.S., *Concepts of God in Africa*, London: SPCK, 1970

Mbiti, J.S., *The Prayer of African Religions*, London: SPCK, 1975

Middleton, J. & E.H. Winter (eds.), *Witchcraft and Sorcery*, London: Routledge and Kegan, 1963

Missionaries of Africa (White Fathers), *Chronique Trimestrielle de la Societé des Missionaries d'Afrique (Pères Blancs)*, Algers: 1880 to 1905), Imprimerie des Pères Blancs

Missionaries of Africa (White Fathers), *Rapports Annuels*, Algers: from 1905 onwards, Imprimerie des Pères Blancs

Mitchell, J.C., "A Note on the African Conception of Causality", in: *The Nyasaland Journal* 5 (1950), no. 2, pp. 51-58

Msonthi, J. D., *Kali Kokha N'kanyama*, Likuni: Likuni Press, 1969

Murray, S.S., *A Handbook of Nyasaland*, London/Zomba: Government of Nyasaland, 1932

Ntara, S.J., *Nthondo*, Nkhoma: Nkhoma Press, 1936

Ntata, S.J., *Mbiri ya Achewa*, Limbe: Nyasaland Education Department, Zomba 1945, new ed. by Malawi Publications and Literature Bureau, 1965

Ntara, S.J., "Miyambo" (a collection on 308 proverbs in Chichewa), Nkhoma, 1958 (polycopied)

Ntara, S.J., *The History of the Chewa*, translation of Mbiri ya Achewa, with commentary by H.W. Langworthy, Wiesbaden: Frank Steiner, 1973

Pachai, B. (ed.), *The Early History of Malawi*, London: Longman, 1971

Paliani, S.A., *Moyo wa kwathu kwa ana a ku Nyasaland*, Likuni: Likuni Press, 1950

Paliani, S.A., *1930 Kunadza Mcape*, Likuni: Likuni Press, 1963

Paradis, E., "A Dossier on the *Nyau*", composed from 1924 to 1928, Archive of the Missionaries of Africa (White Fathers), Rome

Parrinder, E.G., *Religion in an African City*, London: OUP, 1953

Parrinder, E.G., *African Traditional Religion*, London: Sheldon Press, 1954 (new ed., 1974)

Price, T. "Mbona's Water-Hole", in: *Nyasaland Journal* 6 (1953), no. 1, pp. 28-33

Price, T., "Malawi Rain Cults", Paper presented at Seminar "Religion in Africa", Centre of African Studies in Edinburgh," April 1964

Rangeley, W.H.J., "Notes on Chewa Tribal Law", in: *The Nyasaland Journal* 1 (1948), no. 3, pp. 5-68

Rangeley, W.H.J. "*Nyau* in Kotakota District," in: *The Nyasaland Journal* 2 (1949), no. 2, pp. 35-49 (part I); vol. 3 (1950), no. 2, pp. 19-33 (part II)

Rangeley, W.H.J., "Makewana - the Mother of All People", in: *The Nyasalana Journal* 5 (1952), no. 2, pp. 31-50

Rangeley, W.H.J., "Mbona the Rain Maker", in: *The Nyasaland Journal* 6 (1953), no. 1, pp. 8-27

Ranger, T.O., "Mchape and the Study of Witchcraft Eradication", paper read at the conference on the History of Central African Religious Systems, Lusaka, 31 August - 8 September 1972

Ranger, T.O., "Territorial Cults in the History of Central Africa", in: *Journal of African History* (1973), pp. 581-597

Ranger, T.O. & I. Kimambo (eds.), *The Historical Study of African Religion*, London: Heinemann, 1972

Ranger, T.O. & J. Weller (eds.), *Themes in the Christian History of Central Africa*, London: Heinemann, 1975

Rattray, R.S., *Some Folk-Lore Stories and Songs in Chinyanja*, London: Society for Promotion of Christian Knowledge, 1907

Rattray, R.S., *Religion and Art in Ashanti*, London: Oxford University Press, 1927 (reprint 1958)

Richards, A.I., "A Modern Movement of Witch-finders", in: *Africa* (1935), pp. 448-461

Richards, A.I., *Chisungu*, London: Faber & Faber, 1956

Salaun, N., "Notes on the Achewa", polycopied, Lilongwe, nd, 124 pp.

Schoffeleers, J.M., "Symbolic and Social Aspects of Spirits Worship among the Mang'anja", PhD. Dissertation, Oxford, 1968

Schoffeleers, J.M., "The Religious Significance of Bush Fires in Malawi", in: *Cahiers des Religions Africaines* 10 (1971), pp. 271-287

Schoffeleers, J.M., "The Chisumphi and M'Bona Cults in Malawi. A Comparative History", Paper read at the Conference on the History of Central African Religious Systems, Lusaka, 31 August to 8 September 1972

Schoffeleers, J.M., "Myths and Legends of Creation", in: *Vision of Malawi* (1972), last quarter, pp. 13-17

Schoffeleers, J.M., "Towards the Identification of a Proto-Chewa Culture", in: *Journal of Social Science* (University of Malawi) 2 (1973), pp. 47-60

Scott, D.C., *Cyclopaedic Dictionary of the Mang'anja Language*, Edinburgh: Foreign

Mission Committee of the Church of Scotland, 1892

Singano, E. & A.A. Roscoe, *Tales of Old Malawi*, Limbe: Popular Publ., 1974

Smith, E.W. (ed.), *African Ideas of God*, London: Edinburgh House Press, 1950, (2nd ed. revised and edited by E.G. Parrinder, 3rd ed. 1966)

Stannus, H. S., "Notes on some Tribes in British Central Africa", in: *Journal of the Royal Anthropological Institute* 40 (1910), pp. 285-335

Taylor, J.V., *The Primal Vision*, London: SCM Press, 1963

Temples, P., *Bantu Philosophy*, Paris: Presence Africaine, 1953

Tew, M., "People of the Lake Nyasa Region", in: D. Forde (ed.), *Ethnographic Survey of Africa*, London: OUP, 1950

Turner, V.W., *The Forest of Symbols*, Ithaca: Cornell University Press, 1967

Turner, V.W., *The Drums of Affliction*, London: OUP, 1968

Wembah-Rashid, J.A.R., "Isinyago and Midimu. Masked Dancers of Tanzania and Mozambique", in: *African Art* (1971), pp. 37-47

Werner, A., *The Natives of British Central Africa*, London: Constable, 1906

Werner, A., *Myths and Legends of the Bantu*, 1933 (new ed., London: Frank Cass, 1968)

Williamson, J., "Salt and Potashes in the Life of the Chewa", in: *The Nyasaland Journal* 9 (1956), pp. 82-87

Williamson, J., *Useful Plants of Malawi*, Zomba: The Government Press, 1972

Wilson, M., *Good Company*, London: OUP, 1951

Wilson, M., *Rituals of Kinship among the Nyakyusa*, London: OUP, 1957

Wilson, M., *Communal Rituals of the Nyakyusya*, London: OUP, 1959

Wilson, M., *Religion and the Transformation of Society*, Cambridge: Uni Press, 1971

Young, T.C., *African Ways and Wisdom: A Contribution Towards Understanding*, London: United Society for Christian Literature, 1937

Young, T.C., *Contemporary Ancestors*, London: Lutterworth Press, 1940

Young, T.C. & H.K. Banda, *Our African Way of Life*, London: Lutterworth Press, 1946

Young, T.C., "The Idea of God in Northern Nyasaland", in: E.W. Smith (ed.), *African Ideas of God*, London: A Symposium, Edinburgh House Press, 1961, pp. 36-60

Updated Bibliography*

A Short List of Bantu Names for God, ed. by The African Way of Life Club, Kachebere Major Seminary, 1969, 9 pp. (Lists 36 different names for God used in Central Africa and offers a brief explanation of their respective meanings)

Adimoni, Bernard K., "*Nyau* Initiation Rites in Dedza District and Catholicism", 16 pp., CC/TRS/1990/12

Amanze, J., "The Bimbi Cult in Southern Malawi", PhD, University of London, 1986, (forthcoming as Kachere Book, 2001)

Banda, B., "Two Healing Spirit Mediums in Nkhwazi Village: An Assessment of their Ministry", CC/TRS/1996/19

Birch de Aguilar, L., "Masks in Social Roles", in: *Society of Malawi Journal* 47 (1994), no. 2, pp. 15-37

Birch de Aguilar, L., "Masks, Society, and Hierarchy among the Chewa of Central Malawi", in: Anthropos 90 (1994), pp. 407-421

Birch de Aguilar, L., "*Nyau* Masks of the Chewa: An Oral Historical Introduction", in: *Society of Malawi Journal* 47 (1994), no. 2, pp. 4-17

Birch de Aguilar, L., "Masks: Outsider and Socio-historical Experience", in: *Society of Malawi Journal* 47 (1994), no. 2, pp. 37-54

Birch de Aguilar, L., *Inscribing the Mask. Interpretation of Nyau Masks and Ritual Performance among the Chewa of Central Malawi*, Studia Instituti Anthropos, no. 47, Fribourg/Switzerland: University Press, 1996

Boucher, C., "La Dimension Spirituelle des Proverbes Chewa du Malawi", unpublished paper, Mua Mission, 12 pp.

Boucher, C., "Some Interpretations of *Nyau* Societies", M.A., School for Oriental and African Studies, University of London, 1976, 58 pp.

Boucher, C., "The Matrilineal Dilemma: Chewa and Kalulu Symbolic", School for Oriental and African Studies, London 1976, 8 pp.

Boucher, C., "La dimension spirituelle des proverbes Chewa du Malawi", unpubl. typescript, 12 pp.

Boucher, C., "The Burial and Commemoration Rites", paper for St Peter's Major Seminary, nd., 4 pp.

Breugel, J.W.M. van, "The Religious Significance of the *Nyau* among the Chewa

* This updated bibliography contains further publications on Chewa Traditional Religion, mainly from the years 1976 until 2000; the acronym CC/TRS refers to dissertations and papers archived at the Department of Theology and Religious Studies at Chancellor College/Zomba.

of Malawi", in: *Cultures et Développement* 17 (1985), n. 3, pp. 487-517

Brown, W.L., "Response to Chewa Culture: A Comparison Between the Baptists and Other Denominations", CC/TRS/1996/10

Bruwer, J.P., "Die gesin onder die moederregtelike Chewa", M.A., University of Pretoria, 1949

Bwanali, Al-Ahmed K., "Sorcery among *Nyau* Dancers of Nkhoma in Lilongwe", 7 pp., CC/TRS/1993/14

Bwanali, T.C., "The Gule Wamkulu Traditional Religion in the Central Region of Malawi", 15 pp., CC/TRS/1988/8

Chafukira, I.F.W., "The *Nyau* Initiation Ceremonies as at Kangunje Village, West of Lilongwe", 18 pp., CC/TRS/1988/9

Chakanza, J.C., "Some Chewa Concepts of God", in: *Religion in Malawi* 1 (1987), pp. 4-8

Chakanza, J.C., "The Mchape Affair at Liwonde: A Reappraisal", CC/TRS/1995/1

Chakhaza, B., "Witch-Hunting in Africa with Special Reference to Malawi", Theology Research Paper, Chancellor College, 1976, 9 pp.

Chakwawa, S.J., "Death Rituals and Ceremonies among the Chewa of Central Malawi", 17 pp., CC/TRS/1981/13

Chigona, G., "The Problem of Evil: A Study in Contrast Between Western and Malawian Systems", CC/TRS/1995/11

Chigona, G., "The Resurrection of the Dead: A Comparative Study of the Chewa and the Biblical Traditions in John's Gospel", CC/TRS/1993/13

Chilinkhwambe, D.B., "Popular Beliefs amongst the Nyanja People of Nkhotakota District, Tandwe Village, T/A Malengachanzi", CC/TRS/1989/6

Chimbiya, J., "Initiation of Chewa Girls: Pastoral Obstacle of Inculturation, CC/TRS/1996/6

Chingondole S., "The First and Second Funeral Rites in a Mang'anja Traditional Society", CC/TRS/1993/8

Chunda, A., "Euthanasia in the Chewa-Tonga Culture of Malawi", CC/TRS/1994/18

Curran, D., "The Elephant has four Hearts. Nyau Mask and Rituals", in: *Iwalewa Forum 1/2000.* Arbeitspapiere zur Kunst und Kultur Afrikas, Bayreuth: Iwalewa Haus, 2000, pp. 7-15

DeGabriele, J., "Spirit Possession around Sitima Mission", Research Paper, University of Malawi, 1995

DeGabriele, J. "Chisupe: Old Peppers don't Bite", research paper, University of Malawi, 1997, 16 pp., CC/TRS/1997/15

DeGabriele, J., "When Pills don't Work - African Illnesses, Misfortune and Mdulo", in: *Religion in Malawi* 9 (1999), pp. 9-23

Drake, A.M., "Illness, Ritual and Social Relations among the Chewa of Central

Africa", PhD., Duke University, 1976

Englund, H., "Witchcraft, Modernity and the Person: The Morality of Accumulation in Central Malawi", *Critique of Anthropology* 16 (1996), no. 3, pp. 257-279

Faiti, D., "The Mambo Spirits in Chapananga", History Seminar Paper, Chancellor College, 1986/87, 20 pp.

Gaga, E.H., "Bunda Hills", in: *Society of Malawi Journal* 35 (1982), pp. 61-63

Garbutt, H.W., "Witchcraft in Nyasa (Mang'anga, Yao, Achewa) communicated by a Native to Writer", in: *Journal of Religion in Africa* 41 (1911), pp. 301-304

Hargreaves, J.B., "Killing and Curing", in: *Society of Malawi Journal* 31 (1978), no. 2, pp. 21-30

Hopkins, J.M., "Theological Students and Witchcraft Beliefs", in: *Journal of Religion in Africa* 11 (1980), no. 1, pp. 55-66

Johnson, W.P., *Chinyanja Proverbs*, Cardiff: Smith Brothers, 1922

Joshwa, F., "Mmeto/Mpalo among the Chewa of Chidewere area in Dedza district", 24 pp., CC/TRS/1990/11

Kachusa, P.N.K.C., "Initiation to *Nyau* amongst the Chewa in Ntchisi District",.18 pp., CC/TRS/1988/16

Kalilombe, P.A., "An Outline of Chewa Traditional Religion", in: *Africa Theological Journal* 9 (1980), no. 2, pp. 39-51

Kambalame, J., *Our African Way of Life*, ed. by T.C. Young & H.K. Banda, London: Lutterworth Press, 1946

Kambwembwe, H.Y., "The Concept and Practice of *Nyau* among the Chewa of Tandwe Village, T.A Kalumo in Ntchisi District", Research Paper, Chancellor College, Zomba, 1988, 19 pp., CC/TRS/1988/19

Kapombe, E.E.J., "Medicinemen", CC/TRS/1992/11

Kaspin, D., "Chewa Vision and Revisions of Power: Transformation of the *Nyau* Dance in Central Malawi", in: *Jean & John Camaroff, Modernity and its Malcontents. Ritual and Power in Postcolonial Africa*, Uni. of Chicago Press 1993, pp. 34-57

Kathewera, R.E.M., "Religion and its Language: the Use and Interpretation of some Traditional Terminologies in Chichewa", 17 pp., CC/TRS/1982/2

Katutu, N., "The Concept of Life-After-Death among the Chewa Compared with the Scriptural Tradition", CC/TRS/1994/16

Koch, G., "Beiträge zum Mbona-Kult in Malawi", M.A., University of Mainz, 1988/89, 159 pp.

Kubik, G., *Nyau: Maskenbünde im Südlichen Malawi*, (Österreichische Akademie der Wissenschaften. Veröffentl. der ethnol. Komm., no. 4), Vienna, 1987

Kubik, G., *Malisi Nyau Mapiko: Maskentraditionen im Bantu-sprachigen Afrika*, München: Trickster, 1993

Kuppens, J.J.M., "They Discovered the Wonders of God in their Culture. Mortuary Rites and Inculturation in Malawi", Doctoraal Scriptie, Katholieke Universiteit Nijmegen, Feb. 1992, 112 pp.

Kuthemba M.J., "Problems of Research into 'the Reserve': an Attempt to Probe into Gule Wamkulu", *Kalulu - Bulletin of Oral Literature*, University of Malawi, No. 3 (May 1982)

Kuthemba Mwale, J., "Transition and Change: a Study of the Psychological Impact of Gule", *Journal of Social Science* (Zomba) 8 (1980/81), pp. 126-147

Kwapulani, A.M., "Spirit Possession in the Religious History of Mchinji District, Central Malawi, from Pre-colonial times to the Present", History Seminar Paper, 22 pp., CC/TRS/1982/4

Linden, I., "Chewa Initiation Rites and *Nyau* Societies: the Use of Religious Institutions in Local Politics at Mua", in: T.O. Ranger & J. Weller (eds.), *Themes in the Christian History of Central Africa*, London: Heinemann, 1975, pp. 30-44

Linden, I., "Chisumphi Theology and Religion in Central Malawi", in J.M. Schoffeleers (ed.), *Guardians of the Land: Essays on Central African Territorial Cults*, Gweru: Mambo, 1978, pp. 187-208

Linden, I., "Mwali" and the Luba Origin of the Chewa: some Tentative Suggestions, in: *Society of Malawi Journal* 25 (1972), no. 1, pp. 11-19

Linden, I., "The Shrine of the Kalongas of Mankhamba: Some Problems in the Religious History of Central Malawi", Paper presented at the Lusaka Conference on the History of Central African Religious Systems (1972), 32 pp.

Luhanga, T., "The Mwanda Cult", 8 pp., CC/TRS/1982/5

Mackenzie, D.R., *The Spirit-Ridden Konde*, London: Seeley Service, 1925. 318 pp.

Mair, L.P., "Marriage and Family in the Dedza District of Nyasaland", in: *Journal of the Royal Anthropological Institute* 81 (1951), pp. 103-119

Malamulo, S., "Backsliding among Malawian Christians", CC/TRS/1993/12

Malekebu, B.E., *Unkhoswe wa aNyanja*, ed. by G. Atkins, publ. for the School of Oriental and African Studies, Oxford: University Press, 1952

Malele, P.B., "The Social and Religious Impact of the *Nyau* Among the Chewa of Mitundu in Lilongwe", CC/TRS/1993/15

Mapopa, M., "The Drama of Gule Wamkulu. A Study of the *Nyau* as practiced by the Chewa of the Eastern Province of Zambia", M.A. Diss., Univ. of Ghana, nd. (unpublished)

Masinga, G.M., "Mdulo Concept among the Chewa", 12 pp., CC/TRS/1989/7

Mkhola, C.C.A., "Taboos: Their Role and Interaction with Christianity", B.A. (Theology) Dissertation, University of Malawi, 1995, CC/TRS/1995/13

Mkhwimba, I.M., "Initiation of Girls in the Area of Chief Pemba", 9 pp., CC/TRS/1988/6

Mkolokosa, C., "Chisumphi in the Religion of Central Malawi", 6 pp., CC/TRS/1979/2

Morris, B., "Chewa conceptions of desease: symptoms and etiologies", in: *Society of Malawi Journal* 38 (1985), no. 1, pp. 14-43

Morris, B., "Herbalism and divination in Southern Malawi", in: *Society of Science and Medicine* 23 (1986), pp. 367-377

Morris, B., "Medicines and Herbalists in Malawi", in: *Society of Malawi Journal* 42 (1989), no. 1, pp. 34-54

Morris, B., "Changing Conceptions of Nature", in: *Society of Malawi Journal* 44 (1991), no. 2, pp. 9-26

Morris, B., "Hunting and the Gnostic Vision", in: *Journal of Human and Environmental Sciences* 1 (1996), no. 2, pp. 13-39.

Morris, B., *Chewa Medical Botany. A Study of Herbalism in Southern Malawi*, Monographs from the International African Institute, no. 2, Hamburg: LIT 1996

Morris, B., *The Power of Animals. An Ethnography*, Oxford/NY: Berg, 1998

Morris, B., *Animals and Ancestors. An Ethnography*, Oxford/NY: Berg, 2000

M'passou, D.B., "A Theological Interpretation of Certain Aspects of African Traditional Beliefs", Diploma in Ecumenical Studies, The Ecumenical Institute, Bossey, Switzerland, January 1984

Msowoya, S.W.R., "Rain-calling in Chief Kyungu's area of Central Karonga", 38 pp., CC/TRS/1986/2

Mtingiza, A.Z., "*Nyau* and the Initiation Rites of Girls in Lilongwe District", 15 pp., CC/TRS/1990/21

Musopole, A.C. "The Chewa Concept of God and its Implications for the Christian Faith", M.A., University of Malawi, 1984, 187 pp.

Mvula, E.S.T., "Gule Wamkulu Performance as Restored Behaviour", University of Malawi, Zomba, 1986, 24 pp.

Mwakanandi, D.S., "The Role of African Traditional Religion in the Promotion of Christian Faith in Malawi", DTh., University of Stellenbosch, 1990

Mwawa, C., "The Msati Rain Shrine (Mgala and Liganga Shrines)", B.A. (Theology) Dissertation, University of Malawi, 1995, CC/TRS/1995/14

Ndalama, L.J., "The Impact of Christianity on the M'bona Cult", 16 pp., CC/TRS/1987/10

Nditani, C.T., "Common Female Rituals of the Mang'anja of Nsanje District", 11 pp., CC/TRS/1989/11

Ng'oma, H.K.A., "North and West Kasungu: *Nyau* in a Changing Environment, 1890-1960", History Seminar Paper, Chancellor College, Zomba. 1987, 18 pp.

Nkhota, N.I., "The *Nyau* Phenomenon in Bweya Area in Dowa District", Research Paper, Chancellor College, Zomba, 1988, 19 pp., CC/TRS/1988/20

Ott, M., *Dialog der Bilder. Die Begegnung von Evangelium und Kultur in afrikanischer Kunst*, Freiburg: Herder, 1995, pp. 113-166

Ott, M., "Church and Culture on Display. The Opening of the Chamare Museum in Mua", in: *Religion in Malawi* 8 (1998), pp. 41-48

Ott, M. *African Theology in Images* (Kachere Monograph, no. 12), Blantyre: CLAIM, 2000

Pachai, B. (ed.), *The Early History of Malawi*, London: Longman 1972

Pachai, B., *The History of the Nation*, London: Longman 1973

Parratt, J., "The Bimbi Cult and its Impact among the Chewa, Yao and Lomwe of the Upper Shire Valley", 28 pp., CC/TRS/1990/28

Parratt, J., "Whatever is Happening to the *Mizimu?* Some Problems in the Study of African Traditional Religions", 15 pp., CC/TRS/1984/1

Peltzer, K., *Some Contributions of Traditional Practices towards Psychological Health Care in Malawi*, Eschborn: Fachbuchhandlung für Psychologie, 1987

Petermann, W., *Regenkulte und Regenmacher bei bantu-sprachigen Ethnien Ost- und Südafrikas*, Berlin: Reimer 1985

Phiri, K.M., "Chewa History in Central Malawi and the Use of Oral Tradition, 1600-1920", PhD., Univ. of Wisconsin, Madison 1975

Phiri, K.M., "The Historiography of *Nyau*", in: *Kalulu. Bulletin of Oral Literature*, University of Malawi, no. 3, 1982, pp. 55-58

Phiri, K.M., "Some Changes in the Matrilineal Family System among the Chewa of Malawi since the Nineteenth Century", in: *Journal of African History* 24 (1983), pp. 257-274

Phiri, K.M., "Reflections on the Morality and Immorality of a Pre-colonial African Society: The Maravi". Faith and Knowledge Seminar No. 30, Chancellor College, Zomba, 1994, 6 pp.

Phiri, P.H.G. (ed.), *Nsembe ndi Miyambo ya Achewa*, Kachebere Major Seminary, 1972, 45 pp.

Probst, P., "Danser le Sida. Spectacles du *Nyau* et Culture Populaire Chewa dans le Centre du Malawi", in: M. Agier & A. Ricard (eds.), *Les Arts de la Rue dans les Sociétés du Sud* (Special Issue), Autrepart/Cahiers des Sciences Humaines, Nouvelle Série, vol. 1/1 (1997), pp. 91-113

Probst, P., "Picture Dance. Reflections on *Nyau* Image and Experience", in: *Iwalewa Forum 1/2000*. Arbeitspapiere zur Kunst und Kultur Afrikas, Bayreuth: Iwalewa Haus, 2000, pp. 17-32

Probst, P., "Moral Discourses and Ritual Authority in Central Malawi", Sozialanthropol. Arbeitspapiere, vol. 6, Berlin: Das Arabische Buch, 1995

Probst, P., "Expansion and Disclosure. Ritual Landscapes and the Management of Locality in Central Malawi", Paper presented at the conference on Historical and Social Science Research in Malawi, Zomba, June 2000, 20 pp.

Regional Cults in Malawi, Zomba: University of Malawi, Sources for the Study of Religion in Malawi, no. 7, 1983

Schoffeleers, J.M., *Evil Spirits and Rites of Exorcism in the Lower Shire Valley of Malawi*, Blantyre: Montfort Press, 1967

Schofelleers, J.M., "M'bona the Guardian Spirit of the Mang'anja", B.Litt., University of Oxford, 1966, 431 pp.

Schofelleers, J.M., "Symbolic and Social Aspects of Spirit Worship among the Mang'anja", D.Phil., University of Oxford, 1968, 666 pp.

Schoffeleers, J.M., "The Religious Significance of Bush Fires in Malawi", in: *Cahiers des Religions Africaines* 10 (1971), pp. 271-87

Schoffeleers, J.M., "The History and Political Role of the Mbona Cult among the Mang'anja", in T.O. Ranger & I.N. Kimambo (eds.), *The Historical Study of African Religions*, Berkeley: University of California Press, 1972, pp. 73-94

Schoffeleers, J.M. & I. Linden, "The Resistance of *Nyau* Societies to the Roman Catholic Missions in Colonial Malawi", in: T. Ranger & I.N. Kimambo (eds.), *The Historical Study of African Religion*, London: Heinemann, 1972, pp. 252-273

Schoffeleers, J.M. & B. Blackmun, "Masks of Malawi", in: *African Arts* 5 (1972), no. 4, pp. 36-41, 69, 88

Schoffeleers, J.M., "The Chisumphi and Mbona Cults in Malawi: a comparative History", Conference on the history of Central African religious systems, Lusaka, 1972, 50 pp.

Schoffeleers, J.M., "Myths and Legends of Creation", in: *Visions of Malawi*, December 1972, pp. 13-17

Schoffeleers, J.M., "Seven Centuries of Malawian Religion", in: *Visions of Malawi*, March, 1973, pp. 11-14

Schoffeleers, J.M., "Towards the Identification of Proto-Chewa Culture", in: *Journal of Social Science* (Malawi) 2 (1973), pp. 47-60

Schoffeleers, J.M., "Crisis, Criticism and Critique: An Interpretative Model of Territorial Mediumship among the Chewa", in: *Journal of Social Science* (Zomba) 3 (1974), pp. 74-80

Schoffeleers, J.M., "The Interaction of the M'bona Cult and Christianity 1859-1963", in: T.O. Ranger & J. Weller (eds.), *Themes in the Christian History of Central Africa*, London: Heinemann, 1975, pp. 14-29

Schoffeleers, J.M., "An Outline History of Territorial Mediumship in a Malawian District", International Conference on Southern African History, National University of Lesotho, 1977

Schoffeleers, J.M., "The *Nyau* Societies: Our Present Understanding", in: *The Society of Malawi Journal* 29 (1976), no. 1, pp. 59-68

Schoffeleers, J.M., "Cult Idioms and the Dialectics of a Region", in: R. Werbner (ed.), *Regional Cults* (ASA Monograph No. 16) London: Academic Press, 1977, pp. 219-239

Schoffeleers, J.M., "A Martyr Cult as a Reflection on Changes in Production: The Case of the Lower Shire Valley, 1590-1622 A.D.", in: *African Perspectives* (Leiden) 2 (1978), pp. 19-33

Schoffeleers, J.M., "*Nyau* Symbols in Rock Paintings", in: N. Lindgren & M. Schoffeleers, *Rock Art and Nyau Symbolism in Malawi*, Lilongwe: Department of Antiquities of the Government of Malawi (Publ. no. 18), 1978

Schoffeleers, J.M. *Guardians of the Land: Essays on Central African Territorial Cults*, Gweru: Mambo Press, 1979 (reprint as Kachere Text in 1999)

Schoffeleers, J.M., "The Story of M'bona the Martyr", in R. Schefold et al. (eds.), *Man, Meaning and History; Essays in Honour of Prof. H.G. Schulte-Nordholt*, The Hague: Martinus Nijhoff, 1980, pp. 246-263

Schoffeleers, J.M., "Twins and Unilateral Figures in Central and Southern Africa: Symmetry and Asymmetry in the Symbolization of the Sacred", in: *Journal of Religion in Africa* 21 (1991), no. 4, pp. 345-372

Schoffeleers, J.M., *River of Blood. The Genesis of a Martyr Cult in Southern Malawi, c. A.D. 1600*, Madison, Wisconsin: University of Wisconsin Press, 1992

Schoffeleers, J.M., *Religion and the Dramatisaton of Life. Spirit Beliefs and Rituals in Southern and Central Malawi*, Blantyre: CLAIM, 1997

Sembereka, G., "The Place of Gule Wamkulu in Dreams attributed to Spirits, Nominal Reincarnation and Spirit-Possession: The Nankhumba Experience", in: *Society of Malawi Journal* 49 (1996), no. 1, pp. 1-31

Sindima, H.J., "Bondedness, Moyo and Umunthu as Elements of a Chewa Spirituality: Organizing Logic and Principle of Life", in: *Ultimate Reality and Meaning* 14 (1991), no. 1, pp. 5-20

Strumpf, M., "Music Traditions of Malawi", Chancellor College, nd., 17 pp.

Useni, R.B., "Personal Survival in Christian Eschatology and the Nyungwe Tradition", CC/TRS/1993/10

Wendroff, A.P., *Trouble-shooters and Trouble-makers: Witchfinding and Traditional Malawian Medicine*, University of New York: UMI, 1985

Yoshida, K., "Masks and Secrecy among the Chewa", in: *African Arts* 26 (1993), no. 2, pp. 34-45

Yoshida, K., "Masks and Transformation among the Chewa of Eastern Zambia", in: *Senri Ethnological Studies* (Osaka) 31 (1992), pp. 203-273

Zulu, H., "Paul's Eschatology and the Concept of Death in Chewa Culture", CC/TRS/1993/11

Kachere Series Publications

Kachere Series offers a range of books on theology, religion, and society in Malawi. Its publications are grouped in *Kachere Monographs, Kachere Books, Kachere Texts* and *Kachere Studies*. Books in vernacular languages are published as *Mvunguti Books*.

Editors:
J.C. Chakanza, F.L. Chingota, K. Fiedler, P. Kalilombe, S. Mahomed,
H. Mijoga, F.L. Moyo, M. Ott, I.A. Phiri
For book orders and information contact:
The Kachere Series, P.O. Box 1037, Zomba, Malawi
Tel./Fax: (+265) 524 705, e-mail: kachere@sdnp.org.mw

Kachere Monographs

Andrew C. Ross, *Blantyre Mission and the Making of Modern Malawi*, Blantyre: CLAIM, 1996

Kenneth R. Ross (ed.), *God, People and Power in Malawi: Democratization in Theological Perspective*, Blantyre: CLAIM, 1996

Harry Langworthy, *"Africa for the African": The Life of Joseph Booth*, Blantyre: CLAIM, 1996

Isabel Apawo Phiri, *Women, Presbyterianism and Patriarchy: Religious Experience of Chewa Women in Central Malawi*, Blantyre: CLAIM, 1997

Matthew Schoffeleers, *Religion and the Dramatization of Life: Spirit Beliefs and Spirit Possession in Central and Southern Malawi*, Blantyre: CLAIM, 1997

Ernst Wendland, *Buku Loyera: An Introduction to the New Chichewa Bible Translation*, Blantyre: CLAIM, 1998

J.C. Chakanza, *Voices of Preachers in Protest: The Ministry of Two Malawian Prophets: Elliot Kamwana and Wilfred Gudu*, Blantyre: CLAIM, 1998

Klaus Fiedler, *Christianity and African Culture: Conservative German Protestant Missionaries in Tanzania 1900-1940*, Blantyre: CLAIM, 1999

George Shepperson and Thomas Price, *Independent African, John Chilembwe and the Nyasaland Rising of 1915*, Blantyre: CLAIM, 2000

Ernst Wendland, *Preaching that Grabs the Heart: A Rhetorical-Stylistic Study of the Chichewa Revival Sermons of Shadrack Wame*, Blantyre: CLAIM, 2000

Martin Ott, *African Theology in Images*, Blantyre: CLAIM, 2000

John McCracken, *Politics and Christianity in Malawi 1875-1940: The Impact of the Livingstonia Mission in the Northern Province*, Blantyre: CLAIM, 2000

Kachere Books

Matembo S. Nzunda & Kenneth R. Ross (eds.), *Church, Law and Political Transition in Malawi 1992-94*, Gweru: Mambo, 1995

Kenneth R. Ross, *Gospel Ferment in Malawi: Theological Essays*, Gweru: Mambo, 1995

Kenneth R. Ross (ed.), *Christianity in Malawi: A Source Book*, Gweru: Mambo, 1996

Kings M. Phiri & Kenneth R. Ross (eds.), *Democratization in Malawi: A Stocktaking*, Blantyre: CLAIM, 1998

Kenneth R. Ross, *Here Comes Your King! Christ, Church and Nation in Malawi*, Blantyre: CLAIM, 1998

Kenneth R. Ross, *Faith at the Frontiers of Knowledge*, Blantyre: CLAIM, 1998

Patrick A. Kalilombe, *Doing Theology at the Grassroots: Theological Essays from Malawi*, Gweru: Mambo, 1999

Matthew Schoffeleers, *In Search of Truth and Justice: Confrontations between Church and State in Malawi 1960-1994*, Blantyre: CLAIM, 1999

Martin Ott, Kings M. Phiri, Nandini Patel (eds.), *Malawi's Second Democratic Elections: Process, Problems, and Prospects*, Blantyre: CLAIM, 2000

David S. Bone (ed.), *Malawi's Muslims. Historical Perspectives*, Blantyre: CLAIM, 2000

Pádraig Ó Máille, *Living Dangerously. A Memoir of Political Change in Malawi*, Blantyre: CLAIM, 2000

Masauko Chipembere, R. Rotberg (ed.), *Hero of the Nation. Chipembere of Malawi. An Autobiography*, Blantyre: CLAIM, 2001

J.C. Chakanza, *Wisdom of the People. 2000 Nyanja Proverbs*, Blantyre: CLAIM 2001

Kachere Texts

Kenneth R. Ross (ed.), *Church, University and Theological Education in Malawi*, Zomba: Department of TRS, 1995

Matthew Schoffeleers, Ann Nielsen, Hubert Reijnaerts, *Montfortians in Malawi: Their Spirituality and Pastoral Approach*, Balaka: Montfort Media, 1997

Joseph Booth, *Africa for the African*, Blantyre: CLAIM, 1996 (ed. by Laura Perry)

Stephen Kauta Msiska, *Golden Buttons: Christianity and Traditional Religion among the Tumbuka*, Blantyre: CLAIM, 1997

Peggy Owens (ed.), *When Maize and Tobacco are not Enough: A Church Study of Malawi's Agro-Economy*, Blantyre: CLAIM, 1998

J.C. Chakanza and Kenneth R. Ross, *Religion in Malawi: An Annotated Bibliography*, Blantyre: CLAIM, 1998

Silas Ncozana, *Sagaya: A Leader in the Synod of Blantyre Church of Central Africa Presbyterian,* Blantyre: CLAIM, 1999

Yesaya Zerenji Mwasi, *Essential and Paramount Reasons for Working Independently,* Blantyre: CLAIM, 1999

J.M. Schoffeleers (ed.), *Guardians of the Land,* Gweru: Mambo, 1999

Kachere Studies

Dick Gordon, *Transforming Psalms,* Blantyre: CLAIM, 2000

Steven Paas, *Digging Out the Ancestral Church,* Blantyre: CLAIM, 2000

Hilary Mijoga, *Separate, but Same Gospel. Preaching in African Instituted Churches in Southern Malawi,* Blantyre: CLAIM, 2001

Mvunguti Books

Silas Nzozana, *Sangaya,* Blantyre: CLAIM, 1999

Klaus Fiedler & Janet Kholowa, *Pa Chiyambi Anawalenga Chimodzimodzi,* Blantyre: CLAIM, 1999

Klaus Fiedler & Janet Kholowa, *In the Beginning God Created them Equal,* Blantyre: CLAIM, 2000

David Mphande, *Nthanthi za Chitango za Kusambizgiya ndi Kutauliya,* Blantyre: CLAIM, 2001

Books in Preparation

Ian Linden, Catholics, Peasants and Chewa Resistance (reprint)

Silas Ncozana, The Spirit Dimension in African Christianity: A Pastoral Study among Tumbuka People of Northern Malawi

James Amanze, Bimbi Cult

Boston Soko, Chikanga. A Traditional Healer

Klaus Fiedler, Joseph Booth in Melbourne

Beryl Brough, Saint Johnson of Lake Malawi

Owen Mkandawire, Chiswakhata Mkandawire of Livingstonia

www.ingramcontent.com/pod-product-compliance
Lightning Source LLC
Chambersburg PA
CBHW021854020426
42334CB00013B/321